Salt Lake City
Livability in the 21st Century

Photography by Adam Barker
Text by Melissa Fields

A publication of the
Office of Salt Lake City Mayor Ralph Becker

HPNbooks
A division of Lammert Incorporated
San Antonio, Texas

First Edition

Copyright © 2014 HPNbooks

All inquiries should be addressed to HPNbooks, 11535 Galm Road, Suite 101, San Antonio, Texas, 78254. Phone (800) 749-9790, www.hpnbooks.com.

ISBN: 978-1-939300-66-9
Library of Congress: 2014946645

Salt Lake City: Livability in the 21st Century

photography for parts 1-3:	Adam Barker
text:	Melissa Fields
design:	Glenda Tarazon Krouse
contributing writers for Salt Lake City partners:	Melissa Fields, Joe Goodpasture, Marie Beth Jones

HPNbooks

president:	Ron Lammert
project manager:	Bart B. Barica
administration:	Donna M. Mata, Melissa G. Quinn
book sales:	Dee Steidle
production:	Colin Hart, Evelyn Hart, Tim Lippard, Christopher Mitchell, Tony Quinn

PRINTED IN MALAYSIA

Contents

Foreword by Salt Lake City Mayor Ralph Becker 7

Introduction 8

Part **One**   **Mountains Meet Metro** 12

Part **Two**   **Sum of its Parts** 66

Part **Three**   **Urban Aesthetic** 120

Appendix 176

Salt Lake City Partners 178

About the Photographer 310

About the Author 310

Sponsors 311

All Resort Group/All Resort Express
P.O. Box 681780
Park City, UT 84068
800-457-9457 • Fax 435-649-4977
www.allresort.com

America First Credit Union
P.O. Box 9199
Ogden, UT 84409
800-999-3961 • Fax 801-827-8452
www.americafirst.com

ATK Aerospace Group
M/S UT40-X60, P.O. Box 707
Brigham City, UT 84302-0707
435-863-4809 • Fax 435-863-3224
www.atk.com

Boart Longyear
10808 South River Front Parkway, Suite 600
South Jordan, UT 84095
801-972-6430 • Fax 801 977 3374
www.boartlongyear.com

Durham, Jones & Pinegar
111 East Broadway, Suite 900
Salt Lake City, UT 84110
801-415-3000 • Fax 801-415-3500
www.djplaw.com

FLSmidth USA, Inc.
7158 South FLSmidth Drive
Midvale, UT 84047-5559
801-871-7000 • Fax 801-871-7001
www.flsmidth.com

IASIS Healthcare Corporation
117 Seaboard Lane, Building E
Franklin, TN 37067
615-844-2747 • Fax 615-846-3006
www.iasishealthcare.com

Through their generous support, these companies helped to make this project possible. The Mayor's Office expresses appreciation for their participation.

Intermountain Healthcare
36 S. State Street
Salt Lake City, UT 84111
801-442-2000 • Fax 801-442-2857
www.intermountainhealthcare.org

KIRTON | McCONKIE

Kirton McConkie
Kirton McConkie Building
50 East South Temple, Suite 400
Salt Lake City, UT 84111
801-328-3600 • Fax 801-321-4893
www.kmclaw.com

Rio Tinto Kennecott
 Utah Copper Corporation
4700 Daybreak Parkway
South Jordan, UT 84095
801-204-2000 • Fax 801-204-2885
www.riotinto.com

Royce Industries, LC
1355 West 8040 South
West Jordan, UT 84088
800-999-3961 • Fax 801-827-8452
www.buyroyce.com

Salt Lake Chamber
175 E. University Blvd. (400 S.), Suite 600
Salt Lake City, UT 84111
801-364-3631
www.slcchamber.com

SME Steel
5801 West Wells Park Road
West Jordan, UT 84081
801-280-0711 • Fax 801-280-3734
www.smesteel.com

University of Utah Health Care
50 North Medical Drive
Salt Lake City, UT 84132
801-581-2121
www.healthcare.utah.edu

Ralph Becker, thirty-fourth
mayor of Salt Lake City, Utah.

Foreword

By Mayor Ralph Becker

I lived for many years near the mouth of Salt Lake City's City Creek Canyon after I first arrived in Utah in the mid-1970s. One of my favorite ways to shed the workday was taking an evening walk through my neighborhood. Sometimes I'd head east into the foothills, where among the pine, scrub oak and aspen trees, I'd often not encounter another person. On other days I'd set off toward the west, and in just a few minutes, find myself in the heart of Salt Lake City's bustling downtown. Never before had I experienced such an immediate juxtaposition of civilization and wilderness, an experience that remains intact and enjoyed by many Salt Lake City residents to this day. Since then, the roots of my affection for this place have both multiplied and grown deeper. But one continues to tower—literally—above the rest: the Wasatch Mountain Range's unparalleled proximity to the city I love.

Few places in the world are as intricately connected to a landform as is Salt Lake City. Water, the lifeline sustaining almost 500,000 people in the Salt Lake Valley and beyond, is delivered unfalteringly by the Wasatch Mountains, representing one of the purest water sources in the contiguous United States. This abundant watershed enabled the Mormon pioneers to boldly establish an outpost here more than 150 years ago, and it continues to play an integral role in the city's and state's robust modern economy. Through fastidious stewardship, Salt Lake City's water quality has remained relatively the same as it was when water treatment facilities were established at City Creek, Big Cottonwood and Parleys Canyons in the 1950s. What's even more remarkable is that we've managed to protect our pristine water supply while at the same time allowing mountain recreation and access to flourish.

Over the last two decades, due in large part to its unique access to the mountains, Salt Lake City has undergone nothing short of a transformation. Once viewed as little more than a mid-country way station, Utah's capital city is now one of the most dynamic metropolitan areas in the western United States. World-class restaurants, shops and galleries populate the city's neighborhoods and urban core, and recent projects like City Creek Center and the new George S. and Dolores Doré Eccles Theater (scheduled for completion in 2016) are further enhancing downtown Salt Lake City's vibrant commercial, arts and cultural landscape. Lured by the area's unmatched outdoor lifestyle and an affordable cost of living, companies and individuals from around the world have taken up residence in Salt Lake City, fueling one of the country's healthiest economies. In fact, *Fortune Magazine* recognized Salt Lake City as the third best large city for jobs in the U.S., and as one of the top fifteen places for doing business in the entire world.

Key to Salt Lake City's evolution is a long-term and dedicated commitment to developing public transportation. Through light rail, high speed trains, bicycle lanes and shares, and the return of the street car, Salt Lake City is developing public transit infrastructure more vigorously than any other city in North America. And though the Salt Lake City International Airport is already one of the most efficient airports in the country, terminal reconstruction plans call for an even more efficient air travel facility, both logistically and in terms of energy use. Combined, these efforts not only help protect our city's abundant natural beauty but provide the basis for creating a sense of place that's uniquely Salt Lake City.

Utah's population is forecasted to grow by eighty-six percent by 2050. Maintaining and improving upon our unparalleled quality of life is one of the city's biggest challenges and priorities. To this end Salt Lake City government has undertaken a groundbreaking project to adopt the most comprehensive sustainability ordinance revision in the country. The Sustainable City Code Initiative shapes development patterns necessary for Salt Lake City to become the country's most sustainable city. One of the first projects completed under the new code, the country's first net-zero public safety building, was unveiled in 2013.

My hopes and dreams for Salt Lake City and its life-giving Wasatch Mountains are that we leave both just a little bit better than how we found them. I want our city's children to know the pleasure of powder skiing in the backcountry or at one of our top-notch resorts; of drinking water as pure as the mountains from which it came; to easily navigate between urban centers and neighborhoods without having to get in their car; and to take a decompressing walk into the foothills at the end of the work day. My awe for the Wasatch Mountains and Salt Lake City's abundant natural beauty is matched only by my respect and appreciation for the deep sense of community cooperation and greater good inherent throughout our great city. I have confidence that not only will my dreams for Salt Lake City be realized, but that the hopes and dreams of those who come after us will be achieved as well.

Introduction

In the years immediately following the Mormon pioneers' arrival, Salt Lake City's prime mid-country location and abundant resources quickly earned the growing outpost the moniker "Crossroads of the West." Completion of the Trans-Continental Railroad at Utah's Promontory Point in 1869 triggered a migratory flood of various ethnic groups into Salt Lake City from China, Japan, Greece and Central Europe; a diversity that remains today. Hispanics now account for approximately 22 percent of residents, while the Asian population makes up approximately 4.5 percent and the Pacific Islander population, comprised primarily of Samoan and Tongan immigrants, represent roughly 2 percent of the population. And though about roughly half of Salt Lake City's residents are members of the Church of Jesus Christ of Latter-day Saints, a variety of other religions and faiths thrive in Utah's capital city as well, including Catholicism, Buddhism, Judaism, Methodism, Presbyterianism, Unitarianism, Greek/Eastern Orthodox and Baptist.

One of the most indelible—and telling—images of Salt Lake City is the downtown skyline framed against the majestic Wasatch Mountains. Nowhere else in America is an urban area situated within such immediate proximity to a major mountain range. This unique combination of city and wilderness has given rise to one of the most diverse, cosmopolitan, economically solvent, innovative and fastest growing communities in the United States.

Salt Lake City's modern history began on a July afternoon in 1847 when Brigham Young and his party of 148 Mormon pioneers reached the mouth of Emigration Canyon overlooking the Great Salt Lake Valley. After travelling 1,300 miles by wagon train from Illinois, crossing one-third of the continent in search of a place where they could live and worship freely, the pioneers believed they'd finally arrived in Zion. According to legend, Young stood atop his wagon, pointed to the valley and declared, "This is the place."

Though "crossroads" may have been an apt way to describe Salt Lake City's past, "destination" better encapsulates Salt Lake City today. A business-friendly environment and high quality of life has made Salt Lake City the top choice for both new and growing companies. Take just one look around and it's easy to see why: Salt Lake City's banking system is more mature and sophisticated than many other larger Western cities; renowned higher education institutions like the University of Utah, Westminster College and Salt Lake Community College fuel one of the country's most well-educated workforces; and the Salt Lake City International Airport allows ninety-minute access to any city in the Western United States and non-stop access to a slew of international destinations.

Salt Lake City's migratory pull is not limited to corporations alone, however. According to a 2012 Headwaters Economic Study, entrepreneurs, retirees and people who can work remotely are also choosing to relocate to Salt Lake City in droves. As a result, the city's population is projected to grow exponentially over the next fifty years. Preparations for the expected boom are already well underway. For years city planners have collaborated with climatologists, hydrologists and other experts to assess how to best conserve the state's precious Wasatch Mountains' snowpack-based water resources. Salt Lake City is developing mass transit faster than any other municipality in North America, to both alleviate pressure on natural areas close to the city and protect air quality.

Utah's diverse landscape is indeed a study in contrasts, from the lush alpine canyons bisecting the Wasatch Range to the surreal red rock wildernesses found in the state's southern quadrant. But Salt Lake City remains the state's literal and proverbial heart, once a refuge for those persecuted, now the thriving economic, social and cultural center of the Intermountain West.

INTRODUCTION
11

Mountains Meet Metro

No other landform has influenced life in Utah more significantly than the Wasatch Range, a subset of the Rocky Mountains stretching 160 miles from the Utah-Idaho border south to Central Utah. Though not as high or expansive as the Colorado Rockies, the Wasatch is as vital to Salt Lake City now as it was to the settlers in the 1800s.

SALT LAKE CITY—Livability in the 21st Century
14

❖

Salt Lake City's tight proximity to the Wasatch Mountains affords residents a laundry list of recreation and economic benefits as well as headwaters access to an extremely reliable and pristine water source. Diligent, ongoing watershed management has ensured that the drinking water accessed by more than a million Salt Lake Valley residents is among the purest in the U.S.

SALT LAKE CITY—Livability in the 21st Century
16

Throughout the winter months the jet stream pushes storms from the Pacific Ocean across the Nevada desert into Utah where they slam into the Wasatch Mountains and release snow. What's different about this weather pattern in Utah is a phenomenon known as lake effect: just before meeting the mountains, the storms are fortified by the Great Salt Lake, which due to its salinity never freezes, creating snowfall more prolific than other mountain locales. In fact, more than 500 inches of snow accumulate in the Wasatch Mountains every winter, about 30 percent more than most other sections of the Rockies. Multiple river drainages provide 60 percent of the drinking and irrigation water used by the more than one million Salt Lake Valley residents. Eighty-five percent of Utah's population now lives along the Wasatch Range in a series of valleys known as the Wasatch Front.

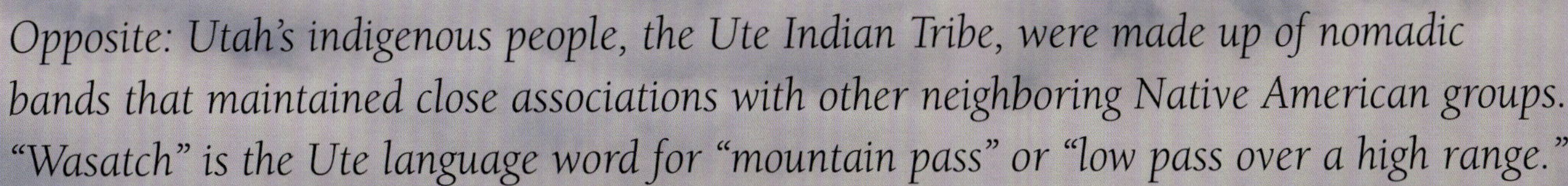

❖

Opposite: Utah's indigenous people, the Ute Indian Tribe, were made up of nomadic bands that maintained close associations with other neighboring Native American groups. "Wasatch" is the Ute language word for "mountain pass" or "low pass over a high range."

This page: Alta and Snowbird in Little Cottonwood Canyon, and Brighton and Solitude in Big Cottonwood Canyon, are among the snowiest ski and snowboard resorts in the Lower 48. All average 500 inches of snow per year, with the exception of Alta, which averages 520 inches per year.

Opposite, left: Technicolor wildflower carpets—bursting with Splitleaf Indian paintbrush, Wasatch penstemon, and Nuttall's Linanthus—are a common mid-summer sight in the canyons and drainages located just east of Salt Lake City.

Opposite, right: Tree species common to the Wasatch Mountains include ponderosa pine, Rocky Mountain Douglas-fir, subalpine fir, Engelmann spruce, quaking aspen, and Gambel oak.

Above: While not the Wasatch Mountains' tallest peak, Mount Olympus is one of the most prominent and recognizable landmarks seen from the Salt Lake Valley.

In the last several decades, however, the role the Wasatch Mountains play in Utah's thriving population has evolved well beyond exclusively watershed. Ask any transplant—or any native who's stayed put—why they have chosen Salt Lake City as home, and the mountains are likely at the top of their list. And it's no wonder. Within just a thirty-minute drive of downtown is hundreds of thousands of acres of wilderness spanning 10,000-foot peaks, alpine meadows and lush old-growth forests. Though it's a part of the larger Uinta-Wasatch-Cache National Forest, four designated wilderness areas—Mount Olympus, Twin Peaks, Lone Peak and Deseret Peak—dominate the backcountry most immediately accessible to the Salt Lake Valley. Recreation opportunities found here include skiing and snowboarding at four resorts within 15 miles of Salt Lake City: Alta, Snowbird, Brighton and Solitude. Park City's three ski and snowboard resorts—Park City Mountain Resort, Deer Valley and Canyons—are located 35 miles east of Salt Lake City along Interstate 80.

Every year hundreds of hikers and alpinists reach Mountain Olympus' craggy 9,026-foot summit by hiking the Mount Olympus Trail, a steep 3.1-mile, 4,800-foot elevation gain route from the parking area at Wasatch Boulevard.

Neffs Canyon, located on the north side of Mount Olympus, is home to one of the deepest caves in the United States. The U.S. Forest Service closed Neffs Cave several years ago due to safety concerns, however, leaving it relatively unexplored.

SALT LAKE CITY—Livability in the 21st Century

Opposite, right: Reynolds Flat, located at the base of Mill D South Fork, is a popular snowshoeing area in Big Cottonwood Canyon.

Above: Cardiac Ridge is the major dividing line between the Big and Little Cottonwood Canyons. The ridge and its associate peak, Mount Superior, are popular with backcountry skiers and are located squarely within the 11.396-acre Twin Peaks Wilderness Area.

❖

Mount Superior, an 11,000-foot peak rising from Highway 210 in Little Cottonwood Canyon, dominates the topography between the Snowbird and Alta resorts.

Pictured here is Superior's knife-like eastern ridge.

❖

Towering high above Honeycomb Canyon, is Fantasy Ridge, a legendary sidecountry area of Solitude Resort.

No lifts exist on this dramatic moraine, requiring skiers and snowboarders to hike the top and then navigate down a series of almost vertical chutes numbered 1 to 26.

Above and opposite: The Town of Alta (located around the base of Alta Ski Area) was founded in 1871 at the height of the silver mining era. A fire destroyed the town in 1878, and an avalanche took out what remained in 1885.

The canyon was relatively dormant until Alta Ski Area (pictured here) opened for business on 1939. Alta is now one of the longest continuously-operating ski areas in North America and is known throughout the world for its prolific snowfall.

SALT LAKE CITY—*Livability in the 21st Century*
28

The Wasatch Mountains are considered the western edge of the greater Rocky Mountains, and the eastern edge of the Great Basin region. Glacial sculpting made the Wasatch much more rugged and dramatic than other sections of the Rocky Mountain Range, though not as tall. Peaks along the Wasatch top out at around 11,000 feet, compared to the 13,000-foot-plus peaks in the nearby Uinta Mountains.

❖

Left and below: Little Cottonwood Canyon's distinct terrain includes broad U-shaped canyons, dramatic headwalls, hanging valleys, and steep gullies.

Opposite: Little Cottonwood's steep, north-facing glacial headwalls—including Devil's Castle, pictured here—capture every possible flake of snow from passing storms, setting the stage for what's widely regarded as the best skiing and snowboarding conditions in the world.

PART ONE
31

❖

Left: Alpenglow illuminates the Wasatch Range, as seen from Salt Lake City's Sugar House Park.

Above and right: The one-mile hike to Little Cottonwood Canyon's Secret Lake (also referred to as Cecret Lake) is a popular hiking destination throughout the summer months.

The popularity of recreating at both the resorts and the surrounding open lands spreads well beyond the winter months, however. Summer activities include hiking, camping, rock climbing and mountain biking. Boating, fishing, sailing, stand-up paddle boarding and other water-related activities are practiced frequently on several small reservoirs and rivers located throughout the Wasatch Mountains as well. All told more than two million people visit the rugged wilderness areas bordering Salt Lake City every year, contributing to Utah's thriving $12 billion per year recreation industry.

Opposite and below: Anglers flock to Big Cottonwood Canyon's Lake Mary and Silver, Blanche, and Florence Lakes,
and Lake Catherine, Twin Lakes, and White Pine and Red Pine Lakes in Little Cottonwood Canyon.

Opposite: Great Salt Lake Marina. The Great Salt Lake is the largest natural lake west of the Mississippi River and, because its only outlet is through evaporation, maintains a salinity level higher than the ocean. Popular lake activities include sailing, sea kayaking, and bird watching.

Below: Multiple reservoirs, peppered within and on both sides of the Wasatch Range, are vital caches for drinking water and irrigation, but also provide a variety of recreational opportunities including fishing, sailing, canoeing, stand-up paddle boarding, sea kayaking, swimming and waterskiing.

❖

At forty-two square miles, Antelope Island is the largest of the ten islands located within the Great Salt Lake. The Mormon pioneers established a sheep and cattle ranch on Antelope Island, named the Fielding Garr Ranch, soon after their arrival in the Salt Lake Valley in the mid-1800s. The entire island was designated a state park in 1981 and is now home to bison, a large big horn and pronghorn sheep herd, coyotes, badgers, and millions of water fowl. Antelope Island activities include bird watching, an annual balloon festival, camping, hiking, mountain biking and wildlife watching.

Opposite, left: An old truck rests at Antelope Island's Fielding Garr Ranch, one of the longest continuously operating ranches in the Western United States.

Opposite, right: Antelope Island as seen from the Great Salt Lake's south shore.

Top, left: Prairie grasslands cover much of Antelope Island making it an idea environment for the large buffalo and sheep herds residing there.

Top, right: The Wasatch Range at sunset, as seen from Antelope Island.

Above and opposite: Picnicking, trail running, hiking and resort-based attractions are just a sample of the popular Wasatch Mountains' day trips pursued in Emigration, Millcreek and Big and Little Cottonwood Canyons.

SALT LAKE CITY—Livability in the 21st Century
44

Ensuring the future of both Salt Lake City's primary water source and the state's booming recreation industry is a delicate balancing act involving city, state and federal interests. In 2012 the Utah Legislature formed the Office of Outdoor Recreation to be a voice for both outdoor recreation businesses and recreationalists. And several entities, both public and private, are working together to form the Mountain Accord, a mountain transportation plan with the goal of alleviating automobile congestion in Salt Lake City area canyons.

SALT LAKE CITY—Livability in the 21st Century

Likely directly attributable to its stone's-throw mountain proximity, in recent years Salt Lake City has earned a slew of awards and accolades, including a No. 3 and No. 4 ranking on Forbes 2012 Best Big Cities for Jobs and 2011 Best Cities for Young Professionals lists, respectively. Salt Lake City also landed a Top 20 ranking of cities responding to climate change by ICLEI-Local Governments for Sustainability in 2013; Salt Lake City is consistently ranked one of the healthiest metro areas in the United States; and in 2012 Salt Lake City was ranked America's 'gayest' city by *The Advocate* magazine. Diverse props for a city barely more than 150 years old.

❖

Opposite: Salt Lake City's climate is relatively rare in that the winters are cold and snowy, and summers are hot and dry. The valley grows lush with greenery in the spring; deep red Gambel oak trees and golden quaking aspens bring the mountains alive with color in the fall. Particularly cold storms have delivered snow to the Salt Lake Valley as early as mid-September and as late as the end of the May.

Whether it's the mountains that make Salt Lake City, or the city that has called attention to the spectacular Wasatch Range, one thing is certain: experiencing such a balanced mix of urban and outdoor sensibilities is exemplified nowhere better than Salt Lake City.

Canyon Primer

The awe-inspiring Wasatch Range runs north and south along the Salt Lake Valley, creating a tight boundary between the city's urban landscape and alpine wilderness. Shaped over millennia by water and snow, dozens of canyons bisect the mountains funneling directly into Salt Lake City proper, including:

City Creek: Once the singular water source for Salt Lake City, this bonafide urban wilderness area is now a favorite walking, hiking and cycling area just east of the State Capitol.

Emigration: The route Brigham Young took to enter the Salt Lake Valley is a popular road cycling route and home to the beloved Ruth's Café.

Parleys: Interstate 80 routes through this canyon as it makes its way east to Park City and eventually Wyoming. The paint-covered Sentinel Rock and the Iron Curtain climbing wall are both found at the canyon mouth.

Millcreek: Snowshoeing, backcountry skiing, hiking, picnicking and mountain biking are prevailing activities here. A Boy Scout camp and the romantic Log Haven Restaurant, located in a restored turn-of-the-century log cabin, are found in this canyon as well.

Canyon Primer

Big Cottonwood: This fifteen-mile-long winding canyon provides excellent hiking, biking picnicking, rock-climbing, camping and fishing in summer. The flat Silver Lake Trail (located at 8,760 feet) is a particular draw for families.The Solitude and Brighton Resorts are this canyon's most visited destinations in winter.

Little Cottonwood: This dramatic canyon is home to one of Utah's most iconic symbols—the Snowbird Tram—and Alta, which at 8,950 feet above sea level is one of Utah's highest municipalities. Skiing and snowboarding are obviously the most popular winter pursuits here (snowboarding is allowed at Snowbird only) while extensive trail systems and wildflower displays attract hikers, cyclists and campers all summer long.

Above: In 2014 the quaking aspen was designated Utah's new state tree. These resilient trees grow in the moist soil common in mountain drainages riddling the Wasatch Mountains as well as many other areas of the state. One of the world's largest living organisms is the Pando clone, a 160-acre aspen thicket located just south of Salt Lake City in Fish Lake National Forest.

❖

Moose are a common sight in the foothills and canyons above Salt Lake City.

Opposite: A moose forages in the boggy wetlands surrounding Willow Lake in Big Cottonwood Canyon.

❖

Streams and waterways located just outside of the Salt Lake City area on the backside of the Wasatch Mountains are a fly-fisherperson's dream come true. Blue Ribbon fisheries include the Jordanelle Reservoir and (pictured at left) the Middle Provo River. On land, the trails noodling throughout the Salt Lake Valley foothills and canyons are ideal terrain for hiking and, in particular, mountain biking.

In the late 1980s Peter Metcalf was looking for a place to relocate Black Diamond Equipment, Ltd, a climbing equipment company he co-founded with Patagonia, Inc., founder Yvon Chouinard. After completing a systematic search of cities and towns across the Western U.S., from Northern California and Montana to Colorado and Nevada, he found that, despite a laundry list of stereotypes and preconceived notions, Salt Lake City was this vibrant, "West Coast facing," sophisticated, small-town-feeling community with all the benefits of a much larger city. The dealmaker, however, was its location in the shadow of one of the most inspiring mountain ranges in America. Today Black Diamond Equipment, Ltd. maintains the bulk of its manufacturing in Utah and is a publically traded company. "I absolutely believe that our location has been an integral and indispensable factor in Black Diamond's success. Salt Lake City has helped define us and I am very proud of the fact that we helped define the city as well," Metcalf says.

GoPro
SPYDER

For Dan Nebecker, Bluehouse Skis co-founder, there is no better place on the planet to launch a ski company than Salt Lake City. The city's proximity to both world-class skiing and a major international airport affords Bluehouse easy access to top quality locally, domestically and internationally sourced ski building materials. And the company enjoys an abundance of extremely talented local skiers who double and often triple as athletes, graphic artists, product testers, web developers, ski builders and a top-notch customer service team. "I would be lying if I claimed that we chose this place. This place chose us. All of the owners of Bluehouse Skis were born and raised near downtown. However, if I had the option to go back and start over, I would definitely choose Salt Lake City to be the home of our company," Nebecker says.

❖

Dan Nebecker,
Bluehouse Skis co-founder.

"In other cities people take two hours to get to work,"
says Carl Fisher, Save Our Canyons executive director.
"Drive two hours from Salt Lake—or even just 30
minutes—and you can be in the middle of nowhere."
Born and raised along the Wasatch Mountain foothills,
Fisher began volunteering with Save Our Canyons—a half-
century-old Salt Lake City-based non-profit organization
dedicated to "protecting the beauty and wildness of the
Wasatch canyons, mountains, and foothills"—in 2001.
Since then Fisher has emerged as one of the most vocal
proponents for protecting the wilderness just beyond Salt
Lake City's borders, not only in terms of the environment,
but in the name of recreationalists and drinking water
quality as well. "Cities and counties have been fairly
receptive to conservation. It's those at the state and
federal level, removed from what we have right here, that
are a little tougher to convince," Fisher says. Save Our
Canyons achievements include designation of the Lone Peak
Wilderness Area in 1978, followed by the Twin Peaks and
Mount Olympus designations in 1984 and most recently,
maintaining public attention for the Wasatch Wilderness
and Watershed Protection Act.

Carl Fisher, Save Our Canyons
executive director.

SALT LAKE CITY—Livability in the 21st Century

Part 2

Sum of its Parts

Utah has had the good fortune of steady growth and a strong economy from virtually the moment the last golden spike was driven into the Transcontinental Railroad at Promontory Point in 1869. But over the last decade or so, Salt Lake City in particular has evolved from a slightly sedate, homogenous professional center deserted after 6 p.m. to a thriving cosmopolitan vortex where people live, recreate and enjoy events, arts and culture. Some credit the 2002 Olympic Winter Games for Salt Lake City's Cinderella story. A more likely catalyst is the state and city's ongoing dedication to infrastructure investment.

By the time the Olympics arrived in Salt Lake in February 2002, the city's 150-year-old utilities were replaced, two light rail lines built and the state's main highway artery, Interstate-15, expanded. More significant, however, are the projects completed since the Games: four additional light rail lines with two more on the way; a commuter rail line running along the Wasatch Front from Ogden to Provo; the architecturally stunning Salt Lake City Main Library building and Library Square; an extensive bicycle lane network and GREENbike bicycle share program; the Sugar House Streetcar; and the Salt Lake City Public Safety Building, the country's first net-zero (generates as much energy as it uses) law enforcement building in the country.

Arguably the biggest project to grace downtown Salt Lake City not only in the last decade, but last half century, is City Creek Center. This mixed use development, funded en total by the Church of Jesus Christ of Latter-day Saints, features an upscale open-air shopping center with a retractable glass roof, swanky office and residential building complex, a two-story fountain and simulated creek stocked with fish and lined with trees and shrubs reminiscent, of course, of the original City Creek that once ran through downtown. According to the CBRE's Economic Benchmark Report of 2013, City Creek Center has added 2,000 jobs and brought more than 16 million visitors into downtown and helped downtown retail sales increase by 36 percent, or $209 million, in 2012. In addition more than 125 new businesses have opened in downtown Salt Lake City since 2009, and residency has jumped 35 percent since 2010.

Opposite: City Creek Center (foreground, left) is a shopping, residential and office center spanning three blocks in downtown Salt Lake City. Temple Square, home to the Salt Lake City Temple and the Mormon worldwide headquarters, is located one block west of City Creek Center.

Above: More than 150 miles of bicycle lanes crisscross Salt Lake City proper allowing both recreation and transportation in the urban core and city neighborhoods, as well as seamless access to bike paths and lanes in adjacent cities and communities. May is Utah's official Bike Month, but cycling-centric events populate the calendar year-round, including June's Road Respect Festival and the Tour of Utah pro-cyclist stage race in August.

SALT LAKE CITY—Livability in the 21st Century

And there's even more to come. The city and county have joined forces to fund construction of the 2,500-seat, $114 million George S. and Dolores Doré Eccles Theater, slated for completion in 2016; a movement is afoot to build a 1,000-room convention center hotel; and another 1,000 condos and apartments are expected to appear in the downtown core in the next few years.

Though the Wasatch Range, located on Salt Lake
City's eastern edge, is most typically associated with
the city's incredible mountain access, the Oquirrh
Mountains frame the city more distantly to the
west. Wildlife abounds in the Oquirrhs, including
healthy populations of deer, mountain lions,
butterflies and bald eagles. Popular hiking trails
are found in Yellow Fork and Butterfield Canyons.
This mountain range is best known, however,
for the rich mineral deposits discovered here and
consequent construction of what is now the world's
largest open pit mine, the Bingham Canyon Mine.

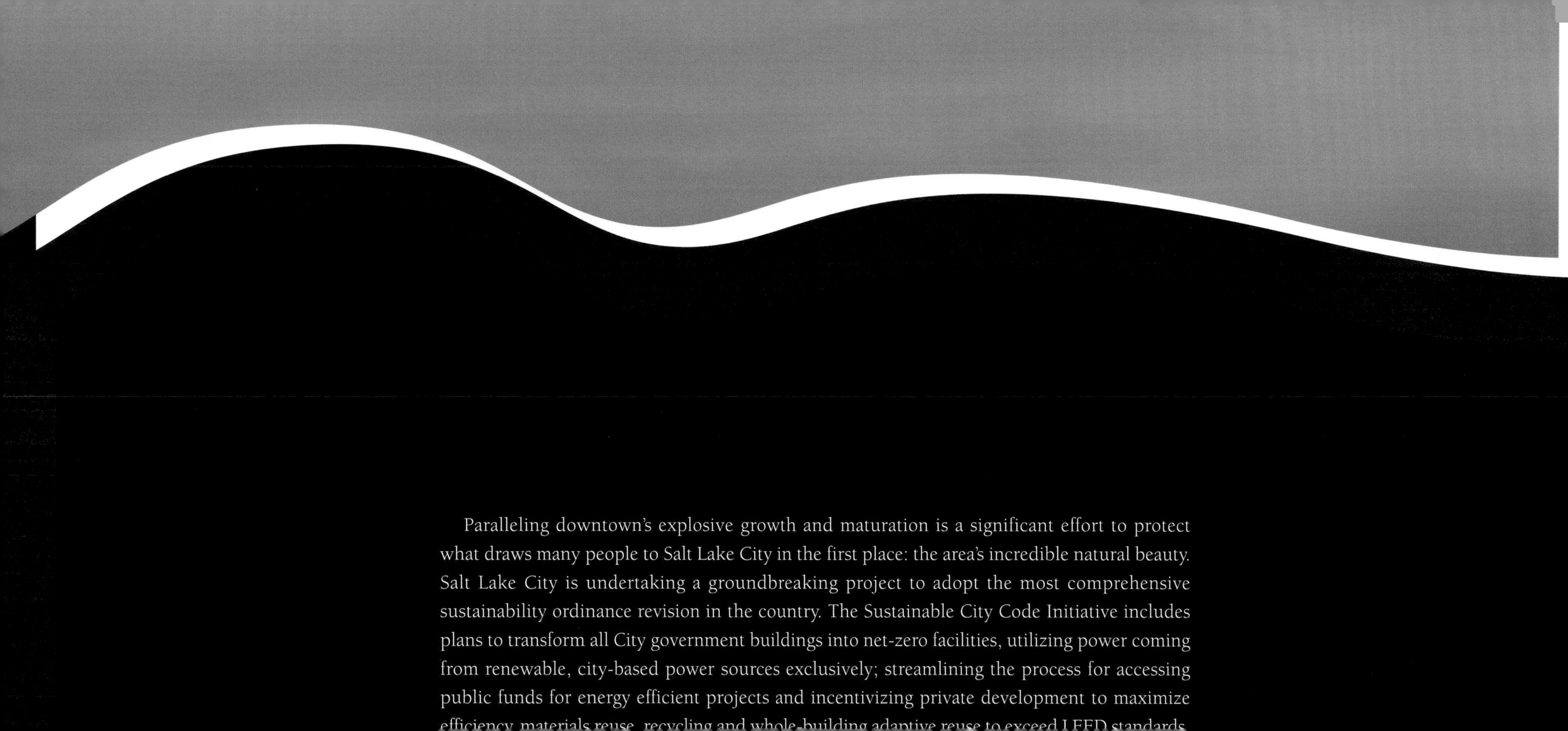

Paralleling downtown's explosive growth and maturation is a significant effort to protect what draws many people to Salt Lake City in the first place: the area's incredible natural beauty. Salt Lake City is undertaking a groundbreaking project to adopt the most comprehensive sustainability ordinance revision in the country. The Sustainable City Code Initiative includes plans to transform all City government buildings into net-zero facilities, utilizing power coming from renewable, city-based power sources exclusively; streamlining the process for accessing public funds for energy efficient projects and incentivizing private development to maximize efficiency materials reuse, recycling and whole-building adaptive reuse to exceed LEED standards.

Salt Lake City's diversity, healthy economy and relative low cost of living have helped shape a variety of micro-communities surrounding Salt Lake City proper, each with its own unique look and personality. The Avenues/Capitol Hill area is characterized by a mix of colorful Victorian and mid-century modern homes, eclectic cafes, mining-era mansions and the Cathedral of the Madeleine, completed in 1909 as the mother church for the Salt Lake City Catholic Diocese. To the west, Rose Park, Poplar Grove and Glendale are the heart of Salt Lake City's diverse immigrant communities, reflected in the well-cared for International Peace Gardens and Jordan River Parkway walking and cycling path. Students, professors and high-tech professionals mingle in the neighborhoods surrounding the University of Utah, an area home to some of the city's most popular attractions including This is the Place Heritage Park, Red Butte Garden & Arboretum, the Natural History Museum of Utah and the Hogle Zoo. Finally, the city's furthest afield neighborhoods, Harvard/Yale, 9th and 9th (named for its 900 South and 900 East locale), Highland Park and Sugar House are each havens for independent restaurants, cafes and boutiques attracting a hip 20- and 30-something demographic residing in the quaint Frank Lloyd Wright-inspired bungalows that are the norm here.

In 1888 Salt Lake City municipal government donated twenty acres of land for the construction of the State Capitol, a parcel then known as Arsenal Hill for its previous function as a private munitions storage area.

PART TWO
79

In 1957 construction plans for the State Office Building (located just north of the capitol and pictured here) began in earnest in response to the state's explosive growth. The office building was completed and dedicated in 1961.

Utah architect Richard K. A. Kletting won a national design competition issued by the Utah State Legislature in 1911 to design the Utah State Capitol Building. Construction of the Neoclassical revival, Corinthian style structure began in 1912 and was completed in 1916. The building was added to the National Register of Historic Places in 1978. A major restoration and seismic upgrade project was completed in 2008, allowing the building to withstand up to a 7.3 magnitude earthquake. A variety of artifacts and artwork are on display within the Capitol and throughout its sweeping grounds.

Within a ten-mile radius of downtown, residents can affordably choose from a variety of living options from a warehouse walkup within walking distance of restaurants, public transit, bars, theaters, shopping and museums to an A-frame on the end of a dirt road at 8,000 feet above sea level; a restored 100-year-old Victorian home with a picket fence to wide open, big-sky horse property. But what all 186,000 Salt Lake City residents get to enjoy, regardless of what part of the city they choose to call home, is the benefits of big-city living sans the big-city hassles.

Though Salt Lake City was founded by Latter-day Saint pioneers in 1847 to be the "New Zion," the city's population quickly diversified. Over the last century Salt Lake City has emerged as a modern secular city, populated by people and faiths from around the world.

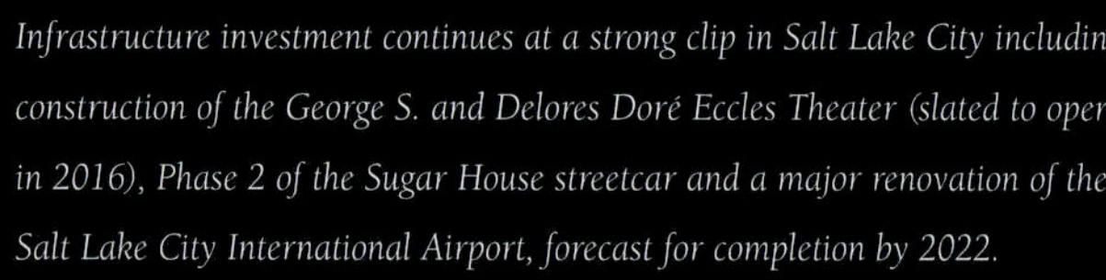

Infrastructure investment continues at a strong clip in Salt Lake City including: construction of the George S. and Delores Doré Eccles Theater (slated to open in 2016), Phase 2 of the Sugar House streetcar and a major renovation of the Salt Lake City International Airport, forecast for completion by 2022.

PART TWO
93

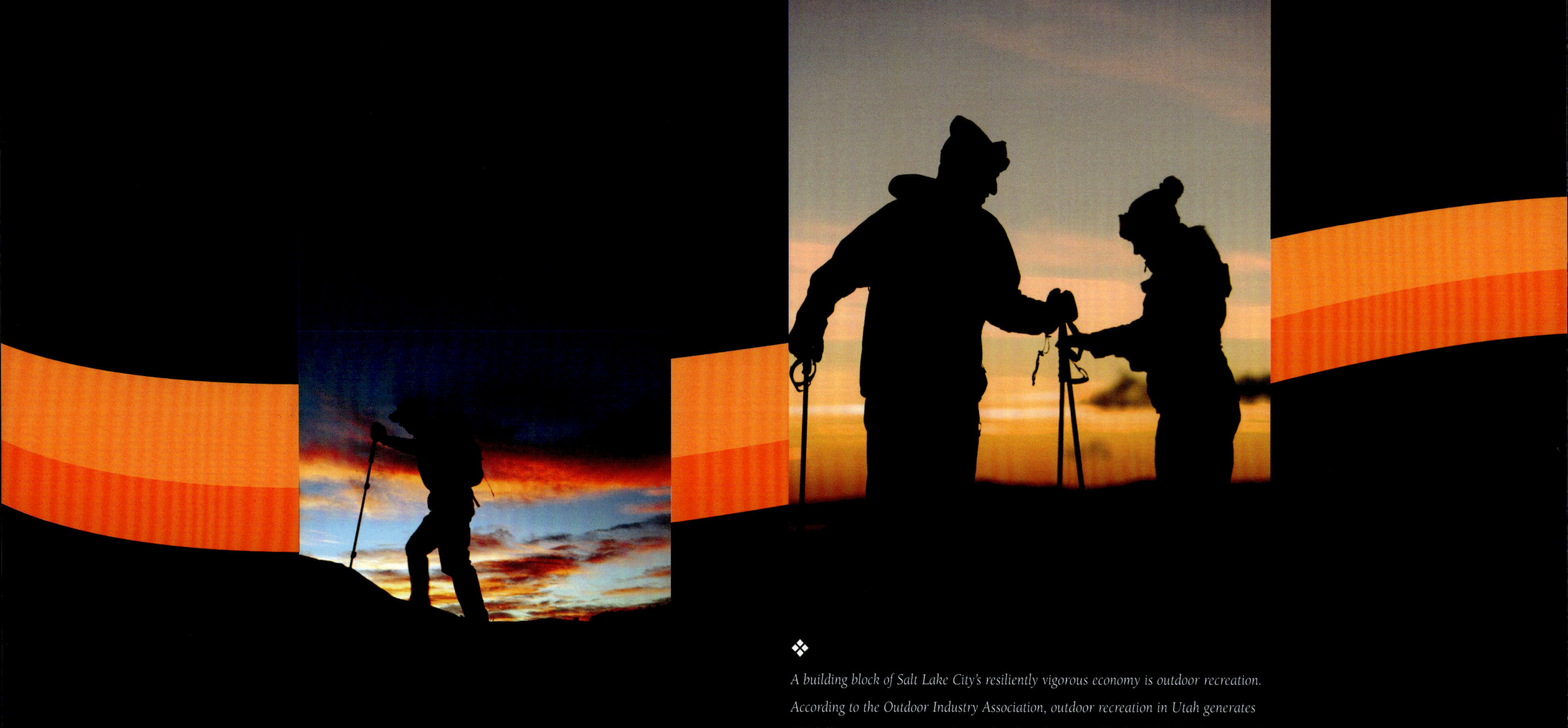

❖

A building block of Salt Lake City's resiliently vigorous economy is outdoor recreation.

According to the Outdoor Industry Association, outdoor recreation in Utah generates

$12 billion in consumer spending and is directly responsible for 122,000 jobs across the state.

SALT LAKE CITY—Livability in the 21st Century

❖

A likely factor of Salt Lake City residents' dedication to getting outside is climate: four distinct seasons occur in Salt Lake City, with a cold, snowy winter, a hot, dry summer, and comfortable, relatively wet transition periods, making the area an ideal venue for a variety of outdoor pursuits. In addition, temperature differences between the mountains and valleys are very distinct, typically varying between 15 to 20 degrees making it possible, for example, to ski mountain powder in the morning and bike or hit the links in the valley in the afternoon.

❖

The University of Utah is a highly regarded research institution and the state's flagship university, offering more than 100 undergraduate majors and 92 graduate degree programs. The U.'s football team, the Utes, won the Fiesta Bowl in 2005 and the Sugar Bowl in 2009. Opening and closing ceremonies for the 2002 Olympic Winter Games were held in the U.'s Rice-Eccles Stadium (pictured right in the foreground).

PART TWO
99

The Salt Lake Valley was formed by Lake Bonneville, a prehistoric pluvial lake existing about 14,500 years ago that once covered much of the eastern Great Basin region. The Great Salt Lake and Utah Lake (found farther south in Utah County) are remnants of this ancient body of water, as are the benches or shelf-like plateaus common along the Wasatch Range foothills.

The Salt Lake City & County Building has served as the seat of city government since 1894, and is the city's finest example of Richardsonian Romanesque architecture.

The building sits between State Street, 200 East, 400 South and 500 South on a block called Washington Square (named for George Washington), site of the Mormon pioneers' original encampment in 1847.

❖

Featuring sweeping windows, a public rooftop garden, a spiral grand staircase and three glass elevators, the main branch of the Salt Lake City Library (pictured here to the right of the Salt Lake City & County Building) was designed by Moshe Safdie and Associates and Salt Lake City's VCBO Architecture, and is one of the city's most architecturally unique buildings.

SALT LAKE CITY—*Livability in the 21st Century*

PART TWO
107

❖

The Salt Lake City Public Safety Building was completed in 2013 and is the first public building in the U.S. to achieve a Net-Zero Energy Emissions ranking; the building produces at least as much emissions-free energy as it consumes. Utah artist Greg Ragland created the striking bronze hands sculpture, entitled To Serve and Protect.

UTA
109
109
UTA

Salt Lake City is developing public transportation more quickly than any other city in North America.

Existing public transit options include the GREENbike bicycle share stations, an extensive local and express bus network,

the TRAX light rail system and FrontRunner commuter rail line.

S-SUGARHOUSE
70
FOR YOUR SAFETY
STAY OFF TRACKS

THE SUGAR HOUSE STREETCAR

Moving toward the future with a nod to the past

Through a partnership between the Federal Department of Transportation, Salt Lake City and South Salt Lake municipalities and the Utah Transit Authority, the $37 million Sugar House Streetcar—dubbed the "S Line"—launched service in December 2013 along a two-mile route between the TRAX Central Pointe Station at 2100 South and 200 West to 2250 South McClelland Avenue (1050 East) in the Sugar House commercial district. The line is reminiscent of streetcars that played a key role in developing Salt Lake City's suburban communities in the early 1900s. The Sugar House Streetcar and accompanying walking and bicycle route greenway not only provide convenient public transit between South Salt Lake, downtown and Sugar House, but also represent a critical link for the Parleys Trail, connecting the Bonneville Shoreline Trail on the east and the Jordan River Parkway on the west.

The Salt Lake City International Airport is serviced by eight

airlines and their affiliates, including Delta Airlines,

for which the airport serves as a major hub.

Salt Lake City native Ken Sanders, owner of Ken Sanders Rare Books, became a bookman while still in high school in the 1960s, when he started a comic and fantasy and science fiction mail order business. In 1975 he co-created the Cosmic Aeroplane Books and Records shop out of the original Cosmic Aeroplane head shop in Salt Lake City's 9th and 9th neighborhood, which quickly became a gathering place for the city's burgeoning avant garde. Sanders founded Dream Garden press in 1980, publisher of many Utah-centric tomes over the years, including the R. Crumb illus-trated edition of Edward Abbey's *The Monkey Wrench Gang*. In 1990, Sanders founded Ken Sanders Rare Books, which has since evolved into a critical component of the city's flourishing literary arts community. "Salt Lake has a vibrant and diverse arts community that in the past and now continues to produce a body of work that we can be rightfully proud of. The depth of cultural and artistic talent here lends more room to breathe here in the city than the sparsely populated geography that surrounds us," Sanders says.

❖

Ken Sanders, owner of
Ken Sanders Rare Books.

Kyong An Millar,
owner of Koo de Ker.

Having worked in shops and boutiques throughout high school and college, by the time Utah native Kyong An Millar opened her first Koo de Ker (French for being smitten or to have a crush) location in Utah County in 2001, she was a retail veteran. So, ten years ago, when her life began to gravitate toward Salt Lake City she knew immediately where to move her hip yet affordable fashion forward boutique: Salt Lake City's thriving 9th and 9th neighborhood. "I wanted to be somewhere close to downtown but in an easily accessible, walkable neighborhood," An Millar says. And though business was a bit challenging during the last decade's economic crisis, An Millar believes the downturn was actually good for independent retailers. "It made people really think about their community and where they spend their money. I don't think it was any kind of coincidence that that was when the Buy Local movement really took off in Salt Lake," she says. With ample, easily accessible parking and friendly, communal vibe, An Millar can not imagine operating Koo de Ker anywhere else. "We have a great local following but also see a lot of visitors as well," she says. "Getting out into neighborhoods like 9th and 9th is a great way to see the true flavor of any town, but Salt Lake in particular."

Left to right: Charlie and Dwight Butler, brothers and co-owners/operators of Wasatch Touring.

Dwight Butler, co-owner of the Avenues neighborhood's iconic backcountry skiing, camping and kayaking store Wasatch Touring, moved to Utah from Minnesota in 1972 after spending a night interlodged at Alta. (On rare occasions when storms and avalanche danger are extreme, Little Cottonwood Canyon guests are asked to stay indoors, a la interlodge. Not nearly as bad as it sounds when you're skiing waist deep powder before anyone else the next day.) But it was Salt Lake City's mountain convenience that converted him from a visitor to a resident. "Based on conditions you can decide in the morning to ski at one of the resorts, go for a quick tour in the backcountry, get out the skate skis and hit a groomed track or even ice climb. And you can be doing any of those things within thirty minutes of taking off from downtown," Butler says.

PART TWO

119

OPPOSITE: PHOTOGRAPH COURTESY OF DAVE BREWER
AND VISIT SALT LAKE.

LEFT: PHOTOGRAPH COURTESY OF EMILY SARGENT
AND VISIT SALT LAKE.

Urban Aesthetic

Awkwardly cool may best encapsulate Salt Lake City's unique urban vibe, a personality punctuated by a thriving local music scene, diverse cultural offerings and year-round events. Rare are the cities that pack as many attractions into such a tight and easily navigable radius as Salt Lake City.

❖

Red Butte Garden is a 100-acre botanical garden on the campus of the University of Utah. The garden's amphitheater is a popular concert venue, hosting regional, national and international bands and soloists throughout the summer months.

PHOTOGRAPH COURTESY OF SEAN BUCKLEY AND VISIT SALT LAKE.

SALT LAKE CITY—*Livability in the 21st Century*

❖

Concerts, festivals, and a holiday market are just a few of the events and activities held at the Gallivan Center Plaza, located in the heart of downtown Salt Lake City.

PHOTOGRAPH COURTESY OF STEVE GREENWOOD AND VISIT SALT LAKE.

Evidence of Salt Lakers' love for art in all forms is strongest throughout the downtown proper. The Utah Museum of Contemporary Art [UMOCA] is Utah's premiere venue for contemporary visual art and was recognized as the state's best museum in 2011. Edgy modern exhibitions are held regularly at downtown newcomer, the Central Utah Art Center [CUAC]. Connections between art and science are fascinatingly made at The Leonardo, a museum brimming with dozens of kid-friendly interactive exhibits and compelling traveling exhibits.

Located slightly outside of the city's urban center on the campus of the University of Utah is the Utah Museum of Fine Arts [UMFA], Utah's primary cultural resource for global visual arts, serving a dual role as a university and state art museum. Also on the U. of U. campus is the Natural History Museum of Utah [NHMU], housed in a stunning LEED Gold-certified building completed in 2011. The stepped design building pays a lovely homage to the mountainside on which it resides while inside ten themed galleries allow visitors to explore nature and science in creative and unexpected ways. NHMU is also a working laboratory; observation galleries allow visitors to observe archaeologists examining and studying actual dinosaur bones and other artifacts.

Opposite: Natural History Museum of Utah at the Rio Tinto Center, The University of Utah.

PART THREE
125

❖

The interactive fountains draw children young and old to Liberty Park, Salt Lake City's second-largest city park, located at 600 East and 900 South. Facilities here are expansive and include an aviary, a large pond with paddleboats, the Chase Home Museum of Utah Folk Art, concessions, multiple playgrounds, tennis and bocce ball courts and a public swimming pool.

Opposite: Abravanel Hall is acoustically engineered to deliver the pure sound of the Utah Symphony.
PHOTOGRAPH COURTESY OF UTAH SYMPHONY | UTAH OPERA.

Below: World renowned Music Director Thierry Fischer conducts the Utah Symphony—one of only fifteen full-time orchestras in the country.
PHOTOGRAPH COURTESY OF UTAH SYMPHONY | UTAH OPERA.

The breadth of support for visual arts in Salt Lake City is matched only by backing for the theater, dance and music. Few other comparably sized cities in the U.S. and around the world can boast not only a local symphony, but ballet and opera as well—all three of which are recognized both nationally and internationally. Abravanel Hall is home to the venerable Utah Symphony, and Ballet West and the Utah Opera perform at the historic Capitol Theatre—arts organizations recognized both across the country and around the world. But the options certainly do not end there. The cutting edge alternative Plan-B Theatre Company, two modern dance companies and the Gina Bauchaur International Piano Foundation are among the performing arts organizations housed at the Rose Wagner Center for the Performing Arts. Both renowned plays and *Saturday's Voyeur*—an annual, good-natured spoof on conservative Utah culture—are presented at the Salt Lake Acting Company. And perhaps Salt Lake City's best-known performers, the Mormon Tabernacle Choir, perform regularly in both the Tabernacle and the Conference Center at Temple Square.

Ballet West boasts a rich and varied repertoire, elegant and versatile artists and an American style and legacy that is as dynamic, expansive and unexpected as the Rocky Mountain region it represents.

ARTISTS OF BALLET WEST PHOTOGRAPH BY LUKE ISLEY.

The Salt Lake City Arts Council's annual Living Traditions Festival, held at the City & County Building in downtown Salt Lake City, celebrates the city's plentiful and diverse folk and ethnic arts.

PHOTOGRAPHS COURTESY OF DAVEBREWERPHOTO.COM.

Opposite and above: Vibrant residential neighborhoods play host to eclectic local businesses that epitomize Salt Lake City's character. The 9th & 9th area and the Granary District are just two of the active, small business nodes that are a boon to locals and great "finds" for visitors.

PHOTOGRAPHS COURTESY OF LANCE TYRELL.

Because of its proximity to the mountains, many locals and visitors think of Salt Lake City
as one of the country's largest ski towns, an attitude that's not exclusively a state of mind.
According to Ski Utah, the marketing arm of the Utah Ski & Snowboard Association, skiing
contributes $1.29 billion to the state's economy and is directly related to more than 20,000 jobs.

SALT LAKE CITY — Livability in the 21st Century
138

Seven ski and snowboard resorts, spanning 18,000 acres of terrain and more than 100 lifts, are located within a thirty minute drive of downtown Salt Lake City.

The same 500 inches-plus of snow that falls on the Salt Lake City area mountains in the winter is the basis for a variety of recreational pursuits at lakes and reservoirs in the summer including water skiing, sailing, fishing and boating. Mountain snows also serve as Salt Lake City's primary drinking water source, which is widely touted as one of the purest in the U.S.

PART THREE
141

SALT LAKE CITY—Livability in the 21st Century
144

SALT LAKE CITY—Livability in the 21st Century
146

❖

The Wasatch Range comes alive in mid-summer with greenery, wildlife and lush carpets of wildflowers. Hiking, trail running and cycling are just a few of the ways Salt Lakers take advantage of the mountains in the warm weather months.

PART THREE
149

The Days of '47 Rodeo is just one of the festivities held on Pioneer Day (July 24) to commemorate the Mormon pioneers' arrival in the Salt Lake Valley in 1847.

Utah's newest performing arts venue is the George S. and Dolores Doré Eccles Theater. Designed by renowned architect Pelli Clarke Pelli Architects, the 2,500-seat, state-of-the-art theater will open to audiences drawn from across the Intermountain West in 2016. Far beyond being just another performance venue, the state-of-the-art theater is designed to enhance the cultural and economic vitality of the region by attracting first-run touring Broadway shows and other nationally prominent music, comedy and family entertainment acts.

Events are another vital part of Salt Lake City's vibrant personae. Visitors from around the world flock to downtown during the holidays to shop, attend Ballet West's annual presentation of *The Nutcracker* and to view stunning light displays at The Gateway, City Creek Center and Temple Square. The Downtown Alliance kicks off each year with EVE, a three-day New Year's celebration packed with music, theater and dining events held throughout the city's urban core. Though the Sundance Film Festival helped put Utah's most famous ski town, Park City, on the international map, Salt Lake City plays an important role in this international event as well, hosting the festival premier at Abravanel Hall every year as well as dozens of screenings at the Salt Lake Film Society's Broadway Cinema downtown and at the Tower Theatre in the 9th and 9th neighborhood.

Events and organizations celebrating the Wasatch Mountains include Snowbird's annual
Oktoberfest, the Wasatch Wildflower Festival, Solitude's Wasatch Mountain Table dining event,
the Cottonwood Canyons Foundation, Alta Community Enrichment and the Wasatch Mountain Club.

PART THREE
153

PART THREE
155

Though winter and summer in the Salt Lake City area mountains receive the lion's share of attention, autumn is one of the most scenic times of the year to visit the area's higher altitudes. A favorite fall drive is through Big Cottonwood Canyon and over Guardsman Pass into Park City.

PART THREE
157

PART THREE
159

Salt Lake City's event schedule reaches its crescendo in the summer months with a series of festivals, concerts and activities filling every weekend from mid-May through mid-October. The Downtown Farmer's Market features produce, meat, cheese and baked goods purveyors from across the state, as well as a variety of food vendors, musicians and artisans every Saturday morning and Tuesday evening in Pioneer Park. For more than thirty years, Twilight Concert Series' organizers at the Salt Lake Arts Council have featured both emerging and established artists as part of their popular (and at $5 a ticket, very affordable) weekly summer concerts. Held on the third weekend of June every year, the Utah Arts Festival is one of the most visited and impressive displays of visual art in the Intermountain West. Cultural celebrations like the Living Traditions Festival and Greek Festival are multi-day, multi-sensory explorations of Utah's various ethnicities. And Pioneer Day, held every year on July 24, commemorates Utah's pioneer beginnings with parades, athletic events, fireworks and a rodeo. Other popular summertime events include Snowbird's Oktoberfest and the Tour of Utah, dubbed America's toughest cycling race.

PART THREE
16

Salt Lake City's mid-country location and well-educated work force has helped it maintain one
of the vigorous economies in the country. In fact, in 2013 Forbes ranked Salt Lake City
as the tenth happiest place in the nation to work, and the third best city for jobs.

❖

Salt Lake City boasts one of the healthiest populations in the country and in 2010, Parenting magazine listed it fourth in the top 10 'Best in Economy' cities for its short commutes and abundance of desirable jobs.

Riding shotgun to Salt Lake's vibrant arts and events offerings is an exploding culinary scene. Eateries like Forage, Pago and The Copper Onion have not only made headlines here in Utah, but have also garnered unprecedented national attention. Salt Lake City nightlife received a much-needed revamp in 2009 when Utah lawmakers finally abandoned pain-in-the-backside membership laws. This fresh liberalism has given rise to a variety of new downtown nightlife options including the Beer Bar, Copper Commons, Beerhive Pub, The Rest and Bar X.

Opposite: A diverse assortment of restaurants populate downtown Salt Lake City and its surrounding neighborhoods. And despite widespread misconceptions about Utah liquor laws, it's as easy to get a drink in Salt Lake City as it is to order a meal.

It is indeed the mountains that attract
people from across the country and around the world.
But once here, Salt Lake City's rich arts, culture, dining and nightlife
is what makes many transplants call Utah's capital city home.

PHOTOGRAPH COURTESY OF VISIT SALT LAKE.

GREYHOUND
AMTRAK
TRAX
FRONTRUNNER
TRAX
FRONTRUNNER
SALT LAKE
CENTRAL
250 South 600 West
GREENbike
B
290 South 600 West
@ The Intermodal Hub
B
station
selecthealth
GREENbike
selecthealth
08615
FrontRunner

In 2010 Salt Lake City was awarded Silver-level Bicycle Friendly Community Status and in 2012 was ranked the twenty-sixth most bike-friendly city in America by *Bicycling* magazine. With all the recent investment in cycling infrastructure over the last several years it's easy to see why. Under Mayor Ralph Becker's administration, funding for bikeways was increased tenfold leading to fifty new bike-lane miles and green, shared lanes downtown. As a result, ridership rose 27 percent from 2010 to 2011. And then in 2012 a group of public and private partners launched the GREENbike bicycle share program. Different from a rental, GREENbike allows anyone to use the distinguishable green bicycles parked at various stations in the downtown area as many times as they like for a small fee. Reception for GREENbike exceeded all expectations. In the first six weeks of operation, 100 bicycles at ten stations made 6,000 trips, a rate outpacing a similar program in Boulder, Colorado. For more information about Salt Lake City bike paths and GREENbike, visit bikeslc.com.

Though Utah as a whole is conservative, it is also
very inclusive. The 2010 Census ranked Salt Lake City
No. 3 for gay-couple households in mid-sized U.S. cities.
One of the state's largest and most well attended annual
events is the Utah Pride Festival, highlighted by the
Gay Pride Parade (pictured here).

PHOTOGRAPH COURTESY OF GRACE CROSBY AND VISIT SALT LAKE.

Brandie Balken,
Equality Utah executive director.

High school is where Brandie Balken first began to develop her penchant for advocacy. Homelessness, food insecurity and the environment where among her early causes. Then in 1996 Balken moved to Salt Lake City and began to shift her focus to LGBT issues. Now, as executive director for Equality Utah, one of the state's most well-known and respected human rights organizations, Balken spends her days working to achieve full equality for all Utahns regardless of their sexual orientation or gender identity. Equality Utah is currently focusing on employment and housing non-discrimination, at both the local and state levels, as well as bullying prevention and relationship recognition. "Salt Lake is a wonderful place to live, and leads the state in fair treatment of LGBT residents. I think people are drawn to Salt Lake City because it has a rich and vibrant culture and is ever increasing in diversity. People are often surprised at how large and active the gay and transgender community is here. While Utah is a very conservative state, Salt Lake is definitely a progressive city," Balken says.

'Institution' is a moniker not often used to describe a restaurant, but in the case of Lucy Cardenas' Red Iguana, the shoe fits. Lured by the promise of work in the Kennecott Utah Copper Mine and good quality of life, the Cardenas family moved to Salt Lake City from San Francisco in 1965. Lucy's parents—Maria and Ramon, Sr.,—opened and closed two restaurants before launching the Red Iguana in 1985. Fueled by the unique combination of Maria's irresistible riffs on traditional Mexican cuisine and her brother Ramon, Jr.'s edgy personality, the Red Iguana evolved into a place where locals and visitors from all walks of life gather to enjoy a satisfying slice of life unique to Salt Lake City. And though Lucy left Salt Lake City for Los Angeles for a brief time, she and husband Bill Coker are back, proudly carrying on the Red Iguana tradition. They operate the Red Iguana at the eatery's iconic original location at 736 West North Temple, as well as at locations just a couple blocks away at Red Iguana 2 (866 West South Temple) and at Taste of Red Iguana downtown in the City Creek Center. "My parents loved the energetic, urban feel of being in the North Temple area and I do too," Cardenas says. "I work every day to honor the legacy my parents built."

Appendix

1800s

1824	Jim Bridger discovers the Great Salt Lake
1841	Captain John Bartleson leads settlers across Utah to California
1843	John C. Fremont and Kit Carson explore the Great Basin
1847	Brigham Young and Mormon pioneers arrive in Salt Lake Valley and establish Great Salt Lake City
1850	Utah becomes U.S. territory
1850	University of Utah founded
1853	Construction begins on Salt Lake City LDS Temple
1857-58	Utah War over polygamy
1861	Telegraph service begins
1863	Gold and silver is discovered in the Wasatch Mountains
1868	'Great' dropped from Salt Lake City's name
1869	Transcontinental railroad completed at Promontory Point
1870	Utah Central Railroad completed allowing rail service from Transcontinental Railroad to downtown Salt Lake City
1870	Utah Territory gives women the right to vote
1873	Polygamy outlawed by Congress
1882	Salt Lake City opens Liberty Park
1890	LDS Church issues Manifesto ending polygamy
1892	Salt Lake City LDS Temple completed
1896	Utah becomes 45th state and Salt Lake City is named state capitol
1896	First football game between the University of Utah and Brigham Young Academy (Later renamed Brigham Young University

1900s

1902	The Salt Lake Collegiate Institute is renamed Westminster College
1906	Copper mining begins in Bingham Canyon
1914	Auto racing starts at the Bonneville Salt Flats
1929	Mormon Tabernacle Choir begins weekly performance radio broadcast, *Music and the Spoken Word*
1930	Utah Ski Club makes first Salt Lake City Winter Olympics bid
1939	Alta Ski Area opens
1941	Streetcar service discontinued
1942	University of Utah Board of Regents approves four-year medical school
1948	Salt Lake Vocation School opens, precursor to Salt Lake Community College
1965	The 220-bed, $15.6 million University Medical Center opens
1979	The NBA Jazz team moves from New Orleans to Salt Lake City
1983	Great Salt Lake floods northern Utah
1992	The Downtown Alliance launches the Downtown Farmer's Market
1995	Salt Lake City wins bid to host the 2002 Olympic Winter Games
1996	Utah celebrates 100th birthday of statehood
1999	Tornado hits downtown Salt Lake City causing more than $100 million in damages
1999	Utah Transit Authority completes first light rail line from Salt Lake City to Sandy

2000s

2002	Olympic Winter Games held in Salt Lake City
2003	New Salt Lake City Main Library completed
2008	Utah State Capitol seismic retrofit and restoration completed
2009	Utah lawmakers eliminate Private Club laws at bars and taverns
2013	Salt Lake City launches GREENbike bicycle share program
2013	Salt Lake City Public Safety Building is completed
2013	Sugar House Streetcar line is completed
2014	Ground broken on construction of the George S. and Dolores Doré Eccles Theater (slated to open in 2016)

Salt Lake City Partners

Profiles of businesses, organizations and families
that have contributed to the development
and economic base of Salt Lake City

Quality of Life 181

The Marketplace 209

Building a Greater Salt Lake City 267

Quality of Life

Healthcare providers, school districts, universities
and other institutions that contribute to the
quality of life in Salt Lake City

Intermountain Healthcare 182
University of Utah Health Care 184
Weber State University...188
ARUP Laboratories 190
SelectHealth® 192
Judge Memorial Catholic High School..194
Canvas by Instructure 196
The Church of Jesus Christ of Latter-day Saints...198
Davis Hospital and Medical Center
    Jordan Valley Medical Center 200
Pioneer Valley Hospital
    Salt Lake Regional Medical Center 201
Hoopes Vision 202
The McGillis School 203
Utah Transit Authority 204
Western Governors University 205
Salt Lake City...206
Visit Salt Lake 207

Intermountain Healthcare

Right: Intermountain Healthcare's Dr. John Carlquist, PhD, participated in the CARDIoGRAM study, an international effort to identify genetic markers associated with coronary artery disease.

Below: Intermountain Healthcare maintains an unwavering focus on improving clinical quality, resulting in fewer medical complications, readmissions, faster recoveries, and reduced healthcare costs.

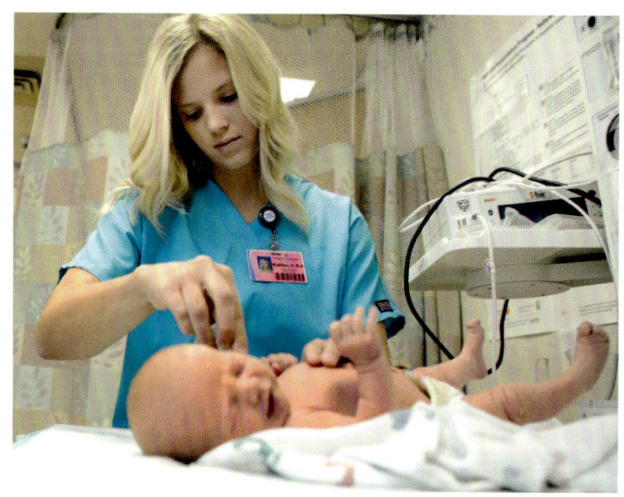

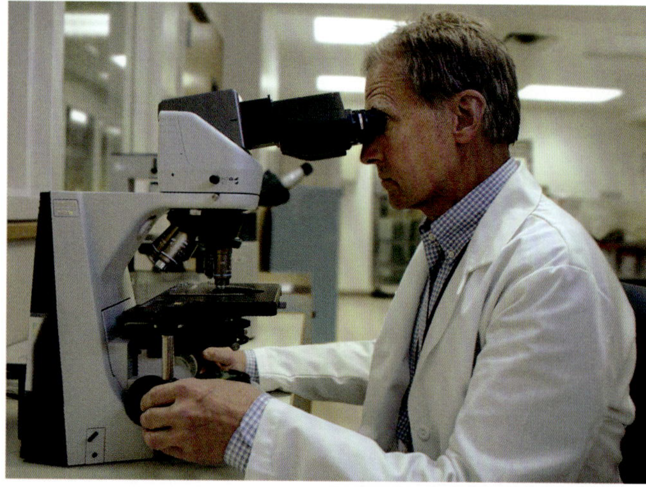

Since its inception in 1975, nonprofit Intermountain Healthcare has provided high-quality healthcare to residents across the Intermountain West. Intermountain employs more than 33,000 people, serving patients at 22 hospitals and more than 185 clinics. In addition, Intermountain owns or financially supports 18 community clinics serving uninsured and low-income patients. Intermountain also operates SelectHealth, a health insurance company providing coverage to more than 550,000 members. Intermountain is governed by a twenty-member board of trustees and more than 400 other trustees who serve on hospital, regional, and foundation boards. These community leaders donate their time to ensure Intermountain fulfills its mission of providing excellent healthcare.

Intermountain recognizes that each person who visits one of its hospitals or clinics for care is unique. Patients are treated as individuals in the physical sense, of course, but also in terms of life stories, outlooks, and personalities. With this premise in mind, Intermountain focuses on a number of key areas to help physicians, nurses, and other caregivers provide the treatments most effective for each patient.

One of these areas is research. Intermountain Healthcare is one of the leading clinical research organizations in the nation and has developed eight clinical programs—cardiovascular; oncology; women and newborns; primary care; surgical services; intensive medicine; pediatric specialties; and behavioral health—to serve as platforms for sharing and implementing medical best practices throughout the Intermountain Healthcare system. Not only are Intermountain physicians, nurses, and other clinicians seeing real results in terms of improving patient care and medical outcomes as a result of these clinical programs, but others outside the organization are taking notice as well. In 2011, *U.S. News and World Report* recognized several Intermountain hospitals for excellence in healthcare delivery in the magazine's annual

"Best Hospitals" ranking, and in the same year Intermountain was chosen to lead the Patients Hospital Engagement Network Initiative, a group of seven health systems contracted by the Centers for Medicare & Medicaid Services to develop and share best practices in clinical quality and patient safety.

A specific example of how research at Intermountain Healthcare is improving patient care and outcomes is the CARDIoGRAM study, an international effort to identify genetic markers associated with coronary artery disease. Intermountain's study contributions included data gleaned from collecting and analyzing samples from willing heart patients for the past eighteen years, led by molecular biologist John Carlquist, PhD. This data helped CARDIoGRAM researchers identify thirteen new markers, effectively doubling the known markers linked to coronary artery disease. While the team is gratified by the new findings, they know they still need to figure out how those markers interact and how they can use that information to create workable treatments. Much more work needs to be done—and is underway. (In fact, Intermountain's extensive use of data mining to directly improve patient outcomes, as utilized in CARDIoGRAM and other studies, was recognized by the College of Healthcare Information Management Executives [CHIME] and the American Hospital Association.)

Intermountain Healthcare is also focused on providing the highest levels of service excellence and promotes an organization-wide culture for delivering extraordinary care. Intermountain's overall "Dimensions of Care" action areas include clinical excellence, patient engagement, physician engagement, operational effectiveness, employee engagement, and community stewardship. These action areas dovetail with a specific framework, called "Healing Commitments," for how department leaders motivate their teams. These commitments create an environment in which patients, guests, and co-workers feel comfort, community, acceptance, inspiration, and peace.

Affordability is another priority at Intermountain Healthcare. Sharing services, focusing on efficient operational processes, and purchasing in volume are a few ways Intermountain keeps costs down. But more important is the organization's unwavering focus on continuously improving clinical quality. In healthcare, higher clinical quality often costs less because there are few medical complications, fewer readmissions, and faster recoveries. Intermountain's efforts play a significant role in Utah's relatively affordable healthcare-cost profile: lower hospital charges, insurance premiums, and per-capita healthcare expenditures.

Despite how affordable healthcare is in Utah, Intermountain recognizes the special role it plays in the communities it serves and works to ensure patients receive the most appropriate, high-quality healthcare regardless of ability to pay. Intermountain directly operates six community clinics serving low-income and uninsured populations. In addition, it financially supports twelve independent community clinics, and the combined patient visits total more than 200,000 per year. In addition, in 2012, Intermountain hospitals and clinics provided more than $300 million in financial assistance.

Intermountain Healthcare also conducts Community Health Needs Assessments, and its Board establishes annual goals for community benefit programs system-wide. One example of Intermountain's public outreach efforts is its LiVe Well teen fitness campaign, which provides free in-school events and resources as well as raising awareness through advertising and other communications.

Intermountain Healthcare has achieved wide recognition as one of the nation's leading healthcare systems by continually learning and seeking to provide extraordinary care. It is an organization that cares as well as cures and benefits not only its patients but also the communities it serves. For more information about Intermountain Healthcare, please visit www.intermountainhealthcare.org.

With twenty-two hospitals and more than 185 clinics, Intermountain Healthcare staff, clinicians, and caregivers provide patients with high quality, highly effective care based on proven medical best practices.

University of Utah Health Care

A New Era in Patient Care: University of Utah Steeped in Deep Traditions and Spirit of Innovation to Guide Health Care into the Future.

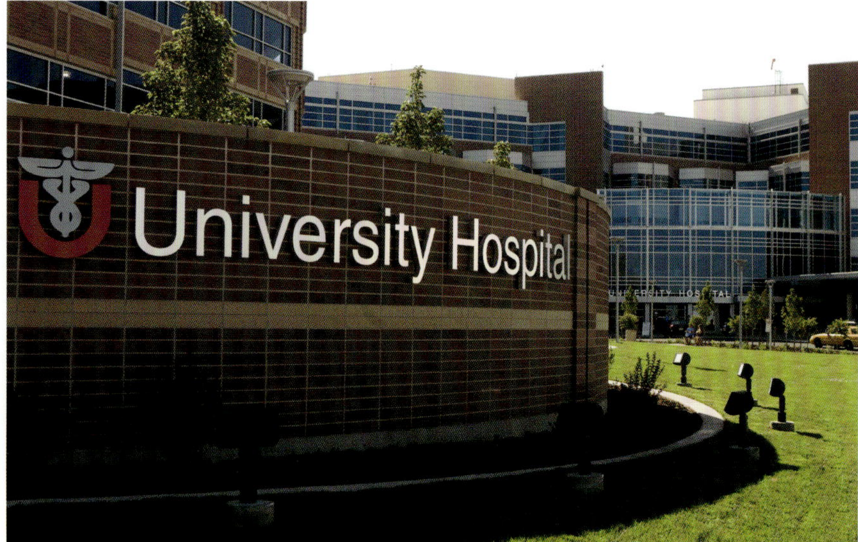

It all began with a human anatomy course and fourteen students.

In 1905 the story of the University of Utah's internationally renowned healthcare system began when a two-year medical course was offered for the first time at the school. New opportunities to formally educate doctors ushered in a new era from a time when frontier doctors, who generally provided herbal remedies to pioneers in need, treated patients without much education.

Over time, as medical practices and procedures advanced from the early days of healthcare in the pioneer West, the University of Utah established itself as a world-class place to seek both healthcare and a medical education.

Today, the University of Utah is proud of its reputation as a place that provides the most comprehensive care in the Intermountain West. As the only academic healthcare system in the region, University of Utah Health Care provides leading and compassionate medicine for Utahns. It also regularly serves a referral area encompassing five states and more than ten percent of the continental United States.

The health system includes four hospitals—University of Utah Hospital; the University of Utah Orthopaedic Center; University Neuropsychiatric Institute; and Huntsman Cancer Hospital—with more than 1,100 physicians who offer more than 135 medical specialties. Recently, University of Utah Health Care ranked No. 1 among all U.S. academic medical centers that participated in the rigorous University HealthSystem Consortium Quality and Accountability study. The University of Utah is also consistently ranked as among the country's best hospitals by *U.S. News and World Report*.

What makes us different? Whether a patient comes to us for a routine visit, a trauma emergency, or a highly specialized treatment, the specialists at University of Utah Health Care are able to offer each person expansive knowledge and experience. Because the institution is an

academic healthcare system, the University of Utah is home to a wide breadth and depth of more than 1,000 medical specialists. Rich partnerships with the University of Utah Schools of Medicine and Dentistry as well as the colleges of Nursing, Pharmacy, and Health set the university apart from other healthcare conglomerates in the region.

University of Utah Health Care aims to improve individual and community health and quality of life. The system provides services available nowhere else in the region, such as University Hospital's Burn Center and the Moran Eye Center. With a strong passion for research, the institution fosters innovation that has led to breakthroughs in artificial organs, cancer treatments, and medical imaging, among others.

The University of Utah is able to recruit some of the finest researchers, doctors, nurses and other professionals from across the U.S. based on its excellent reputation for fulfilling its mission of providing compassionate care without compromise, educating scientists and healthcare professionals for the future, and engaging in research to advance knowledge and well-being.

University of Utah Health Care thrives on its values of compassion, collaboration, innovation, responsibility and diversity and is constantly reevaluating how it meets these values in delivery of care.

In addition to an exceptional healthcare system, the University of Utah conducts groundbreaking research. The university advances knowledge through innovative, basic and clinical research and translates discoveries into applications that help people.

From Nobel laureate Mario Capecchi's landmark work in gene targeting to pioneering investigations in areas as diverse as neural interfaces and using stem cells to regenerate healthy tissue in diseased hearts, the University of Utah School of Medicine is internationally regarded for its innovative basic science and biomedical research. With almost $160 million in annual research funding, the School of Medicine also has earned a well-deserved reputation among physicians and scientists as a place where faculty and students can pursue creative and novel ideas in a collaborative and supportive environment.

University of Utah Health Care thrives because of our values of compassion, collaboration, innovation, responsibility and diversity.

The University of Utah is ranked among the top thirty public research universities in the nation with particular distinctions in medicine and genetics.

Already a prestigious presence in the medical community, University of Utah Health Care's future will be even brighter as the campus and outreach efforts expand in the rapidly changing world of medicine.

In 2013, Governor Gary Herbert signed a bill into law which expanded the University of Utah's School of Medicine class size from eighty-two students to 122 by the year 2015.

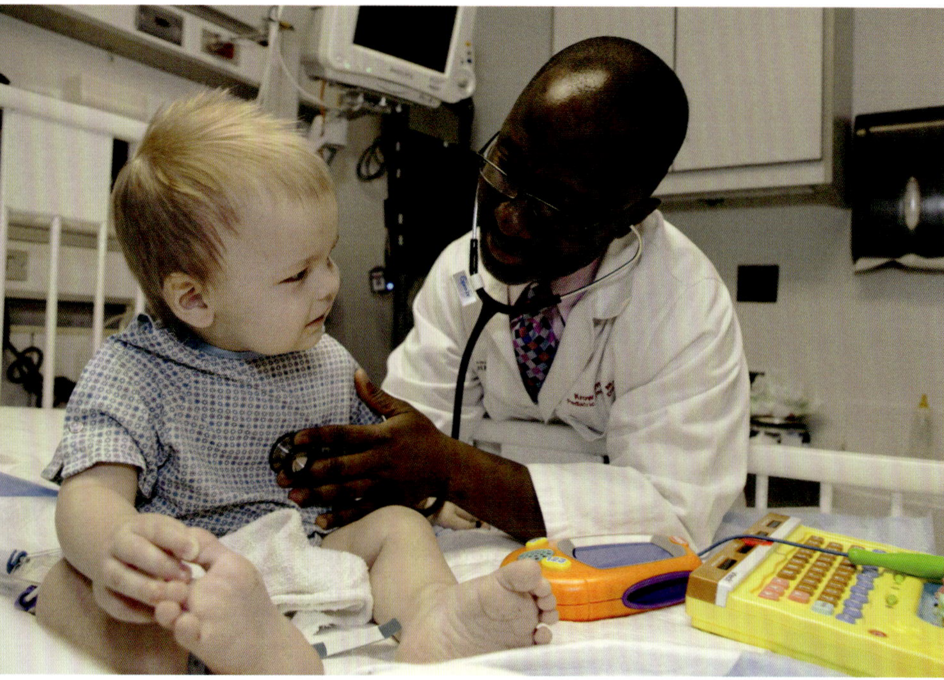

During the signing ceremony, which took place in a classroom laboratory, Herbert told the crowd that an important role of government is to improve the lives of people, and that the bill would do that by ensuring Utahns would have better access to healthcare by increasing the number of providers. The University of Utah is central to the role of giving people the care they need, Herbert noted.

The University of Utah is also home to the Utah Genome Project, an exciting large-scale initiative to advance the development of better disease prevention, diagnosis and treatment methods through discovery of new genetic signatures for human disease and response to drug therapies, using genome sequence analysis.

While genome sequence analysis is becoming routine in biomedical research, the Utah Genome Project is different. Unlike genome initiatives that study unrelated groups of

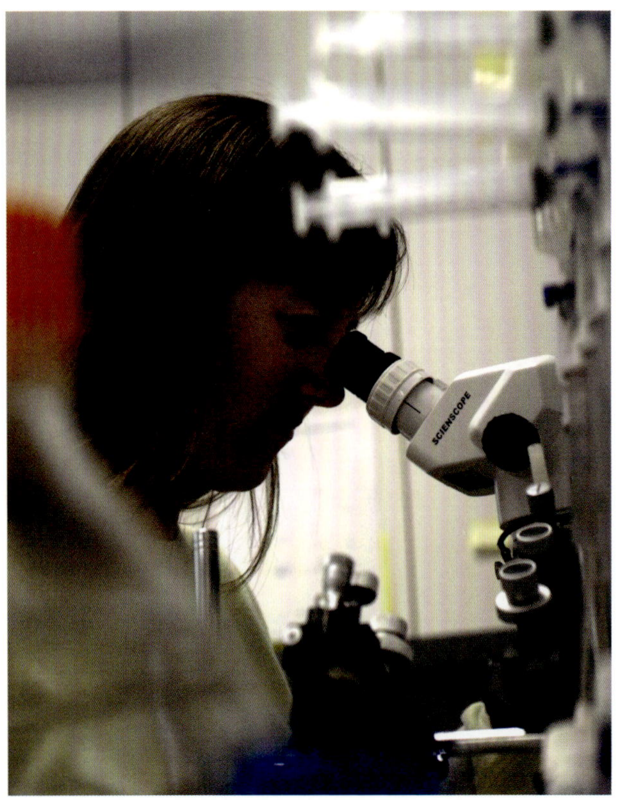

people, the Utah Genome Project will investigate genetic signatures of disease and drug response in large families. Only in Utah is a family-based approach of this scale possible, thanks to the decades-long legacy of unrivaled support and participation of many Utah families in research, and to the Utah Population Database, one of the world's richest sources of in-depth information that supports genetic, epidemiology, demography and public health research.

Another cutting-edge program at the University of Utah is the Center for Medical Innovation, which serves as a place for students and faculty from diverse areas to collaborate and turn innovative ideas into actual medical products for the market. Researchers work with students to help them through the process of prototyping, verification testing and commercialization phases where they can translate their ideas to improvements in patient care.

Besides making innovative strides forward in genetics, the University of Utah is also celebrating new facilities to help researchers and clinicians in other fields of science.

In 2013 the University of Utah also unveiled its breathtakingly beautiful new pharmacy building and broke ground on the country's first new dental school in almost forty years.

The pharmacy building, named in honor of L. S. "Sam" Skaggs, stands as a tribute to Skaggs' dedication to scientific discovery and many years of friendship to the University's College of Pharmacy. A businessman and philanthropist who revolutionized U.S. shopping habits and led one of the country's largest food and drugstore chains, American Stores, Skaggs and charitable organizations he created donated more than $50 million to help construct the 150,000 square foot Institute.

The School of Dentistry is a similarly impressive building. Anticipated for completion in 2014, the $30 million school is possible because of donations from Ray and Tye Noorda and their children. The nearly 80,000 square foot building in the university's Research Park will provide state-of-the-art lab and classroom facilities, administrative and faculty offices, and a dental clinic.

More growth is on the horizon as new projects—which will undoubtedly be home to future groundbreaking discoveries—find roots at the University of Utah.

Interesting achievements from University of Utah Health Sciences:

- The University Health Systems Consortium has ranked the University of Utah in the top ten in the nation in quality among 110 academic medical centers.
- For twenty years running, *U.S. News & World Report* has ranked the University of Utah as one of the top performing health systems in the country.
- In 2013, *Consumer Reports* named the University of Utah number ten in the nation for quality and safety, among 450 academic medical centers.
- In 2013, *Becker's Hospital Review* named the University of Utah one of 100 "Great Hospitals in America."
- The field of biomedical informatics was developed at the University of Utah. The Department of Biomedical Informatics was created in 1964. It was the first in the nation and today remains one of the most renowned programs of its kind in the world.
- In 1970, University Hospital established the first cerebrovascular disease unit in the U.S. west of the Mississippi River.
- On December 1, 1982, the first artificial heart implant was performed at the University of Utah.
- Utah is known throughout the world as a leader in the study of human genetics. The school has been involved in some of the most valuable research in field, such as the sequencing of the tumor suppressor genes responsible for breast cancer in the 1990s.
- WebPath, the world's most popular pathology education website, was created in 1994 by Edward C. Klatt, a professor in the Department of Pathology at the time.
- Advanced Wilderness Life Support (AWLS) is a certification course created at the University of Utah in 1997. AWLS is the gold standard program—both nationally and internationally—for teaching management of medical emergencies in wilderness situations.
- The John A. Moran Eye Center annually ranks among national leaders in research grants from the National Institutes of Health.
- From 2000 to 2012, the residency training program in diagnostic radiology has been ranked No. 1 in the world by the American Board of Radiology.

More growth is on the horizon as new projects—which will undoubtedly lead to groundbreaking discoveries—find roots at University of Utah Health Sciences.

WEBER STATE UNIVERSITY

For more than 125 years, Weber State University has been helping students achieve their dreams.

In 1889, the Church of Jesus Christ of Latter-day Saints converted an Ogden meetinghouse into an academy open to male and female students of all nationalities and religious denominations. For $125 a month, Louis F. Moench was hired as principal. A German-born educator, he believed education was important for everyone—young students and adults—even inviting community members to attend classes for an hour each day to improve a skill or learn a new subject.

Soon, the meetinghouse could no longer accommodate the growing number of students, so the academy's founders mortgaged their homes to guarantee construction of a new campus. By 1923, the school was housed in a larger building in downtown Ogden and had adopted a "college attitude," dropping its high school courses.

In 1933, the church transferred the college's ownership to the state. That same year, during the midst of the Great Depression, state salaries were slashed. With 170,000 Utahans out of work, many families could not afford to send their children to college. In lieu of tuition, Weber accepted in-kind donations of meat and produce.

To cut the budget in 1953, the state Legislature voted to stop funding Utah's junior colleges. A campus and community "Save Weber" campaign defeated the measure through a public referendum, forging a lasting bond. One year later, Weber, with its ever-growing enrollment, moved to Harrison Boulevard. It became a four-year state college in the early 1960s, retaining its commitment to its core principles and personalized teaching.

Today, Weber State University offers its 25,000 students more than 225 degree programs—the most comprehensive undergraduate selection in Utah—while eleven master's degree programs provide additional training.

Abundant classrooms, laboratories, computing centers, performing and visual arts facilities, a spacious library, and a newly renovated health and fitness complex occupy some of the sixty buildings on Ogden's 526-acre mountainside campus. WSU Davis, a modern, growing, high-tech campus in Layton, serves Hill Air Force Base. Courses at schools, health facilities, off-campus centers, and work sites throughout Utah, plus more than 250 courses online, are all designed to make a college education available and affordable for any student.

WSU's large nontraditional student population, multiple campuses, flexible schedules and extensive list of online courses exemplify the ideals of open access, continuing education, lifelong learning and engaging the greater community. It is large and complex enough to offer stimulating educational challenges but small enough to care about individuals. Principal Moench's vision has guided it for 125 years and helped hundreds of thousands of students achieve their dreams.

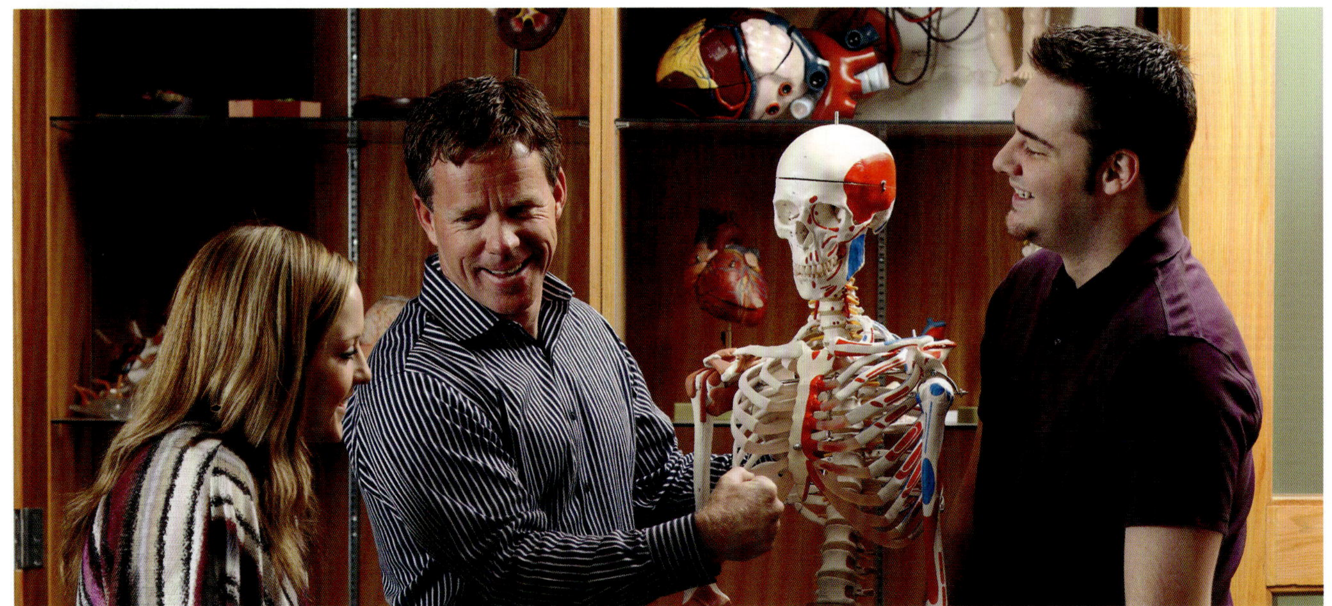

ARUP Laboratories

ARUP Laboratories is a national clinical and anatomic pathology reference laboratory and a nonprofit enterprise of the University of Utah and its Department of Pathology. It offers in excess of 3,000 tests and test combinations, ranging from routine screening to esoteric molecular and genetic assays. Rather than competing with its clients for physician office business, ARUP supports clients' existing test menus by offering those that are complex and unique, along with accompanying consultative support, thereby providing local and regional laboratory services through outreach programs.

Since its formation in 1984, ARUP has founded its reputation on reliable and consistent laboratory testing and innovative healthcare information. This simple strategy

contributes significantly to client satisfaction. Clients who respond to surveys regularly rate ARUP highly and state that they would recommend ARUP to others.

Elected officials, healthcare leaders, physicians and patients, all of whom are placing more emphasis on accountability, integration, and efficiency, find that ARUP's philosophy of putting patients' needs first and doing what is right is just what the doctor ordered.

"As the most responsive source of quality information and knowledge, we strive to be the reference laboratory of choice for community healthcare systems," says Edward R. Ashwood, MD, ARUP's president and chief executive officer. "We help our clients meet the customized needs of their unique communities and provide guidance and support to navigate the changes in the shifting healthcare terrain. Together, ARUP and its clients will improve patient care today and in the future."

ARUP funds various initiatives to adapt emerging technologies to laboratory medicine. Bridging the gap between research and application can be difficult, but ARUP maximizes the use of new advances. Not only does it implement

new tools for diagnostic tests, but its methods are actively shared with the world through scientific publications, presentations, open-source databases, free multimedia based education, and technology licenses.

One of the nation's top reference laboratories, ARUP is nationally recognized for excellence. Their teams of genetic counselors works with ordering physicians to ensure tests are properly ordered, saving clients thousands of dollars per month. In addition, its products and services are designed to help clients implement new healthcare delivery models, including ACOIs, patient-centered medical homes, and other variations. It offers diagnostic lab testing services to more than one thousand clients, including academic hospitals, children's hospitals, multi-hospital groups, major commercial laboratories, group-purchasing organizations, military and government facilities, and major clinics in all fifty states.

ARUP's eighty medical directors are all faculty members at the University of Utah School of Medicine, and most hold academic appointments within the Department of Pathology. Centrally located in Salt Lake City, ARUP has one of the fastest, most consistent result turnaround times in the industry. It performs 99 percent of all testing on-site in one central location, operating 24 hours a day, 7 days per week and processing an average of 30,000 to 55,000 specimens of blood, body fluid, and tissue biopsies daily. ARUP's Specimen Processing Division, which is comprised of both human operators and automated systems, records an error rate of less than one per 8,000 and is working to reduce that number.

ARUP's state-of-the-art Blood Bank and Transfusion Center is the sole source of blood and blood components for the University of Utah Hospital, Huntsman Cancer Hospital, Shriners Hospital for Children, and Primary Children's Medical Center, and provides twenty-five percent of all blood transfused in Utah.

The ARUP Institute for Clinical and Experimental Pathology®, which was founded in 1996, is charged with providing R&D services to ARUP. The institute improves current lab tests, evaluates new technologies, creates original methods and reagents, and conducts numerous research projects.

Noting that ARUP is unique in many ways, Ashwood notes that ARUP clients "value our patient-comes-first philosophy and are extremely loyal, providing us with stability in an unstable economy."

He emphasizes that ARUP cares about its clients and its employees, adding, "We don't compete with our clients for physician-office business, choosing instead to support clients' existing test menus by offering esoteric, highly complex tests and accompanying consultative support, so that they can provide local and regional laboratory services in their communities."

With a focus on integrity and service, ARUP creates a culture of trust and respect for its employees, who are provided with training, support, empowerment, assistance in developing a healthy work/live balance, and a safe and progressive work environment, Ashwood says. "We offer an excellent, award-winning benefit package, including a free on-site health clinic and fitness center, as well as a profit-sharing retirement plan and tuition reimbursement," he points out. "Our employees regularly vote ARUP one of the best places in the state to work. We realize that every employee is an integral part of the ARUP family and remain dedicated to their success."

SELECTHEALTH®

SelectHealth® has been helping Utah families and businesses get healthcare since 1984. A nonprofit health insurance carrier, SelectHealth works to improve the health of not just its members but the entire community.

As a subsidiary of Intermountain Healthcare®, SelectHealth is part of one of the nation's top-ranked integrated health systems. Studies have shown that integrated systems—where doctors, members, and insurance companies work together—achieve better outcomes at lower costs.

Because health insurance can be complicated, SelectHealth helps its members every step of the way—from finding the right doctor to understanding their benefits. Here are just a few of the services SelectHealth offers:

- Member Advocates—Representatives help members find a doctor and schedule the next available appointment.
- Online Tools—Members can access their medical records, review claims, and estimate the cost of medical procedures.
- Care Management—Trained registered nurses provide one-on-one support to members with chronic or urgent conditions.
- Healthy Living Program—Members and doctors work together and members are rewarded for making healthy changes, saving everyone money over the long-term.
- Pharmacy Benefits Manager—SelectHealth Prescriptions®, a full-service PBM, offers industry-leading generic dispensing rates and evidence-based formularies.
- Transparent Doctor Ratings—The online provider search allows members to view clinics' quality scores and patient satisfaction ratings.
- Help for Expecting Moms—Healthy Beginnings®, a prenatal program, provides support and resources for pregnant women, and includes a cash incentive for completion.

To provide the best possible care and service for its members, SelectHealth works closely with clinical partners, including Intermountain Healthcare. Whether through clinical programs or treatment of chronic diseases, SelectHealth and Intermountain share best medical practices and raise the standards of clinical excellence. Patient billing is simplified and members are able to access their insurance information and medical records online.

In a vertically integrated organization like Intermountain, costs are not just reduced through economies of scale and efficient management. Significant cost reductions are achieved by improving the total process of medical care. With hospitals, physician clinics, health plans, home health agencies, occupational medicine clinics, and other services, Intermountain provides a relatively seamless continuum of care.

In 2013, SelectHealth expanded its offerings in Idaho through an alliance with St. Luke's Health System, Idaho's largest and only locally governed healthcare system. St. Luke's and SelectHealth will work together to better serve the healthcare needs of the community through a model of data sharing, innovative insurance plan designs, and physician and patient engagement.

Offering a wide variety of plans and services, SelectHealth meets the needs of individuals, families, and employers:

- Medical Plans;
- Dental Plans;
- Pharmacy Benefits;
- Government Plans (Medicaid, Children's Health Insurance Program);
- Federal Employee Plans;
- Medicare Advantage Plans;
- Wellness Plans;
- Life and Disability Coverage; and
- Eyewear Coverage.

SelectHealth is consistently rated Utah's top HMO plan by state and national organizations, receiving top scores in both member satisfaction and clinical performance.

Each of the past four years, SelectHealth has ranked highest in member satisfaction among health plans in the Mountain region, according to the J.D.Power and Associates® 2013 U.S. Member Health Insurance Plan Study[SM].

SelectHealth maintains "Commendable" accreditation status from NCQA, a nonprofit organization dedicated to improving healthcare quality. Results show that NCQA-accredited plans outperform non-accredited plans in all measures of clinical care and member satisfaction.

SelectHealth is also known for its workplace culture, earning the *Utah Business* "Best Companies to Work For" award each year since 2007.

SelectHealth wants to improve the health of the communities where its members and employees live, work, and play. The organization is actively involved in programs that improve health and promote education.

To fight childhood obesity, SelectHealth created a free fitness program for fourth graders. The STEP Express program includes lesson plans, PE activities, and a fitness challenge where students track their minutes of exercise. SelectHealth

provides all of the necessary exercise equipment and materials. The program is in more than 100 Utah schools and has been completed by more than 30,000 students. See www.stepexpress.org for more information.

Each year, SelectHealth recognizes twenty-five Utah nonprofits that are improving health or serving those with special needs. Each organization receives $2,500 to further its mission. Winners are selected from all areas of the state and represent a wide range of causes. Past winners include exercise programs for the elderly, afterschool programs for underserved youth, and nutrition classes for Navajo families. See www.select25.org for more information.

SelectHealth is proud to be the title sponsor of GREENbike, the bike share program in Salt Lake City. Riders can pick up a bike at any sharing station in the downtown area and then drop it off when they are done. It is an easy and affordable way to get some exercise and help keep the air clean. See www.greenbikeslc.org for more information.

SelectHealth supports local farmers and vendors by sponsoring the Downtown Farmers Market in Salt Lake City. Throughout the summer, SelectHealth provides thousands of free health screenings to market goers.

Find out more about SelectHealth programs at www.selecthealth.org.

Judge Memorial Catholic High School

Judge Memorial Catholic High School partners with parents to foster the integration of each student's spiritual, intellectual, emotional, physical, and social development. In this safe, caring, respectful environment, students are empowered to become builders of a more just society. The school's mission is to create a community through Catholic faith and education that will foster the development of each student's inherent gifts.

Judge Memorial, founded in 1921, has provided an outstanding educational experience firmly rooted in a faith tradition for nearly a century. Teachers, students, parents, and alumni have consistently fostered and sustained a tradition of excellence. Since its opening, the school has operated at 650 South 1100 East in downtown Salt Lake City, Utah.

Its 95 employees, 60 percent of whom have advanced degrees, include 61 faculty members bringing a faith commitment and depth of knowledge, generosity of time, talent, and personal caring to the learning environment. The school's 751 students in grades ninth through twelfth are also served by five school counselors and two college counselors, all dedicated to viewing each individual as a child of God endowed with many gifts.

In the fall of 2013, Judge Memorial opened the JM Learning Commons program, replacing the library. This leap into the future offers a new and innovative approach to research and learning. It is designed to provide students, teachers, and staff with access to current and appropriate information resources, and to ensure that they are effective users of information.

The school's building originally housed Judge Mercy Home, a hospital for Catholic coal miners who suffered from Black Lung. As coal mining east of Salt Lake declined, so did the need for a hospital dedicated to this cause. Mary Judge, who with her deceased husband, John, was the hospital's benefactor, had expressed the wish that the facility be used as a school, but passed away before it opened. It was originally named Cathedral High School and Catholic Grammar School, with Bishop John J. Mitty changing the name to Judge Memorial School in 1929. The Congregation of the Sisters of the Holy Cross was responsible for starting Judge Memorial in 1920 when the Judge family decided to turn the building from a miner's hospital to a school. It was coeducational until 1964, when Bishop Joseph Lennox Federal brought in the Oblates of Saint Francis de Sales to operate it as an all-boys' school. At that time girls attended St. Mary of the Wasatch Academy. After St. Mary closed in 1970, girls again joined the boys at Judge, and the school added the word "Catholic" to its name.

With the present-day guidance of Bishop John C. Wester and a committed administrative staff, the school continues to build upon the legacy of Catholic education begun by Mary Judge and fostered by all members of the Judge community. The school boasts a 100 percent graduation rate, with 99 percent of students going on to college immediately following their senior year. Judge Memorial exemplifies academic excellence, with its graduates going on to matriculate at many top colleges and universities.

In recognition of the outstanding education offered at Judge Memorial, graduating classes routinely earn between $10-$16 million in scholarships and renewable grants.

Key individuals in the school's early days include Monsignor James T. Kenny, a teacher, coach, and administrator who also served the diocese as Superintendent of Catholic Schools; and Monsignor J. Terrence Fitzgerald, a 1954 Judge Memorial alumnus, who as the school's principal and president in the 1990s, brought it to financial solvency and restored its strong Catholic identity. Sister Louise Marie, a Holy Cross sister who taught at both St. Mary of the Wasatch and Judge Memorial for many years, is a beloved former faculty member. Marjorie Pierce who, for over twenty year, taught at both St. Mary's and Judge, was a champion for women's sports long before it was fashionable to be one. Roy and Teru Okamoto, who, in 1945, began work in the cafeteria and caring for the grounds. After Teru's death in 1975, Roy continued to live and work at Judge until his retirement in 1987.

The school's tradition of both excellence in education and service to others continues. Current students volunteer within the school, the Diocese, across the Salt Lake Valley, and throughout the country and the world. The mission of the Christian Service program at Judge Memorial is to engage students in service to others. Senior students annually contribute over 21,000 hours of service, with over forty of them typically honored with the Presidential Service Award each year for community service.

Judge Memorial is well-known for its commitment to academic excellence, character building, sportsmanship, and for producing well-rounded graduates who are ready to make a difference. Students learn the value of hard work, generosity toward others, and respect. Judge Memorial is recognized and respected for challenging students of all races and socioeconomic backgrounds to reach their full potential; to prepare for the rigors of a university education; to participate in community service; and, ultimately, to return a full measure of value and character to society. Simply put, Judge Memorial students are prepared for success.

Canvas by Instructure

Instructure, Inc., was founded in 2008 by Brian Whitmer and Devlin Daley, two graduate students in the computer science program at Brigham Young University, who wanted to develop an easy-to-use software application to facilitate online learning. So that is exactly what they did.

But before they wrote any code, Whitmer and Daley launched a "product validation tour" to learn more about the needs of their stakeholders. In a Geo Metro with no air conditioning, they drove throughout the West, visiting seventeen universities and gathering critical feedback from students, faculty, and administrators that would lay the groundwork for their

Canvas by Instructure learning management system or LMS. Not bad for a couple of college students on a road trip.

Instructure's first investor was Josh Coates, the technology entrepreneur who founded the cloud-based file backup service called Mozy, and who joined Instructure as CEO in 2010. That year, Coates and his skeleton crew of twenty employees had landed just a handful of customers when they won a major contract with the Utah Education Network (UEN) to provide Canvas as the statewide LMS at all Utah public schools and state-funded colleges and universities. Selected as the most innovative of eight systems in a highly-competitive evaluation process, Canvas became the new online learning platform for more than 100,000 Utah students.

Following its success with UEN, Instructure formally launched Canvas in February 2011. As open-source software and the only true, native cloud LMS, it set a new, open standard for education technology. In 2012, Cisco Networking Academy, known as "the world's largest classroom," announced it would use Canvas to deliver online IT courses to more than a million students worldwide.

Between 2010 and 2013, Instructure secured more than $100 million in contracts and the Canvas community grew to more than 500 colleges, universities, and K-12 schools with 9 million cumulative users. Continuing as a pioneer in twenty-first century education technology, the company recently launched Canvas Network, an index of open, online courses taught by educators and institutions from around the world. In 2014, Instructure will expand its Canvas LMS into international and corporate markets.

In addition to its fast-growing client base, Instructure is backed by private investment. In June 2013, it raised $30 million in Series-D funding, which brought its lifetime funding total to $50 million. Current investors include Bessemer Venture Partners (BVP), EPIC Ventures, OpenView Venture Partners, and TomorrowVentures.

Located in Salt Lake City's Old Mill Corporate Center, Instructure had just over 250 employees in September 2013. Through the Governor's Office of Economic Development (GOED) incentive program, it expects to nearly triple that number by 2019, bringing an estimated 655 new jobs to Utah.

Asked about Instructure's overwhelming success, Coates said, "Education is universally accepted and admired because it's so powerful. At Instructure, we're solving a problem in education with technology and building the foundation for a company that can grow to hundreds or possibly thousands of employees and effect change all over the world. It's about real, permanent change."

As a good corporate citizen, Instructure has partnered with the Salt Lake Chamber of Commerce in the Governor's 2020 Initiative, and has joined other organizations, such as the Utah Technology Council, in their efforts to improve Utah schools. Through its own grant program, it also awards $100,000 annually to cultivate innovation in K-12 and higher education.

To learn more, visit www.instructure.com.

❖

Above: Nobody at Instructure has an office. Not even the CEO. That's what they mean by "open."

Left: Instructure's office is a flurry of activity, including employees buzzing around on scooters, all to help make teaching and learning easier.

The Church of Jesus Christ of Latter-day Saints

❖

Right: Historic Temple Square is one of Utah's most visited attractions, drawing millions of visitors a year, and is part of the thirty-five-acre world headquarters of The Church of Jesus Christ of Latter-day Saints. Temple Square consists of the Salt Lake Temple, the Tabernacle (home of the Mormon Tabernacle Choir), the Assembly Hall and two visitors' centers.

Below: Inside the 21,000-seat Conference Center, where members of the Church gather twice yearly for General Conference.

Millions of people from around the world visit Salt Lake City each year. Some come for the skiing, others for the spectacular national parks. Many come to visit the world headquarters of The Church of Jesus Christ of Latter-day Saints.

Situated in the heart of downtown, the Church's thirty-five acre main campus draws visitors from all over the world because of its renowned research libraries, cultural activities and historic buildings—most notably the Salt Lake Temple at the center of Temple Square. Volunteer tour guides on Temple Square come from fifty-one nations and speak more than thirty languages to accommodate foreign guests.

Some visitors also come to see the Church's Humanitarian Center and to learn how it partners locally and internationally with other faiths and nonprofit organizations to minister to those in need. For example, Salt Lake City is a refugee relocation center, and the Church offers refugees, regardless of religious affiliation, an opportunity to work in its international Humanitarian Center in Salt Lake City, providing them with food, clothing, job training, and English, computer, and cultural adaptation classes. They also receive medical, educational, and emotional support through the Church and its interfaith partners. The training programs normally last up to eighteen months, after which participants are helped to find long-term employment.

The Church's Humanitarian Center was established in 1991 to provide emergency supplies to those who were suffering in the wake of natural and man-made disasters. Humanitarian leaders work together globally with Catholic Relief Services, the American Red Cross, the Red Crescent, among others to provide services and supplies in disaster zones.

Typically the Humanitarian Center will ship approximately 8 million pounds of shoes and clothing, 500,000 hygiene and school kits, and 20,000 quilts to relieve suffering in more than 50 countries every year. The Church of Jesus Christ of Latter-day Saints has provided over $1 billion in financial and material assistance to individuals in more than 170 countries since 1985, when the Church began tracking such information. Relief supplies are provided locally and internationally to relieve suffering without regard for ethnicity, religion, or political persuasion.

Internationally the Church's humanitarian efforts focus on emergency response, clean water, neonatal resuscitation training, wheelchairs, vision care, immunization, and food production. Church members and others fund these projects through cash and in-kind donations, 100 percent of which are directly used in helping those in need, with the Church absorbing its own overhead costs.

The Church of Jesus Christ of Latter-day Saints also operates a welfare system through Bishop Storehouses strategically located throughout the United States, Canada and around the world. These facilities have often been compared to supermarkets without tills.

The Welfare Program is designed to help recipients make it through the tough times, simultaneously teaching them to become self-reliant, allowing them to retain their self-respect. It is available to all who are in need, regardless of religious affiliation and funding is provided by donations from Church members. One Sunday a month, members of the Church go without two meals and give the money they would have spent on food to the Church. Local bishops identify those who need assistance.

In some locations with high concentrations of Church members, welfare facilities may be substantial. Welfare Square near Church headquarters in Salt Lake City, Utah, is the largest concentration of such facilities. Buildings on the square include a cannery, a milk-processing plant, a Bishops Storehouse, a thrift store, an employment center and silos where wheat and other grains are stored. Recipients of commodities are given opportunities to work for what they receive, to the extent of their ability. There are currently 129 bishops' storehouses.

In addition, the Church operates 259 employment resource service centers around the world where people can receive job training, learn how to enhance their résumés and find job opportunities. It also operates a private, nonprofit organization called LDS Family Services that provides counseling, adoption services, addiction recovery support groups and resources for social, emotional and spiritual challenges, and operates nonprofit thrift stores throughout the western United States with the main purpose of providing job training. All thrift stores are open to the public.

❖

Above: The Church of Jesus Christ of Latter-day Saints provides relief and development projects for humanitarian purposes in countries all over the world. Pictured above, the Church partnered with Islamic Relief Worldwide to provide immediate humanitarian assistance to the tsunami-hit areas of Indonesia, Thailand and Sri Lanka in December 2004. Other humanitarian partners include Catholic Relief Services, the American Red Cross and the Red Crescent among others.

Left: Members of The Church of Jesus Christ of Latter-day Saints worldwide gather twice yearly to watch what they call General Conference, which originates in the 21-000 seat Conference Center in Salt Lake City. This is in addition to their weekly worship services each Sunday. Conference proceedings are transmitted in real time in ninety-three languages globally through state-of-the-art broadcast, interpretation, and translation facilities in the building.

Davis Hospital and Medical Center

Since 1976, Davis Hospital and Medical Center has been providing high-quality healthcare in Layton and its surrounding communities. Davis Hospital is equipped with advanced medical technology and offers comprehensive services, including:

- Two convenient ER locations to treat a wide range of emergencies, from stroke treatment to broken bones, with some of the shortest emergency wait times in Utah.
- Highly skilled cardiologists providing interventional heart care and cardiac catheterization.
- Women's care, including a breast health center, mid- to late-life gynecological surgery, maternity care with private labor and delivery suites and a Level III NICU.
- Comprehensive cancer services, including leading-edge radiation technologies such as TomoTherapy® and Brachytherapy. Personal certified patient navigators are available to assist all patients through their journeys.
- Advanced surgical procedures and imaging capabilities, including 128-Slice CT scanner.

Davis Hospital is a 2013 HealthInsight Quality Award recipient. This award recognizes hospitals ranking in or above the seventy-fifth percentile in HealthInsight national rankings. Davis Hospital is committed to providing quality care in a friendly environment. For more information, visit DavisHospital.com or call 1-866-431-WELL (9355).

Jordan Valley Medical Center

Jordan Valley Medical Center is a 183 bed, state-of-the-art hospital located in West Jordan. It is equipped with advanced medical technology and offers comprehensive services, including:

- Emergency medical services for major emergencies, including a certified stroke treatment center for specialized care, and a fast track for less-serious cases.
- Heart care from an experienced team includes testing for early diagnosis and interventional treatments.
- Women's care for all stages of life, including breast health and gynecological services. Maternity care includes labor and delivery, postpartum, and a Level III NICU nursery.
- Breast care center offering digital mammography, MRI, advanced stereotactic procedures, specially trained nurse navigators, know error® technology and more.
- Comprehensive orthopedic services including joint replacement and repair for knees, hips and shoulders, spine surgery and sports medicine. Includes inpatient orthopedic center and outpatient services, such as aquatic, physical, occupational and speech therapies.

Jordan Valley is a 2013 recipient of the HealthInsight Quality Award for its rank in or above the seventy-fifth percentile in HealthInsight national rankings and the Women's Choice Award for America's 100 Best Hospitals for Patient Experience from WomenCertified®. For more information, visit JordanValleyMC.com or call 1-866-431-WELL (9355).

Pioneer Valley Hospital is a 139 bed, state-of-the-art hospital located in West Valley City. Equipped with advanced medical technology, Pioneer Valley's comprehensive services include:

- Emergency medical services for major emergencies, including a certified stroke treatment center for specialized care, and a fast track for less-serious cases.
- Heart care from an experienced team includes testing for early diagnosis and interventional treatments.
- Women's health, including maternity care with labor and delivery, postpartum, nursery, breast health and gynecological services.
- Orthopedic services including joint replacement and repair for knees, hips and shoulders, spine surgery and sports medicine.
- Behavioral health services providing psychiatric care for adults, with inpatient services available 24/7. An outpatient clinic is also available.
- Advanced surgical procedures and imaging capabilities.

Pioneer Valley is a 2013 recipient of the HealthInsight Quality Award for its rank in or above the seventy-fifth percentile in HealthInsight national rankings and the Women's Choice Award for America's 100 Best Hospitals for Patient Experience from WomenCertified®. For more information, visit PioneerValleyHospital.com or call 1-866-431-WELL (9355).

PIONEER VALLEY HOSPITAL

Davis Hospital and Medical Center, Jordan Valley Medical Center, Pioneer Valley Hospital and Salt Lake Regional Medical Center are directly or indirectly owned by an entity that proudly includes physician owners, including certain members of the hospitals' medical staffs.

As one of Salt Lake Valley's first hospitals, Salt Lake Regional Medical Center has been providing quality care for residents for 140 years. Salt Lake Regional is equipped with advanced medical technology, and offers comprehensive services, including:

- Emergency services for major emergencies, including certification as a Stemi/PCI receiving facility. Call ahead using InQuicker for non-life-threatening emergencies.
- Orthopedic services include the Center for Precision Joint Replacement, providing partial and total joint replacements for hip, knee and shoulder; spine surgery; sports medicine; and inpatient/outpatient therapy, including acute rehabilitation and an aquatic pool.
- Women's care for all stages of a woman's life, including gynecological care utilizing robotic assisted surgery, breast health and complete maternity care.
- Heart care, including cardiac catheterization and open heart surgery.
- Specialized geriatric care, including inpatient and outpatient senior behavioral health for adults.
- Center of Excellence bariatric program, advanced surgical procedures and diagnostic imaging.

Salt Lake Regional Medical Center is a 2013 HealthInsight Quality Award recipient, which recognizes hospitals ranking in or above the seventy-fifth percentile of HealthInsight national rankings. With a knowledgeable and compassionate staff, patients are sure to find the kind of comfort and caring Salt Lake Regional is known for. For more information, visit SaltLakeRegional.com or call 1-866-431-WELL (9355).

SALT LAKE REGIONAL MEDICAL CENTER

HOOPES VISION

Founded in the Salt Lake City area in 2000, Hoopes Vision provides LASIK, PRK, ICL, custom laser cataract surgery, clear lens exchange, and corneal transplants. Its founder, Dr. Phillip C. Hoopes relocated to Utah from Kansas City, where he had established an innovative and successful surgery practice.

Hoopes Vision is in the forefront of vision correction technology, offering the safest, most effective vision correction procedures available. Hoopes Vision has pioneered every major advance in eye surgery technology—from LASIK to blade-free IntraLASIK, to wavefront-guided and wavefront-optimized laser treatments, ICL lens implants, and laser cataract surgery. It dedicates an entire department to clinical research, and is involved in multiple FDA studies.

Formerly in Sandy, Utah, the main office and surgical center is now located at 11820 South State Street in Draper, Utah, fulfilling Dr. Phillip C. Hoopes' dream to create a laser vision correction facility combining advanced technology and a warm environment.

Patients who travel to the Salt Lake City area for the superior treatment provided by an acclaimed team of eye care professionals find a welcoming atmosphere with clean, beautiful architecture, massage chairs, artwork and even complimentary fresh-baked cookies.

The Draper building also houses an ambulatory surgical center, EyeSurg of Utah; one of the world's first designed specifically for laser cataract surgery. It was the first center to have two cataract lasers, Optimedica Catalys™ and Alcon LenSx™. ICL, corneal transplants and pterygium surgeries are also performed here among one of the country's best-equipped, most technologically advanced eye surgery centers.

A second location at 105 East South Temple allows delivery of advanced technology and world-class patient care to more people across a greater area. The Eagle Gate clinic focuses on post-operative care, testing and examinations for new cataract patients. All surgery, as well as pre-operative testing and examinations for LASIK patients, is at the Draper facility, which recently added an Oculoplastics specialist, offering a broader range of procedures.

Several factors, including the surgeons' experience, clinical research center, and patient care set Hoopes apart from other centers. With a staff of seventy, it is proud to be the official eye care and LASIK provider of the Utah Jazz, Salt Lake Bees, Real Salt Lake, and Miller Motorsports Park.

"We have developed great working relationships with hundreds of optometrists in Utah and surrounding states," Dr. Hoopes says. "Gaining their trust is critical, as they refer patients to our center. We will continue offering educational seminars and materials to them and our patients, and developing new ideas to improve patients' experiences, as 'word of mouth' is our top source of patient referrals."

The mission of The McGillis School is simple but vital: to educate children and instill in its students a love of learning and the abilities to think critically, live ethically, and appreciate the value of each individual. The school's singular focus on the K-8 years defines it, but of far more importance, it defines its students.

The school was originally formed as an extension of the Salt Lake Jewish Community Center Preschool and Kindergarten. In 2003 the school became its own independent 501(c)3 named in honor of its primary benefactors Joanne and Dick McGillis. Its doors were opened in the historic Douglas School to 129 students in grades first through seventh. In 2010 the school opened expansion spaces as the first LEED Gold K-8 School in the state of Utah. Now in 2013, the school enrollment stands at 365 students in grades K-8. The school strives to develop curiosity, creativity, global awareness, critical thinking skills, and an ethical foundation to prepare McGillis students for success as they aspire to change the world.

The McGillis School believes that these are the years when the whole child—emotionally, academically, and socially—can be nurtured to learn not just how, but why. Not only what, but to what end. Not merely the reason, but the reasoning. Their goal as educators is to provide this start for each child at The McGillis School.

This is the start of a lifetime of learning and laughing and asking and engaging with those around them—the start of a lifetime of something greater than themselves, curious about the opportunities ahead and ultimately, the start of a lifetime influential to the world. This could be your child at The McGillis School. Welcome to the start of a lifetime.

For more information on The McGillis School, please visit www.mcgillisschool.org.

Utah Transit Authority

Public transportation plays an important role in Utah's economic development and improving the quality of life. The Utah Transit Authority's vision is to provide an integrated system of innovative, accessible and efficient public transportation services that offer increased access to opportunities and a healthy environment for all people of the Wasatch region. UTA operates bus, TRAX light rail, FrontRunner commuter rail, streetcar, and vanpool services that transported more than 44 million people in 2013.

In 1968 one of the last public transportation providers in Salt Lake County, Salt Lake City Lines, ended its services.

Salt Lake City Corporation, Union Street Railway and Salt Lake County successfully lobbied the Utah State Legislature to pass a bill allowing individual localities to address their public transportation needs by forming local transit districts. In 1970 residents of Salt Lake City and the surrounding communities of Murray, Midvale, Sandy and Bingham voted to form a public transit district, and created the Utah Transit Authority.

For years, UTA primarily provided bus services along the Wasatch Front. That all changed in 1999, when UTA opened its first TRAX light rail line. The new TRAX line inaugurated a proud tradition of delivering major capital projects ahead of schedule and on budget. UTA has since completed seven additional TRAX lines servicing the greater Salt Lake metropolitan area, and constructed two major FrontRunner commuter rail lines servicing the Wasatch Front. In 2013, UTA also opened its first streetcar project, the S-Line, servicing the Sugar House area of Salt Lake City and the City of South Salt Lake. UTA now operates 44.8 miles of light rail, 89 miles of commuter rail and 2 miles of streetcar services.

Administrative offices for UTA are located at 669 West 200 South in Salt Lake City. UTA also has vehicle maintenance facilities in Ogden, Midvale, South Salt Lake and Orem. UTA has 2,248 employees, including 794 in administration; and 1, 454 in operations, maintenance and support roles.

UTA services cover 1,600 square miles in Box Elder, Davis, Salt Lake, Tooele, Utah, and Weber Counties and offers limited service to Park City in Summit County. More than eighty percent of the state's population has access to UTA services. UTA has won the "Outstanding Public Transportation System," award from the American Public Transportation Association three times, placing it among the most respected agencies in the industry.

For more information, please visit rideuta.com.

Based in Salt Lake City, nonprofit, online Western Governors University (WGU) has grown into a nationally recognized university in just over fifteen years. One of the largest online universities in the country, the idea for WGU began during a meeting of the Western Governors Association in 1995. Its chairman, then-Utah Governor Mike Leavitt, noted that distance learning technologies had the power to tackle one of the western states' most-pressing problems: rapid population growth compounded by limited public funds for educational services.

That discussion eventually led this bipartisan group of governors to create Western Governors University, a first-of-its-kind university with a mission "to improve quality and expand access to post-secondary educational opportunities by providing a means for individuals to learn independent of time and place and to earn competency-based degrees and other credentials credible to both academic institutions and employers."

Incorporated as a private, nonprofit university in 1997, WGU has grown to a national university with more than 40,000 students and more than 26,000 graduates in all fifty states, with more than 3,000 students and 2,500 graduates living in the state of Utah alone.

WGU is the first exclusively online and nonprofit university in the country that offers accredited competency-based degree programs. Its more than fifty undergraduate and graduate degree programs are available to adult learners who need flexibility to achieve their educational and career goals in the fields of business, kindergarten through twelfth grade teacher education, information technology, and health professions, including nursing. Tuition is affordable at about $6,000 per year and has not increased since 2008.

WGU has garnered attention and praise from the nation's leaders in higher education and public policy, including Utah Governor Gary Herbert, U.S. Secretary of Education Arne Duncan, and Bill Gates. Remarking on WGU's innovative competency-based programs, Secretary Duncan said, "While such programs [like Western Governors University] are now the exception, I want them to be the norm."

In 2013, WGU was named to *Fast Company*'s list of The World's Most Innovative Companies, a recognition that highlights the fact that WGU's programs are developed with input from leading employers and emphasizes the ways WGU uses innovative technologies to improve learning while keeping tuition low.

Now as a leading employer in the state; more than 830 of WGU's nearly 2,300 employees live in the Beehive State, where the university's national headquarters is located. Helping adults return to college to fulfill their dreams of a bachelor's or master's degree, WGU has become an integral part of the educational landscape of Utah. What was once just a blue-sky idea has turned out to be a visionary reality.

Additional information is available on the Internet at www.wgu.edu.

WESTERN GOVERNORS UNIVERSITY

Based in Salt Lake City, Western Governors University serves more than 40,000 students in all fifty states.

Salt Lake City

Salt Lake City is the center of one of the best business climates in the country. With a resilient and diversified economy, Utah's capital embodies a livable city. A combination of local, national and international industries continues to be the envy of much of the country and supports a solid education system, renowned cultural and recreational assets and a strong social safety net.

Mobility gives Salt Lake City momentum and is the "circulatory system" that keeps the city connected and vibrant. The City's multi-modal mobility, including bike lanes, light rail, streetcars and trains, offers connections for residents and visitors; connections to the downtown core, to distinct neighborhoods, other municipalities throughout the region, and to adjacent natural spaces like City Creek Canyon and the Jordan River, as well as to the world-class assets of the Wasatch Mountains and Great Salt Lake.

To maintain the remarkable assets that distinguish the Capital City, Salt Lake City continues a strong tradition of careful stewardship and provides an array of outdoor experiences much valued by residents and visitors alike. The City is surrounded by natural treasures and is committed to providing the use and access that sustains a valued quality of life while protecting the abundant resources that place Salt Lake City in a rarified place for a large urban area.

Salt Lake City is the beneficiary of tremendous assets that provide a foundation for the development of a world-class education system and workforce. The City boasts an immense concentration of post-secondary and higher education institutions (including the University of Utah, Westminster College, Salt Lake Community College, a growing BYU Downtown campus, Utah State University extension and a plethora of trade schools and certification programs). Currently, these institutions are seeing record enrollment levels as more and more students pick Salt Lake City as their higher education destination.

Salt Lake City government continues to elevate the protection of basic human rights for all Salt Lake City residents through policy, education, advocacy and celebration. Principles of diversity, equal protection and accessibility are all critical to a well-functioning municipal government and are fundamental elements of a livable city.

Residents and visitors are attracted to the City's plentiful artistic and cultural offerings and sophisticated, cosmopolitan feel. The Utah Symphony & Opera, Mormon Tabernacle Choir and Ballet West anchor a myriad of acclaimed dance and theater companies, choral groups and galleries. Salt Lake City recognizes the value of these cultural amenities. The arts not only lift the human spirit, but also stimulate economic activity, support business recruitment and retention, and enhance the livability of the region's vibrant hub.

The world is quickly discovering what Salt Lake locals have known for the past few years: Salt Lake's urban scene is on the rise, fast-becoming one of the nation's most desirable places to live and a "must visit" destination. In recent years, articles in nationally acclaimed publications have offered a glimpse of the revolution happening in Utah's capital city, celebrating the changing landscape of Salt Lake's restaurants, nightspots, and neighborhoods.

Residents and visitors alike are truly enjoying the renaissance that has been taking place recently throughout the city, the centerpiece of which was the opening of City Creek, the $2 billion redevelopment project. Located in the heart of downtown, City Creek's sustainably designed mixed-use development of retail stores, restaurants, residences and offices has already proven to be a game changer for those who frequent the downtown business district. City Creek, combined with the opening of two groundbreaking museums—the Natural History Museum of Utah and The Leonardo—and scores of restaurants and bars in the downtown core alone, Salt Lake's urban renaissance truly positions this "Crossroads of the West" into one of the nation's most desirable cities in which to live and visit. Taking it one step further, on tap for 2016 is the opening of the new performing arts center, the Eccles Theater, a 2,500-seat, state-of-the-art facility also located in the heart of downtown, fully complementing Salt Lake's Capitol Theater, Abravanel Hall and Rose Wagner Theater.

This sizeable shift within Salt Lake included not only brick-and-mortar improvements, but those of the culinary and nightlife variety as well. For such a compact downtown, dozens of new restaurants, bars and nightclubs have infused the city with a vibrancy sure to astonish the first-time visitor (or anyone who has not visited Salt Lake in the past five years). From a celebrity-owned Euro-style beer bar and nightclub to an exciting and ardent music scene, Salt Lake is pleasantly surprising many long-time visitors and, in all honesty, some locals as well.

Further adding to Salt Lake's reputation as being one of the most user-friendly cities in terms of getting around, the much-anticipated airport TRAX line now whisks travelers from SLC International Airport to downtown in just twenty minutes. Running every fifteen minutes, the airport TRAX line connects with Salt Lake valley's existing vast network of TRAX lines, bus lines and FrontRunner trains to Provo and Ogden, making for a seamless experience regardless of your final destination. And the city's bike share program, GREENbike, has exceeded all expectations, recently doubling the number of bikes and bike stations available throughout the city after just one year.

These exciting changes are merely the beginning of what city planners and community leaders have in store for Utah's capital city. Additional community enhancements to benefit locals and visitors alike are constantly being discussed, moving from the idea phase to the drawing table and to reality before our very eyes. It is definitely an exciting time to be in Salt Lake City, with even more wondrous changes on the horizon.

Top, left: Downtown Salt Lake and the Wasatch Mountains.
PHOTO BY SEAN BUCKLEY.

Above: City Creek Center, in the heart of Salt Lake City.
PHOTO BY SEAN BUCKLEY.

The Marketplace

Salt Lake City's retail and commercial establishments offer an impressive variety of choices

Royce Industries, L.C. 210
Red Iguana 214
America First Credit Union 216
Deseret Management Corporation 218
Lewis Stages 220
Creative Bioscience 222
First Utah Bank 224
Durham Jones & Pinegar 226
Utah Paper Box 228
Strong Automotive Group 230
Regional Supply 232
Sportsman's Warehouse 234
Beijer Electronics 236
Sysco Intermountain 238
Christopher's Prime Steak House & Grill 240
Alsco Inc. 242
Peak Alarm Company, Inc. 244

Salt Lake Chamber 246
Nicholas & Company 248
Kirton McConkie 250
ConsultNet 252
Mountain West Small Business Finance 254
Wintersteiger Inc. 255
A&Z Produce Company 256
Himalayan Kitchen 257
The Salt Lake Tribune 258
VLCM 259
Rhodes Bake-N-Serv™ 260
Mountain Land Design 261
Adam Barker Photography 262
IDFL Laboratory and Institute 263
Harmons Grocery 264
Rocky Mountain Water Company 265

ROYCE INDUSTRIES, L.C.

❖

Right: Royce is proud to work with his sons and sons-in-law. Top row, from left to right: Tommy Troske, Chad, Clint and R. Calvin Rasmussen. Bottom row, from left to right: Brian Hardman, Casey and Royce C. Rasmussen, Jerrod McCall and Cliff Rasmussen.

Below: Founders Royce and Julie Rasmussen.

Cleaning services and cleaning equipment have been the means of success for Royce Industries, L.C. over the past thirty years. Committed not only to solutions for customers' needs, but also to the community and the environment, the company has achieved a stellar reputation for partnering with business and industry of all kinds when it comes to cleaning.

"Businesses turn to Royce Industries, L.C. because we are known for solving the toughest cleaning challenges," says R. Calvin Rasmussen, the company's CEO. "We provide the best selection of pressure washers; steam cleaners; parts washers; floor scrubbers; floor sweepers; car, truck, bus, and railcar-washers; water recycling; water treatment; infra-red heaters; detergents; cleaning equipment accessories; parts; service; warranty and more."

The business was founded in 1984 by Royce Rasmussen, a native of Salina, Utah. Royce, who was told when he was twelve years old that he would not amount to much and should "learn his place," was motivated to be "better than expected." During his active childhood he took part in Boy Scouting and earned his Eagle Scout rank, was a drum major, participated in wrestling, All-State Band, was president of Boys' League, and was even a rodeo clown.

Royce began work at age thirteen, cleaning restrooms at a Texaco station, and worked at several jobs through the years. A 1967 graduate of North Sevier High School, he married his high school sweetheart, Julie. They have been married 45 years and have 8 children and 25 grandchildren.

Working primarily as a truck driver, Royce logged over two million miles accident free, transporting mostly gasoline and propane. At the end of one long, tiring day he told Julie he did not have time to clean his semi-truck. She suggested that he act on an idea he had mentioned previously, starting a mobile truck wash service.

Royce convinced his parents to loan him $4,000 to purchase the equipment, and Royce & Sons Mobile Truck Wash was born. It operated out of his home, employing only himself and two sons, Calvin and Casey. The company, which grew rapidly, originally focused on mobile truck cleaning but Royce soon recognized the need for a company versed in all aspects of the cleaning industry. He envisioned building a company that would be a leader in industrial cleaning. With a strong work ethic and the help and support of his family, he began the journey to realizing his dream.

"Back when Royce Industries, L.C. offered only cleaning services, one of our best customers asked about buying similar equipment to clean their own trucks and how much that would cost," Calvin says. "Because we hadn't yet learned how to 'buy right' we offered them the equipment for the same price we had paid for it. That was the start of our equipment sales business."

After saving enough to buy some new machines, Royce bought four new machines from a California manufacturer, not realizing that the company had been sold and these four machines were about the last of those available with the current technology. As a result, Royce Industries, L.C. began its sales business with the previous year's model.

Money for growth was scarce, and the next few years were extremely difficult. Not many people wanted to do business with an unknown company. Access to cash was difficult and Royce had to wait for customers to pay before he could buy equipment and supplies. He ran the business part time for two years, because he still needed his truck driving paycheck. He refinanced his home, Julie tended neighbor kids for money and Royce still drove trucks at night. When he came home one day and told Julie how much money he needed to purchase a water tank for his trailer unit, she recommended that he sell her car for cash to buy the tank. For the next two years their travels—even family trips with seven children—were made in a pickup truck. "Cash flow is still an ever-present problem for growth," Calvin says. "Every time Royce Industries, L.C. grows, it's followed by a period when cash is a problem."

Although many years have passed since washing that first truck, Royce's intense desire "to be better" has never changed. Although he describes himself as just a simple guy from rural Utah who worked hard and got lucky, his employees and friends disagree. They call him one of the most honest, hardworking people they know. His ability to surround himself with the right people, train them and then have the insight to direct them has led to the company's tremendous success. Even though Royce deflects much of the credit to others, his leadership, innovation and persistence have built the company to become the one of the largest pressure washer distributors in the world.

Today, Royce Industries, L.C. is a recognized leader in the field of industrial cleaning equipment, car wash equipment and railroad/railcar services in the Intermountain area. With 4 locations and growing, it serves 7 states, and employs nearly 50 people with a vast and varied base of knowledge. In addition to specializing in cleaning equipment, consulting and sales, Royce Industries, L.C. offers extensive repair and maintenance programs with comprehensive parts inventories, mobile service, warranty services, factory-trained technicians, complete "turn-key" installations and more, continuing its commitment to remaining on the cutting edge of the cleaning industry.

In its journey from its humble beginnings to today's position of strength in the industry, one constant remains—the commitment to providing customers with the finest products and the highest quality service available in the marketplace today. As "Your partner in a cleaner environment," Royce Industries, L.C. is a trusted name in industrial, commercial, manufacturing, construction, fleets, earthmoving, mining, petroleum/refinery, military, aerospace, aircraft, railroads, marine, automobile, food processing, golf, and agriculture. Its car wash experts are well versed in design, construction, equipment, installation, and car wash supplies.

Royce Industries, L.C. meets cleaning needs throughout the western U.S., with locations in Salt Lake City, Utah; Denver, Colorado; Boise, Idaho; and Las Vegas, Nevada, and service provided to parts of California, Montana, Oregon and Wyoming.

❖

Above: Royce Industries, L.C. railroad crew assembling components to build railcar covers in Western Utah.

Below: Left to right, Chief Executive Officer R. Calvin Rasmussen and Royce Industries, L.C. founder Royce C. Rasmussen at headquarters in West Jordan, Utah.

❖

Above: Royce Industries, L.C. construction and car wash crew working at a new site in Nevada.

Right: Royce Industries, L.C. Parts and Service Manager, Cliff Rasmussen, putting the final touches on a bus wash in Salt Lake County.

Below: Royce Industries, L.C. installing bus wash equipment in Salt Lake County.

Royce Industries, L.C. has always utilized a variety of innovative strategies. Its motivation and uncompromising high standards have transformed segments of several industries to a modern business model to become more successful. Long before environmentally friendly practices became popular, Royce Industries, L.C. was using them.

Its computerized contact management and tracking systems revolutionized the cleaning industry. Calvin and company employees have taught at seminars and conferences to help others automate and become more profitable. The company is revered for its part in improving distribution and service. It has also invested in training the right people, resulting in better-trained employees and higher wages than industry norms.

The company has undertaken a number of "people initiatives," participating in its employees' personal development for success, creating an innovative, progressive, clean, world-class company in an industry known for dirt, smells, uneducated employees, and low tech operations. It also provides health and retirement benefits to employees and utilizes progressive incentive pay to raise wages above the industry standard. Recognized as an innovator in the cleaning industry, Royce Industries, L.C. has grown every year since inception, and now serves over 7,600 customers throughout its operations.

Royce has been granted patents for two of his inventions, a portable equipment wash station in 1997 and a fluid retention station in 1998. He has also received the 2005 Cleaning Equipment Trade Association (CETA) Lifetime Achievement Award, and was a finalist for the Utah Ernst and Young Entrepreneur of the Year Award in 2006. The company has also received a lengthy list

of awards from industry-related, community, civic, and charitable groups, magazines, youth organizations, church and sports groups, and more.

"Because we are a family company and have a drive to continue servicing our customers and industry, the future of Royce Industries looks bright," Calvin says. "We embrace the obligation to stay current in all applicable areas and continue to grow. Our strategy for growth and sustainability will be attained through organic growth, mergers and acquisitions. Ultimately our goals include better coverage of the Intermountain West, including the eleven Western States. We plan to reach this goal through expansion of physical facilities, staff, infrastructure and technology."

He points out that the groundwork for this growth was set in motion years ago by Royce, whose vision includes empowering others. "He has allowed his family and others within the organization to excel in their own areas of expertise," Calvin says. "He has encouraged and paid for continuing education in these areas, improving the company's position as an industry leader and further fostering confidence among others. His vision is focused not only on this generation but also on future generations. The company not only has an ownership succession plan, but a management succession plan, as well, further ensuring its future success.

"Royce Industries' products, themselves, are indicative of our approach to the environment," Calvin says. "Historically,

people and companies have used their garden hoses hooked to their home or business to perform all types of cleaning functions. This not only wastes over ten gallons of water per minute, the lack of heat and pressure makes the work take longer, further wasting both water and people's time. Furthermore, all this water historically goes into storm water drains, then to rivers, streams and lakes, or directly into the environment where it is used."

Royce Industries, L.C. works to minimize this waste. Cleaning equipment uses a fraction of the gallons of water per minute, the higher pressures and temperatures make any cleaning application more efficient and safer, and the company's recovery products redirect the runoff to approved areas and/or treatment equipment with advanced technology to prepare it for reuse. In addition, GPS technology and route planning software minimize fuel consumption; the detergents used are "green" products; sales and service personnel are trained in the best practice use of waste water recycling equipment and patented wash-containment pads.

With the same ability to diversify, recognize and embrace change that has marked its history, Royce Industries, L.C. continues today to look toward expanding into other areas, as well as improving service to the areas it currently serves.

Top, left: Royce Industries, L.C. facility in Boise, Idaho.

Top, right: Royce Industries, L.C. facility in Las Vegas, Nevada.

Below: Royce Industries, L.C. General Manager, Chad Rasmussen, working with a customer.

RED IGUANA

Below: Red Iguana founders Maria and Ramon Cardenas, Sr., came to the United States from Chihuahua and San Luis Potosi, respectively. The menu the couple offered diners when they opened the Red Iguana in 1985 is very similar to what is served there today: authentic, savory Mexican dishes created from the heart.

Right: Red Iguana co-owners, Lucy Cardenas and Bill Coker, take their stewardship of one of Salt Lake City's most iconic eateries very seriously. They look forward to enriching and enhancing the Red Iguana experience for many years to come.

Opposite: The Red Iguana menu is as much an anthem to ancient Pre-Hispanic cuisine as it is a Cardenas' family legacy. Each item, from the popular moles to this mouth-watering Chile Relleno, is a delicious riff on traditional Mexican food you will not find anywhere else.

Describing the Red Iguana's place in the Salt Lake community is no easy task. Iconic, homey, cool are all apt descriptors. None alone, however, completely encapsulate the Red Iguana's truly inimitable vibe. "It's like being at a wedding reception," Co-owner Bill Coker says. "Everyone is a different age and from often wildly different backgrounds but they've come together for a singular event. But rather than celebrating a marriage, they're celebrating Red Iguana's food and atmosphere, together, in close proximity, like extended family. Regardless of who they are, or who's sitting at the next table, that shared purpose gives them permission to thoroughly enjoy themselves."

Stop by the Red Iguana any day for lunch or dinner and you will see what Coker means. The crowd assembled outside waiting for a table is made up of equal parts suit-and-tie clad convention goers, twenty-something hipsters and families. Inside, Red Iguana's colorful atmosphere reflects its homespun yet complex family dishes—somehow comforting and a bit edgy at the same time. Diners leave feeling like they have visited a friend's home, rather than a restaurant.

Maria and Ramon Cardenas, Sr., opened the original Red Iguana in a tiny space at 300 West and 300 South in 1985. Serving up an endearing mix of original Cardenas family Mexican food and their larger-than-life personalities, the couple quickly gained a loyal following in the eighteen seat eatery. When a fire destroyed the building after just a year, the Cardenas moved the Red Iguana to its current location on North Temple.

Through the 1980s and 1990s, the Cardenas' son, Ramon, Jr., played a pivotal role both in the Red Iguana's operation and in defining its incomparable culture. "Ramon, Jr., was very tied into the local music scene, hosting many musicians at the restaurant as they passed through Salt Lake, helping shape the place's funky, alternative personality," Coker says. One look at the front door, covered with stickers from every corner of the world, is all it takes to get a sense of how far and wide the Red Iguana's reach is felt. Over the years the Red Iguana has received dozens of

awards and recognitions, including a feature on the popular Food Network program, *Diners, Drive Ins and Dives in 2008.*

Today, the Red Iguana remains a family affair. Lucy Cardenas—Maria and Ramon, Sr.'s daughter—with her husband Coker, run the original Red Iguana, Red Iguana 2 (866 West South Temple) and Taste of Red Iguana (City Creek Center). "Both Lucy and I feel it's an honor being the caretakers of such a wonderful community experience. We look forward to preserving and enriching that experience for many years to come," Coker says. For more about the Red Iguana, please visit www.rediguana.com.

America First Credit Union

America First Credit Union is one of the largest, most stable and most progressive credit unions in the country and has remained a member-owned, not-for-profit cooperative financial institution since its inception over seven decades ago. From low-rate loans and free online services, to mortgages and free checking accounts, America First offers a vast array of tools allowing members to manage their money, in the manner they desire. America First operates 104 branches, with assets exceeding $5.8 billion, is the thirteenth largest credit union in country and the seventh most substantial in membership with more than 607,000.

America First operates 104 branches in Utah and Nevada, including the credit union's newest location in downtown Salt Lake's City Creek Center.

It was founded on March 16, 1939 at the Hotel Newhouse in Salt Lake City, Utah. Among the fifty-nine who attended the charter meeting of what was then the Fort Douglas Civilian Employees Credit Union was R. D. (Ray) Hagen, a volunteer who eventually become the organization's first full-time employee (treasurer/manager) and later president and chief executive officer (CEO). The founders established the credit union in a small office housed in Fort Douglas' Building 207, with service hours on Fridays only from 3:30 to 4 p.m. A Prince Albert tobacco can was used to hold all cash deposits at the time; total assets and membership were $788 and 79, respectively.

On June 23, 1947, the finance office of the U.S. Army at Fort Douglas was moved to the Utah General Distribution Depot in Ogden, Utah, and the credit union went with it.

The name was appropriately changed to Federal Employees Credit Union and the organization steadily grew. Then, in 1984, Utah-chartered credit unions expanded service from federal employees to all state residents. The name was changed to America First Credit Union to reflect its growing membership and mission. It was headquartered in Ogden and branched out primarily to serve the Wasatch Front (Box Elder, Weber, Davis, Salt Lake and Utah Counties). Today, America First maintains five headquarter buildings in Riverdale, Utah.

Over the last fifteen years, America First has experienced significant operating challenges and has met each with professionalism and in the spirit of cooperation. In 1998, when local and national banks sued to invalidate America First's charter to serve all of the state's residents, America First worked with the Utah Legislature to broker a compromise: restricting its field of membership to five counties along the Wasatch Front. Then, in 2003, the banks struck again by writing, sponsoring and funding legislation to eliminate business lending by sizable state-chartered credit unions and limiting whom they could serve.

America First took action to protect its members a second time and converted its charter from state to federal, thereby providing a reasonable field of membership and maintaining its ability to make loans to business members. As a result of these and other efforts that keep the interests of its members firmly in focus, the company won the Outstanding Political Action award from the *Credit Union Times* in 2007.

A unique and defining characteristic of America First is that, in seventy-four years, the credit union has had just four presidents/CEOs: the aforementioned Ray Hagen, James (Jim) Dawson, Olin (Rick) Craig, and now John B. Lund, who was appointed to the top post in 2012 after thirty-seven years of service. In 2012, the National Credit Union Foundation (NCUF) presented Craig with its 2013 Herb S. Wegner Memorial Award for Lifetime Achievement; he is one of only twenty-four credit union leaders in history to receive this award and the only Utahn ever to have such an honor.

America First's mission of service is not limited to helping people develop and maintain financial well-being. In fact, it emanates throughout the community. America First's employee volunteer program, dubbed the Greater Good, offers a planned, managed framework that motivates staff members to effectively donate time and resources to the communities where they live. Quarterly Greater Good activities are focused on four specific areas: health and human services, community beautification, education and Warm the Soles of Kids, a program sponsored by America First and other credit unions, providing new shoes to disadvantaged kids during the holiday season.

Other philanthropic activities engaged in by America First staff members include mentoring students at Lakeview

Elementary School in Roy, encouraging the children to excel, achieve and succeed; and fundraising for the Community Assistance Program (CAP), which benefits organizations working to end homelessness and help the impoverished, including the Ogden Rescue Mission, St. Anne's Shelter, Catholic Community Services, the Cathedral of the Madeleine, Christmas Box International, the Assistance League of Salt Lake, the SHARE food bank in Ogden and Safe Nest in Las Vegas, Nevada.

Far beyond simply a place to deposit money, America First Credit Union is dedicated to creating lifetime relationships with each and every member served. No matter the life stage they have reached, America First provides the right products, services, assistance and support to maintain and improve members' financial health. For more information about America First Credit Union, please visit www.americafirst.com. America First is federally insured by NCUA and an Equal Housing & Opportunity Lender.

Meeting the financial needs of its members is priority number one at America First Credit Union, which includes day-to-day services, as well as free consumer education and counseling.

Deseret Management Corporation

Above: Salt Lake City is a global leader in fields ranging from cancer research to digital communications. Deseret Management Corporation is an integral part of Utah's growing global influence.

Opposite, left: The Triad Center, in downtown Salt Lake City, is home to a number of Deseret Management companies including Bonneville International, Beneficial Life Insurance Company, The Deseret News and Deseret Digital Media.

Opposite, right: One of Deseret Management Corporation's most well-known companies is Deseret Book, a market leader in faith-based books, DVDs, home décor and religious art.

The diverse companies making up Deseret Management Corporation (DMC) provide vital products and services for individuals and families here in Utah, across the country and around the world. Many began as fledgling pioneer businesses founded to address the needs of growing frontier communities and today are national leaders in a variety of fields and industries including media and hospitality, all of which adhere to DMC's enduring mission: to be trusted voices of light and truth reaching hundreds of millions of people worldwide.

Founded in 1966, Deseret Management Corporation is a parent company operating commercial for-profit businesses affiliated with The Church of Jesus Christ of Latter-day Saints. DMC's family of companies includes:

- Bonneville International: KSL Radio first went on the air in Utah in 1922 as KZN. KSL-TV debuted to Utah audiences in 1949. In the years since, the KSL brand has achieved unprecedented reach and continues to reinforce, connect, inform and celebrate Utah communities and families every day. Bonneville International also operates FM100 (KSFI) and The Arrow 103.5 (KRSP) in Utah, as well as radio stations and websites serving the Los Angeles, Seattle and Phoenix markets.
- *The Deseret News*: First published on June 15, 1850, *The Deseret News* is Utah's oldest and most stalwart provider of news, analysis and commentary on issues impacting families including faith, education, values in the media, care for the needy and financial responsibility. *The Deseret News* also publishes a national edition covering stories through the lens of faith and family.
- Deseret Book: Since 1866, Deseret Book Company has been the market leader in faith-based books, DVDs, home décor and religious art, serving primarily members of The Church of Jesus Christ of Latter-day Saints. The company is rapidly growing its digital media and lifestyle products to better serve families and individuals around the world.
- Deseret Digital Media: With almost 13 million unique visits and over 300 million page views per month, the network of websites making up Deseret Digital Media represents the largest digital network in the Intermountain West market. The network's premier sites include ksl.com and deseretnews.com. In addition, the company is working on digital global reach initiatives to help families and individuals worldwide.
- Beneficial Life Insurance Company: Founded by Heber J. Grant in 1905, Beneficial Life is the oldest life insurance company domiciled in the Intermountain West. Though the company discontinued expansion of its insurance and annuity policy base in 2009, it continues to service existing policies in a professional, service-oriented manner.
- Temple Square Hospitality: Traces its roots back to 1911 with the launch of food service operations at the Hotel Utah. Temple Square Hospitality now serves more than 600,000 meals every year at four Temple Square restaurants—The Roof, The Garden, The Nauvoo Café and the Lion House Pantry—and at two catering facilities, The Lion House and the Joseph Smith Memorial Building.

When the Transcontinental Railroad was completed in 1867, Utah became known as "the crossroads of the west." Since then, the state has emerged as a leader in a range of fields including computer analytics, cancer research and digital technology. At its center is Salt Lake City, a thriving and multi-layered cosmopolitan city, home to a world-renowned symphony and opera, museums and theaters and an NBA basketball team. "We at Deseret Management Corporation believe that what has been both within our company and in Utah as a whole is merely a prologue, a laying of the foundation, for what is yet to be," says DMC's President and CEO Keith B. McMullin. "As strong as we are individually, our strength increases exponentially as we work together, all of us with

compatible desires, aims, purposes and vision. Deseret Management Corporation is excited to be part of this important growth. We look forward to helping Utah evolve from the crossroads of the west to the crossroads of the nations."

For more information about Deseret Management Corporation and its family of outstanding companies, please visit deseretmanagement.com.

1850: First published on June 15, 1850, The Deseret News is *not only the oldest newspaper but the longest continuously operating business in the State of Utah.*

1866: Deseret Book Company is launched and since then has been the market leader in publishing and distributing faith-based books, music, DVD's, religious art and home décor, and other lifestyle products.

1905: Heber J. Grant, the seventh president of The Church of Jesus Christ of Latter-day Saints, founds the Beneficial Life Insurance Company with the intent of protecting widows and orphans and helping people attain financial security.

1911: Temple Square Hospitality traces its roots back to 1911 with the launch of food service operations at the Hotel Utah. Temple Square Hospitality consists of four restaurants—The Roof, The Garden, The Nauvoo Café and the Lion House— and two catering facilities—The Lion House and Joseph Smith Memorial Building.

1922: KZN, precursor to KSL Radio, hits the Utah airwaves sowing the seeds of a media holding company now known as Bonneville International Corporation (1964), which spans radio and television stations in the Salt Lake City, Phoenix, Seattle and Los Angeles markets.

1966: Deseret Management Corporation is formed to operate several commercial for-profit companies affiliated with The Church of Jesus Christ of Latter-day Saints.

2010: DMC launches Deseret Digital Media, a company creating and managing digital environments to elevate, inspire and inform families and individuals worldwide.

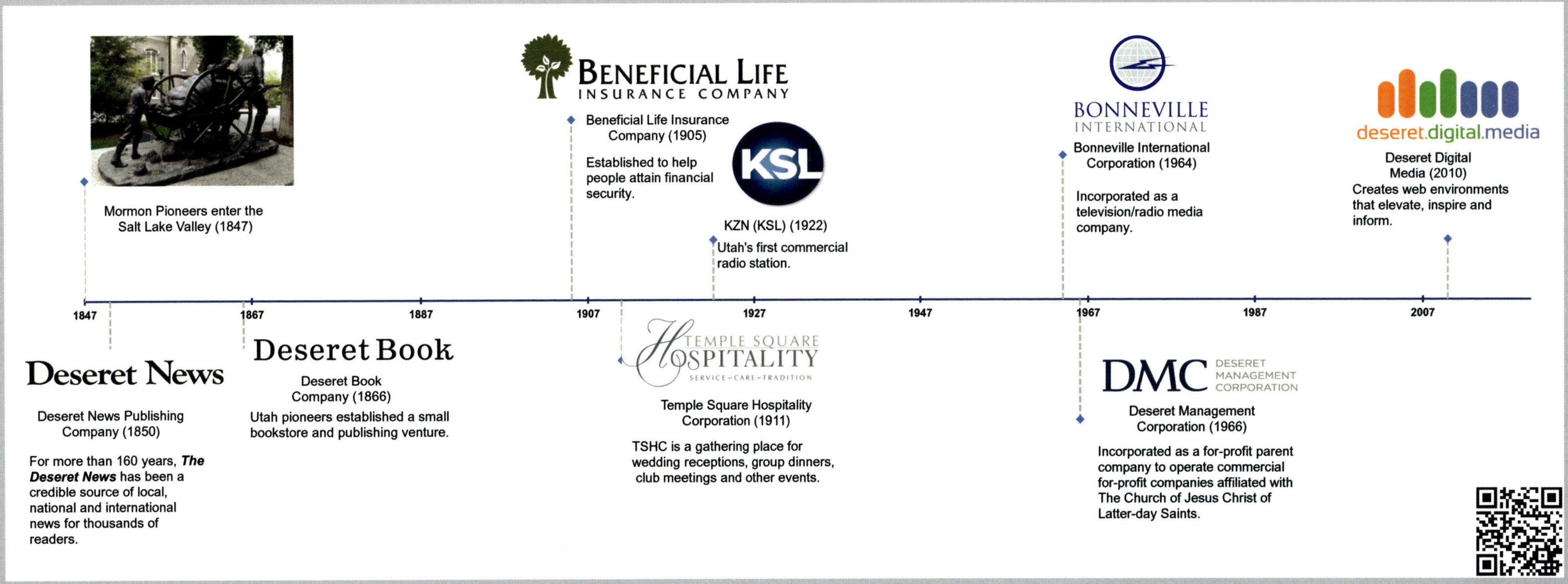

Deseret Book

BENEFICIAL LIFE
INSURANCE COMPANY

Beneficial Life Insurance Company (1905)

Established to help people attain financial security.

KSL

KZN (KSL) (1922)
Utah's first commercial radio station.

BONNEVILLE INTERNATIONAL

Bonneville International Corporation (1964)

Incorporated as a television/radio media company.

deseret.digital.media

Deseret Digital Media (2010)
Creates web environments that elevate, inspire and inform.

Mormon Pioneers enter the Salt Lake Valley (1847)

1847   1867   1887   1907   1927   1947   1967   1987   2007

Deseret News

Deseret News Publishing Company (1850)

For more than 160 years, *The Deseret News* has been a credible source of local, national and international news for thousands of readers.

Deseret Book

Deseret Book Company (1866)

Utah pioneers established a small bookstore and publishing venture.

TEMPLE SQUARE HOSPITALITY
SERVICE~CARE~TRADITION

Temple Square Hospitality Corporation (1911)

TSHC is a gathering place for wedding receptions, group dinners, club meetings and other events.

DMC DESERET MANAGEMENT CORPORATION

Deseret Management Corporation (1966)

Incorporated as a for-profit parent company to operate commercial for-profit companies affiliated with The Church of Jesus Christ of Latter-day Saints.

LEWIS STAGES

From transport via Model "T" Ford in 1914 to today's modern fleet of motor coaches, transit buses, mini-coaches, vans and a new fleet of CNG (Compressed Natural Gas) buses, All Resort Coach, Inc., d/b/a Lewis Stages boasts a century of outstanding service. The company provides charter, tour and contract transportation services in Utah, Nevada, and throughout the Western United States.

At age sixteen, Orson Lewis earned enough money shoveling boxcars of salt at Morton's Great Salt Lake ponds to purchase a Model "T" Ford. Securing one of the first chauffeur's licenses in Utah, he began transporting miners twenty-five miles between the Bingham Canyon Copper Mine and Salt Lake City and called his company "Bingham Stage Lines." A century later, Lewis Stages is again transporting miners at the Bingham Canyon Mine for Kennecott Utah Copper, LLC.

When six of his brothers joined Orson in the business, the company was renamed, "Lewis Bros. Stages, Inc.," and they built a vital network of scheduled routes connecting otherwise isolated farming communities between Pocatello, Idaho and Las Vegas, Nevada.

Booming growth of passenger routes in the "Roaring Twenties," ended with the Great Depression, which weeded out dozens of competing jitney operators. During those hard times, Orson bought gas and paid drivers with cash from each day's fares, taking home what little was left to feed his family.

In the late 1930s, when the drums of war were beating in Europe, Orson put up everything he had to get a loan. One Sunday a friendly banker made a "kitchen-table deal" that financed the purchase of a fleet of used school buses. That loan enabled Orson to win his first arms-plant worker shuttle contract, beating out a competitor who did not yet have the needed equipment.

The used school buses, held together during World War II with "bailing wire and bubblegum," were golden when no new buses could be found, because manufacturing was devoted to the war effort. Those buses moved thousands of newly minted pilots from Camp Kearns, the Army Air Corps' western training center, to Salt Lake City for their precious few days of leave before shipping out.

When the brakes failed on one of those buses, a seasoned driver used the gears to time stoplights and made it all the way downtown without incident but could not stop when he pulled into the depot. He ran into the back wall at ten miles per hour ripping the seats, jammed with GIs, out of the floor. Running towards the crash, Orson was nearly trampled by stampeding pilots rushing towards the red light district. Not one stopped to file an injury claim.

After WWII, the company's operations passed to Orson's son, Joe, just returned after three years in Patton's Army. With scheduled routes giving way to America's love affair with the automobile, Joe reshaped the company as a charter specialist. The foundations of the revitalized company were decades-long relationships with the Utah Symphony, University of Utah, Brigham Young University (including moving the 200 member cast of the Palmyra Pageant to New York each summer for twenty-five years), Utah Jazz, and the growing National Park tour market led by Tauck Tours.

Between the mid-1970s and early 2000s, Joe's son, Steve, grew the company, broadening its focus, winning long-term shuttle contracts with Wendover, Nevada, Bryce Canyon National Park, the Department of Defense, and a dozen others, including the 2002 Winter Olympics. In 2006, Richard Bizzaro and Gordon Cummins of All Resort Express (now part of their growing All Resort Group) bought and reenergized Lewis Stages, doubling its fleet, expanding its tour operations and contract business, and adding a very successful facility in Las Vegas.

Undoubtedly, the most unique service ever provided by Lewis Stages was its Department of Defense contract for Russian Missile Inspectors under the Intermediate-Range Nuclear Forces Treaty from 1988-2001. This one-of-a-kind contract required Lewis Stages to transport, escort and monitor two dozen Russians, whose official job was to make sure the Hercules (now Alliant-Tech) missile plant at Magna did not make anything that violated the treaty.

"Our company sent daily reports to the Pentagon," says Steve Lewis, vice chairman of Lewis Stages. "The challenge was to keep the Russians from succeeding in their covert mission of snooping on local military sites as we hosted their social and shopping expeditions into the unknown wilds of U.S. capitalism. The company's unofficial mission was to show them the heart and hospitality of their Cold War enemy and the vitality of our system."

Steve notes this definitely worked. "Their initial hostility and misconceptions soon softened," he says. "They carried a different 'truth' back to the USSR. Initially, they thought Kmart (their favorite stop) was a staged propaganda shopping-feast, just to impress them. Later, we witnessed 'Glasnost' and the meltdown of the Soviet Union through the frightened eyes of Russian inspectors who didn't know if they would be employed or imprisoned when they returned home."

Lewis Stages' 250 employees operate from the Salt Lake Bus Depot, 549 West 500 South, Salt Lake City, Utah; the Las Vegas Bus Depot, 2880 North Nellis Boulevard, Las Vegas, Nevada; and Executive Offices, 1500 Kearns Boulevard, Park City, Utah.

The company's charitable activities include support of Rotary International, Boys and Girls Clubs of America, Muscular Dystrophy Association, The Road Home, Friends of Animals and many others.

Creative Bioscience

As one of the world's largest suppliers and marketers of high quality, branded nutritional supplements, Creative Bioscience has emphasized innovation, quality and customer service, making it a widely recognized brand among customers of health and natural food stores throughout North America.

"You don't have to feel deprived, starved and tired in order to trim a few inches and get back in your skinny jeans," says Ike Blackmon, executive director of Creative Bioscience. "Diet smart with our weight loss aids and get there faster. Improving your health and appearance is a great goal and when you get help from Mother Nature, it's easier than you might think."

Easy instructions, diet charts and free, unlimited diet support from a team of trained diet specialists are all available with each purchase of Creative Bioscience products.

"This means not only questions about hCG drops but questions about any diet," Blackmon says. "If you have a question you can ask an expert, and the company's philosophy is that when you reach your goal, so does the company."

To fulfill its mission Creative Bioscience pledges to combine research, innovation and technology in order to offer safe, effective diet supplements for every dieter. In addition to producing premier diet aids the company is committed to providing excellent quality with live, personalized weight loss coaching to help dieters achieve their goals and maintain their success.

The company was founded by Ike and Megan Blackmon in April of 2010 and focuses on providing free, 24/7 live diet support with every product sold. The goal is to help customers achieve their goals.

"We are dedicated to weight loss and our products are constantly in the top ten of the SPINS Topline data report for weight loss and diet products," Ike says. "We pride ourselves on providing exceptional products without the use of any starches or fillers." He emphasizes that the products offered by Creative Bioscience are free of gluten, dairy, soy and shellfish.

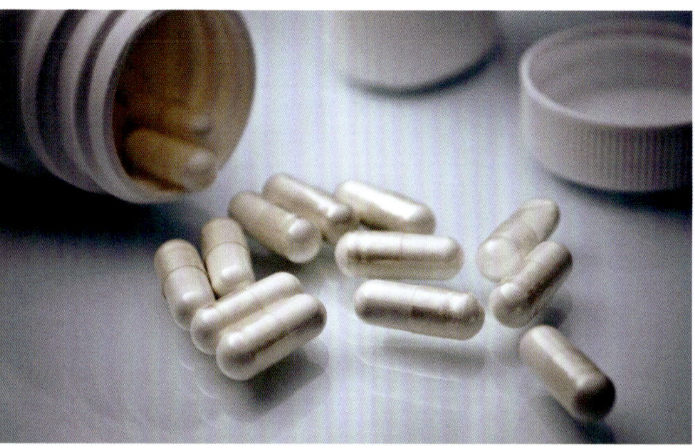

"All of them are manufactured in the United States in FDA-inspected and GMP-approved facilities," he explains. "In addition, Creative Bioscience customers can receive unlimited diet support via phone, email or social media. A store locator feature provides a great tool for retailers to drive customers into their stores."

As the company's Internet presence and reputation have grown so has its retail experience. Its products are now sold in over 30,000 locations in the United States and have been shipped to over eighty countries throughout the world.

"In the early days, Megan and I would personally take orders, package the diet supplements and deliver them in our car while taking care of a newborn baby," Ike recalls. "Now, eighteen wheelers take turns being loaded at our docks. Our staff has grown from two to forty and everyone is a key part of our company's development."

Ike says the company began as a manufacturer of premium hCG drops, helping hundreds of thousands of dieters lose weight rapidly with Dr. Simeons' Protocol…and keep the weight off.

"Those who buy hCG drops from us receive unlimited diet support from our experienced support specialists and experience greater weight loss as a result," he says. "Since the early days, our portfolio has grown in response to customer feedback. It now includes such heavy hitters as Raspberry Ketones, African Mango, Green Coffee Bean, Day & Night Diets, Energy and Appetite Control and more, without losing the core dieters' favorite hCG drops. When scientists and celebrities give rave reviews of an amazing new weight loss wonder in the media, odds are we already offer that ingredient." Originally an Internet-based company that sold one unit a day, Creative Bioscience's volume increased to twenty units daily and then to hundreds of units. Employees were hired and the company was departmentalized to help manage the exponential growth, both on the Internet and through the 30,000 U.S. and Canadian-based retailers to which the company supplies its products.

"Growth statistics are phenomenal, with double to quadruple sales percentages from year to year," Ike says. The company's plan for the future is to be of service to as many people as possible who have the desire to lose weight. Retail partners include Sprouts, The Vitamin Shoppe, GNC, Walgreens, Costco Wholesale and CVS Pharmacy, among others. Creative Bioscience, which has its headquarters at 4530 South 300 West, Murray, Utah, is available online at www.creativebioscience.com.

A key beneficiary of the company's community and charitable participation is Housing for America, a nonprofit corporation that buys properties in edge neighborhoods, invests in renovations and offers the properties at an affordable monthly rent to homeless and potentially homeless individuals. Other charities to which the company contributes include Girl Scouts of Utah, The Road Home and the Utah Chapter of the National Multiple Sclerosis Society.

First Utah Bank

Despite tremendous growth in facilities, employees, and assets, First Utah Bank has retained its personal interest in providing services that will enhance the financial welfare of each person and company that banks there.

"Our mission reflects our continuing dedication to our customers, shareholders, communities, and employees," says Chairman Scott M. Browning. "We strive to deliver state-of-the-art, unparalleled products and services to our customers through avenues of choice; goodwill to the communities in which we serve; and an enriching experience to our employees."

He noted that the bank continuously works to enhance its products and services, and to remain technologically competitive in the marketplace.

Beginning as Cottonwood Security Bank in September of 1978, First Utah Bank has grown from a single location to seven full-service banking offices and a mortgage division located within the Salt Lake Valley.

These include:

- Main Office branch and headquarters, 3826 South 2300 East, Salt Lake City;
- Midvale, 7070 South State Street, Midvale;
- Centennial, 1991 South 3600 West, Salt Lake City;
- Sandy, 11100 South State Street, Sandy;
- City Center, 115 East 1300 South, Salt Lake City;
- Riverton, 4168 West 12600 South, Riverton;
- International, 3123 South Redwood Road, West Valley City; and
- Mortgage, 8915 South 700 East, Sandy.

Now staffed by approximately 112 employees, the corporation has reached $275 million in total asset size.

"At First Utah Bank we believe that building long-term, values-based relationships is the key to our success," says Vice President of Administration, Jean John. "As a community bank, one of our strengths is experienced local management with customer accessibility to decision makers. We are 100 percent locally owned.

"The bank's personnel understand the importance of giving customers easy access to their banker for resources and information," John says, adding, "that this has always been important and is especially true in today's challenging economy."

She urges that customers "feel free to contact us at any time" for advice and ideas that will help them succeed today and in the years to come.

"Your success is our success," she says.

The bank is in the forefront of energy conservation efforts. A lighting retrofit project is nearing completion. This will convert all interior and exterior lights of its buildings, corporate-wide, to LED to conserve energy. The bank also promotes e-Statements, online, and mobile banking in an effort to decrease paper usage and to eliminate the need for clients to travel to a branch location to conduct their banking business.

As an active community partner, First Utah Bank supports various charitable activities. For a number of years, the bank was a top contributor to the annual March of Dimes fundraising walk-a-thon. More recently, First Utah Bank has made generous donations to assist the International Rescue Committee with its New Roots Farm in West Valley City. This project helps teach refugees how to grow much of their own food, as well as how to sell the excess produce at farm stands.

More information about First Utah Bank is available on Internet at www.firstutahbank.com.

FIRST UTAH BANK
DRIVE UP ATM
FIRST UTAH BANK

Durham Jones & Pinegar

❖

Top, left: Looking toward the Utah State Capital building,
Durham Jones & Pinegar's corporate office is located on the corner of
State Street and Broadway.

Top, right: The firm's three partners, left to right: Managing Partner Kevin R.
Pinegar, Founder and General Counsel Paul M. Durham, and Director and
Shareholder Jeffrey M. Jones. Durham founded the firm in June 1991.

Since it was founded nearly a quarter century ago, Durham Jones & Pinegar has become one of the largest law firms in Utah. The firm operates from offices in Salt Lake City, Provo, Ogden, St. George and Las Vegas, and its attorneys advise clients around the world in a spectrum of legal fields including complex business and finance, securities law, mergers and acquisitions, banking, commercial litigation, intellectual property, bankruptcy, real estate, tax, estate planning, elder law, employment, family law and more.

The firm and its lawyers have received significant accolades in its relatively short existence including: frequent recognition in *U.S. News & World Report*'s Best Lawyers Ranking (which in 2013 named the firm's Managing Partner Kevin Pinegar as Utah Lawyer of the Year in Corporate Compliance); and consistently high rankings in Chambers USA America's Leading Lawyers for Business; the Mountain States *Super Lawyers®*, and *Utah Business Magazine*'s "Legal Elite."

Most D|J|P shareholders have earned the coveted Martindale-Hubbell "AV" peer review rating (the highest rating awarded to attorneys for professional competence and ethics), and in 2013, The American College of Bankruptcy inducted D|J|P Shareholder Kenneth L. Cannon II as a fellow in recognition of his professional contributions in the fields of bankruptcy and insolvency. Steven J. McCardell, a member of D|J|P's board of directors is also a fellow of the College.

D|J|P is actively involved in attracting new business to Utah and helping existing Utah companies succeed. The firm supports: chambers of commerce throughout the state; the Economic Development Corporation of Utah; the National Association of Women Business Owners; and MountainWest Capital Network, to name a few. Shareholder Jeff Jones serves as general counsel for the Utah Technology Council, a resource for emerging Utah high-tech companies. The firm deepened its commitment to the state's thriving high-tech sector with the launch of an intellectual property group in 2010, which includes patent prosecution, trademark and copyright, as well as intellectual property litigation expertise.

Though D|J|P is firmly invested in the communities in which its attorneys practice, the firm's influence is realized well beyond the Intermountain West. The firm employs talented attorneys who are admitted to practice in Arizona, California, Connecticut, Colorado, Hawaii, Idaho, Maine, Minnesota, Nevada, New York, Washington, Wisconsin, Texas, Utah and Washington, D.C. The firm is also the sole representative for legal services in Utah and Nevada for the prestigious World Services Group, the second largest professional services network in the world.

D|J|P was founded by Paul Durham, a member of the firm's board of directors and the firm's General Counsel.

After his admission to the bar in 1980, Durham worked for ten years for what was then the largest law firm in Utah. Durham ventured out to build his own firm in 1991, employing from day one what he describes as the "no jerk" rule. "Our focus is hiring and retaining attorneys who not only produce high quality legal work, but who are also great people," Durham says. The firm's high civility standards apply not only to how the firm's attorneys conduct themselves when representing D|J|P and its clients, but to how they treat one another and the firm's employees. "The sense of teamwork we enjoy here is quite remarkable," Durham says. Others have apparently taken notice as well. In 2013 the Utah State Bar Association presented Durham its prestigious Professionalism Award. Also, *Super Lawyers* Magazine has named him one of the top 100 lawyers in the Mountain States, and he is listed in *Best Lawyers in America* in litigation, corporate and real estate law.

In addition to providing the highest quality legal services, D|J|P philosophy is strongly rooted in giving back to the communities in which each office operates. The firm is committed to supporting organizations that benefit the arts, community wellness, health and humanitarian services. Some of the nonprofit corporations and other organizations attorneys have served include: Pioneer Theatre Company, Utah Regional Ballet, Hale Centre Theatre, Salt Lake City Gallery Stroll, Make-A-Wish Foundation of Utah, Muscular Dystrophy Association of Utah, American Cancer Society, Amicus International, the Ogden School Foundation, Utah Heritage Foundation, Utah Food Bank, Rescue Mission of Salt Lake, United Way and more.

D|J|P's commitment to community is further demonstrated by the firm's generous ongoing contributions to "And Justice For All," a fundraising organization sanctioned by the Utah Supreme Court to support worthwhile organizations that provide legal services directly to poor and disadvantaged individuals throughout the state of Utah. These organizations include Legal Aid Society of Salt Lake, Utah Legal Services, the Disability Law Center and the Multi-Cultural Legal Center.

For more information about the law firm of Durham Jones & Pinegar, please visit djplaw.com.

Above: Durham Jones & Pinegar focuses its community efforts on improving education and economic development, and in enhancing the arts, zoos, parks and recreation in the firm's areas of operation. Pictured here is one of the nonprofit organizations supported by the firm—Wasatch Community Gardens.

Left: Durham Jones & Pinegar is one of the largest law firms in Utah, with more than twenty practice areas and about 100 attorneys. It has offices in Salt Lake City, Provo, St. George, Ogden, and also in Las Vegas.

UTAH PAPER BOX

❖

Above: Utah Paper Box, 920 South 700 West—our LEED Gold headquarters building.

Right: Senior management: Teri Jensen, vice president, finance; Mike Salazar, vice president, operations; Steve Keyser, president; Paul Keyser, chairman of the board, 2013.

Below: Left to right, Wayne Sanford and Jim Keyser next to our first big truck.

After a century in business, Utah Paper Box (UPB) is sharing its history, including colorful stories from its past and looking forward to many years of growth and continued success. The company produces innovative, high quality, sustainable packaging solutions and strives to meet customers' quality and timeline expectations while treating them and UPB employees with integrity and as family.

Opened in 1914, UPB mostly made boxes for laundry services until receiving an order from Glade Candy Company for single bar candy boxes, then later for rigid setup boxes. Thereafter, it made both folding cartons and rigid boxes, for sales of about $4,500 that year. Employees worked on a piece-work basis and made ten to fifteen cents per hour.

When the Keyser Company, composed of Aaron Keyser's children, George D., Malcolm, Paul, and Helen, bought UPB in 1922, George, was elected president. His brothers, along with Al Merrill and Jim Ingebretsen, were directors. Using original capitalization of $50,000, operations began at the site of today's Salt Palace, with Kirt (KD) Young as manager. Several years later George's son, James F. (Jim) Keyser became a director, then secretary-treasurer and in 1946, manager. Early foremen were Neil Soderburg and Cliff Peck. Jim's son, Paul, is currently chairman and his son, Steve, is president.

UPB's history is colorful. In 1915 and 1916, material shortages and cost increases brought shirt box prices up from thirty-nine to sixty cents each. Women were hired to assemble the rigid boxes in the early 1920s, and still do the majority of production. UPB closed at noon on Christmas Eve, with boxed dinners from the Doll House Restaurant served to employees. Spouses and partners were invited in later years, and the party was held in the manufacturing plant. The cooking was done by Roy Peck and Wayne Sanford. This and a summer party that was added later are still held today.

Machinery shortages after WWII led UPB to add a night shift. Day workers' hours were 7 a.m.-3:30 p.m. To keep costs down, Jim Keyser, Ralph Bean, Wayne Sanford and most production employees worked nine-hour days during the week and five on Saturdays.

"During the 2002 Olympics, the Secret Service used the east parking lot, and we shuttled employees to work from other parking lots," says Steve. "Everyone showed photo IDs to pass the check point."

In 1991, UPB purchased the former 7Up bottling plant at 959 South 800 West. This became the finishing plant and later the central site for all UPB production. After a building

addition in 2009, rigid box production was moved there. In 2013 the office and printing plant has been built and connected to the existing buildings, putting all production and offices in one location.

"UPB's new headquarters and printing operation demonstrates our company's commitment to Salt Lake City's future and to UPB's customers," Keyser says. "By committing to LEED certification and obtaining LEED Gold, UPB has invested in the community's quality of life and the value of our products."

UPB reinvests seventy percent of its profits and spends thirty percent on profit sharing. Since 2006, over $25 million in the company's future has been invested through machinery, buildings and people. Strong partnerships with customers and equally strong partnerships with equipment and board suppliers are maintained. Overcrowding at the downtown central location in 2009 brought expansion of buildings on the west side of Salt Lake City.

In 2009, UPB committed to a thirty-three percent reduction in its carbon footprint by 2017. Solar energy production, minimized truck routes, specialty lighting, low energy heating and air conditioning systems reduced the UPB footprint by thirty percent as of August 2013. Utilizing low and high

air compressor systems, as well as large storage tanks, and employing new state-of-the-art variable speed compressors, has reduced UPB's energy consumption for compressed air by sixty percent. UPB also committed to LEED guidelines in the new office and print building. LEED emphasizes sustainable sites to reduce energy consumption and emissions from commuting while promoting connections with the community. This process identifies opportunities to build an efficient facility, utilizing items such as a white roof, recycled steel building frame, insulated wall panels, low flow plumbing, evaporative cooling in manufacturing, and an upgraded HVAC system for the offices. The goal was for a basic building design that would be efficient for the next century.

In an effort to reduce automotive pollution, UPB has installed bicycle racks and five electric vehicle (EV) charging stations for employees. Building the new headquarters displaced a tire recycler, required brownfield redevelopment, and helped convert an abandoned rail spur to a bike and pedestrian trail. UPB's roof is reinforced for initial and future solar panel installations.

UPB's growth continues. In 1965 the company produced mainly rigid boxes, had thirty employees and sales of $443,000. In fiscal 2013, it had 230 employees, sales of about $33 million, producing rigid, folding, litho lam, and plastic boxes.

Today, the Keyser family and employees participate in a host of charitable and community causes and organizations, and share their commitment to continued growth within Salt Lake City in UPB's second century of operation.

Above: Utah Paper Box employees.

Left: Some of the current customer boxes we make: Uinta Brewery (SLC), Smith Optics, Sweet Candy Company (SLC), Rocky Mountain Chocolate Factory, Scott and Fran's Chocolate.

Below: The newly constructed printing plant, 2013.

STRONG AUTOMOTIVE GROUP

In Utah, the Strong name is synonymous with the state's earliest car dealership and the quality of the familial bonds in this more than eighty year old family owned and operated business. It all started during the midst of the Great Depression in the mid-1930s when L. H. "Roy" Strong had the foresight to know cars would play a big role in the country's future. He opened a Studebaker franchise in Logan, and later moved to Ogden to operate a Packard dealership. In the 1940s, he purchased property in downtown Salt Lake City and built a showroom where he began selling Hudson automobiles.

Dave Strong began working for his father, Roy, at the age of fourteen, starting with washing and detailing cars and mopping the showroom floors. He moved up to selling parts and learning more about what it takes to run a dealership. At eighteen, Dave went to the University of Utah where he was in the basketball program. He soon married his high school sweetheart, Merle Jackson, and continued pulling double duty with work and school.

When Roy retired for health reasons, Dave left school to run the dealership, which was facing its biggest challenge yet. The manufacturing of Packards, Hudsons and Studebakers ceased. But Roy had one more card up his sleeve. Prior to his retirement, Roy took the opportunity to purchase a Volkswagen franchise in the mid-1950s. The VW Beetle became an instant hit in Salt Lake City shortly after its release in the U.S., and Strong Volkswagen was born, one of the first VW dealerships in the nation.

Yes, cars are in the blood of the Strong family and Dave added the Porsche franchise in 1960 and the Audi franchise in 1969, after purchasing and remodeling an old laundry building to house the Audi line. Together, Dave and Merle were both business partners and household partners. They began building their family, ultimately having five children. Being a man dedicated to finishing what he started, Dave completed his education at the University of Utah and Brigham Young University at the same time his dealerships prospered. Dave's reputation for honesty and integrity, combined with not a small amount of hard work, contributed to the success of all three franchises in Utah and neighboring states.

Sons Brad and Blake Strong literally grew up in the car business and, like their father, they began working at the dealerships washing cars in their early teens. As time went on, they learned about all the responsibilities involved in owning and operating car dealerships by holding almost every position in the business at one time or another. By 2002, Brad and Blake bought the VW dealership from their father and subsequently acquired the Audi and Porsche locations in 2004 and 2011, respectively. The brothers continue to be owners and partners today with Brad running the Volkswagen dealership and Blake over the Audi and Porsche dealerships.

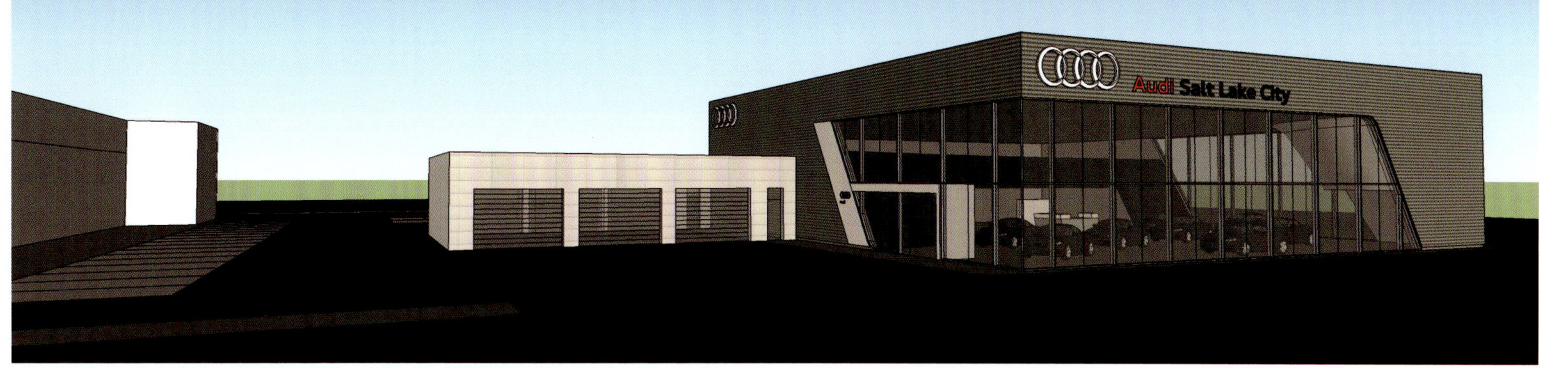

Not only are the Strong dealerships an important part of Utah's history from a business and economic standpoint and as an early provider of personal vehicles, but they have received numerous regional and national awards. A few examples: *Time* magazine named Dave Strong with their highly prestigious "Quality Dealer for Utah Award" in 1997 for "outstanding performance as an automobile dealer and a valued citizen in the community" in recognition of the Porsche, Audi and Volkswagen dealerships. This honor is part of a permanent display in the National Automobile Hall of Fame in Dearborn, Michigan. In addition, Audi, Inc., ranked Strong Audi Number 1 among all U.S. Audi dealerships in customer loyalty. Finally, during Volkswagen of America's fiftieth anniversary in 2005, Strong VW was one of only thirteen dealerships in the country still owned and operated by the original founding family.

From its humble beginnings, the Strong dealerships have grown from ten employees to over 170 as each location continues to thrive due to outstanding leadership and the teamwork of every single person in their various departments, including sales, service, parts, administration, and yes, car washers, too. Other members of the family, including the fourth generation of Strongs, work at the dealerships and at their newest venture, Porsche Design, a retail store which opened in 2012 at the City Creek Center and features everything from fashion to eyewear to luggage and more.

Involved in the larger community, the Strong family of dealerships is continually interested and active in community development and a huge supporter of the University of Utah sports programs, the Utah JAZZ, the Real, and Bees as well as Ballet West, Big Brothers Big Sisters and more. They also sponsor various 5Ks and other events in support of an impressive number of nonprofit organizations and youth sporting groups.

Today, Strong Automotive Group, headed by Brad and Blake, is thriving and consistently among the top dealerships in the nation in sales volume and customer loyalty, despite being a small family-owned business rather than a multi-state or national corporation. From its humble beginnings during the Great Depression through today, Strong has remained one of Salt Lake City's most dependable employers and an example of what a family owned and operated business really means.

REGIONAL SUPPLY

Regional Supply, one of the largest sign, screen print and plastic supply wholesalers in the Western United States, is a division of Fisher Group, Inc. Regional Supply was founded in 1946 by Art Mendenhall and was originally called Regional Electric Works. At that time, they repaired electric motors and rebuilt neon transformers for the electric sign industry, with Young Electric Sign Company (YESCO) as its main customer. By 1951, Art and his team had expanded their business into a full-service sign supply business.

As the years passed, Regional Supply's business continued to expand and become more recognized in the sign industry, supplying product and services to most of the area's leading sign manufacturers. In the 1960s the company continued to diversify and expand as the market changed, further developing the product line to include screen-printing equipment and supplies. The late 1990s brought about digital imaging and printing as another new and emerging trend for the sign and graphics industry. Regional Supply embraced this new technology and has become a leader in the sales of digital printers, inks and media.

After many years of successful operation, Art retired in 1978 and was succeeded by his son, Dwain C. Mendenhall, who owned and operated the company for thirty years. In 2008, Dwain sold his companies to his son-in-law, David L. Fisher, who had been the company's vice president for many years. David's company, Fisher Group Inc., now acts as a holding company for four businesses, including Regional Supply.

"We take pride in the deep roots of our history and value the relationships we have cultivated over the last sixty plus years," Fisher says. "We don't just sell products we take care of our customers through technical support, daily delivery, and a personal sales staff. When you purchase supplies and equipment from Regional Supply, we want you to know that you're not alone. Your purchase will be backed by experts with years of experience in the field."

Fisher noted that the sales team is trained in the latest technology, and its members also have a vast working knowledge of each piece of equipment the company sells.

Regional Supply specializes in wholesale supply to screen printers, large format digital printers, electric and vinyl sign makers and installers and a wide variety of plastics users. It carries more than 10,000 items for customers' businesses, from vinyl, inks and neon to plastic sheets, transformers, screens and lamps.

"If you need it, we have it," Fishers says. "We take pride in keeping our customers up-to-date on the latest breakthrough technology and knowledge the industry has, by offering continuing education courses on many different subjects and products."

Regional Supply is backed by some of the largest names in the industry, and sells only the best products and materials. Custom mixing of screen print inks and sign paints is available, plus custom-cut plastics and many other substrates. Regional prides itself on its vast inventory, including fully custom, hard-to-find items.

"In the last sixty plus years, we have learned what our customers want, and more importantly, what they need to be successful," Fisher says. "Our staff has many years of experience in the industries we serve, and we know our products, materials, and equipment. We will continue to nurture our past business relationships and look forward to the new opportunities that lie ahead."

Regional Supply is one of four unique companies that comprise Fisher Group, Inc., a holding company established in 2007. Others in the group are American Label, Plastic Fabricating, and Fisher Fulfillment. Like Regional, each has a rich heritage, a long history, and roots that grow deep into the soil of Salt Lake City, Utah. Each has established a tradition of quality and excellence throughout the Western United States and across the country.

Fisher Group, Inc., seeks, develops and capitalizes on profitable opportunities, leveraging its diverse knowledge, skills and experience of its wholesale and retail distribution, fabrication, printing and fulfillment to provide valued goods and services. Recognizing that its employees are the core of its success, Fisher Group is committed to their growth and development. It also strives to be the company of choice by nurturing relationships with its employees, customers, vendors and the community.

Regional Supply is currently headquartered at 3571 South 300 West, Salt Lake City, and has approximately sixty employees. They are active members of the community, contributing to a wide variety of charitable and community improvement efforts including numerous contributions and projects through the Salt Lake City Rotary Club and other organizations.

For more information about Regional Supply, visit www.regionalsupply.com or telephone 801-262-6451 or 800-365-8920 (toll free).

SPORTSMAN'S WAREHOUSE

With a trademark proclaiming that Sportsman's Warehouse is "America's Premier Outfitter," the over fifty Sportsman's Warehouse stores in eighteen states across the U.S. provide hunting, fishing, camping and shooting enthusiasts with quality, brand-name merchandise within a comfortable shopping environment.

Passionate, enthusiastic associates create a memorable shopping experience as they help outdoor sports enthusiasts find the right equipment for their activities, with brand-name products ranging from apparel and footwear to the specific gear needed for hunting, shooting, reloading, camping, backpacking, fishing, and other activities.

"This combination of the right products, a friendly shopping environment, and knowledgeable staff has made Sportsman's Warehouse the place to go for all outdoor sports activities," says John Schaefer, the company's chief executive officer.

Those who prefer to shop online will enjoy the Sportsman's Warehouse e-commerce site, www.sportsmanswarehouse.com. The online store sells products, offers product reviews and sales, videos and an interactive section in which customers can post pictures and descriptions of successful outdoor adventures.

"Both our regular stores and our e-commerce site have one clear mission—to provide a great shopping experience," Schaefer says.

The fifty plus Sportsman's Warehouse brick-and-mortar stores operate in eighteen states throughout the West, Southwest and Southeast, as well as Alaska and Iowa. Many businesses find it difficult to compete with web-based companies, but the Sportsman's Warehouse stores continue to thrive. This is due in large part to the expertise and passion of the stores' employees, who are both knowledgeable and

enthusiastic about outdoor sports. In recent years, Sportsman's Warehouse has opened three to four new locations each year, a rate of growth it plans to maintain while expanding to both the west and east. In each new location, it seeks employees who are outdoor sportsmen or sportswomen.

"Many of our customers rely on the proficiency of our associates when making product selections," Schaefer says. "We appreciate their work and take pride in the positive customer feedback we receive about them. Our success is driven by this expertise and passion. We receive an impressive amount of positive feedback about the great job they do, and appreciate their contributions to Sportsman's Warehouse."

Founded by Bill Hayes and Scott Neilsen in 1986 as Sports Warehouse, the company's name changed soon afterward to Sportsman's Warehouse. It employs a total of 3,350 people, including 105 at the corporate headquarters in Midvale, Utah.

Marketing is driven by new product lines and use of the Internet, with the stores and e-commerce site having a clear mission to provide a great shopping experience. The stores' footprints—averaging 48,000 square feet—are sometimes smaller than certain other big box outfitters, but their size allows customers to find the national brands they know and trust quickly and easily. The Sportsman's Warehouse loyalty program rewards frequent shoppers with gift cards and specific offers catered to their favorite outdoor activities.

Plans for the future include adding to offerings on the e-commerce site. Since it opened in 2010, improvements to design, content and usability have brought a significant increase in use. Among the most recent improvements has been the addition of a mobile site for easier shopping from phones and tablets along with the continued focus on content as well as with additions to the products offered online, with corresponding multiple-image views and enhanced descriptions.

Although guns will not be sold online, the company is creating a library of guns and safes on the site. This is designed to aid consumer research and to give customers information about what is available in the brick-and-mortar stores. Plans also call for equipping the site with enhanced reporting tools so consumers can access details concerning their purchase and location.

"Hands-on testing will be done in the stores to determine how people use the site," Schaefer said, along with promotional offers in areas where the company's stores are located, and marketing of the e-site inside the stores. Plans also call for Sportsman's Warehouse to sponsor five or six national television programs, along with advertisements in such national publications as *Outdoor Life* and *Field and Stream*, with QR codes on each ad.

Special events offered by Sportsman's Warehouse are geared to the specific areas in which they are scheduled. These include classes, seminars and presentations, and events. Most stores offer a "Ladies Nights" to engage more females interested in fishing, camping and hunting in a friendly and educational environment. In Alaska, some sites hosted an Easter Egg Extravanza, a Basics of Rainwear presentation and introduction to archery. Classes in California have covered topics ranging from deep-frying turkeys to hunter safety, and from Dutch oven cooking to a pistol reloading seminar.

It is all designed to provide the information and products the customer wants, and to make the entire process an enjoyable one.

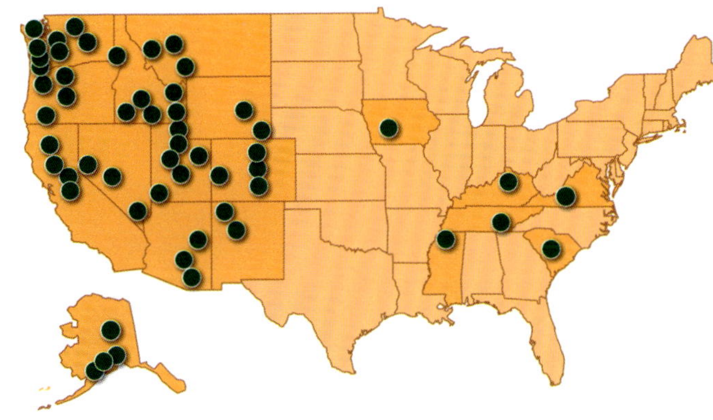

BEIJER ELECTRONICS

A leading provider of user-friendly automation solutions on a global basis, Beijer Electronics is driven by a strong commitment to people and technology while providing innovative and reliable automation and communications solutions to improve its customers' businesses.

In 1983 twin brothers Jim and John Elwell, both electrical engineers, began making battery-operated computers as QSI. Both worked in fields needing such computers, Jim with sounding rockets and John with down-hole oil well instrumentation. Utilizing a private "blue sky" stock offering from individuals, they raised the entire $60,000 capital to start their business.

Jim, originally the only employee, was soon joined by a part-time secretary, then by John Coffee, a university student who designed many of the company's products before moving on. John Elwell worked there briefly before leaving to work for one of QSI's customers, but retained his stock ownership.

Extremely tight finances and long hours marked QSI's early days. For two years, Jim worked eighty hour weeks with few days off. When the company almost ran out of money in 1984, a secondary offering raised another $54,000, augmented by occasional family loans. Sales during the first year totaled $50,000, gradually increasing to $780,000 in 1988.

After a large order from Thiokol Corporation (now ATK) in 1988, QSI was overstaffed and left with inadequate funds. An ill-advised move from an industrial park in South Salt Lake to the USU Research Park in Logan tripled the rent and placed the company ninety minutes from many suppliers. From thirteen employees, QSI scaled back to three, moved back to South Salt Lake, and rebuilt the business.

"QSI operated nearly twenty-nine years from founding to selling, and spent eleven years learning how to run a business," Jim says. "In 1994, we released a support product—a small, inexpensive, handheld terminal (20 keys, 4 x 20 character display) that our low-power computer board used to set up and check systems in the field. By 1990 it was bringing in more than the low-power computers, so QSI became a terminal manufacturer. We hired our first marketing/sales professional when sales reached $1 million. In the fairly rapid growth that followed, we reached $20 million in 2008."

Initially, the company designed some of the lowest-power computer boards available, often going into systems that would be field-deployed for six months with a set of flashlight batteries, Jim said, adding, "Later we developed very strong expertise in making LCD displays function in very nasty environments. At no point did the company ever file for or receive a patent on any of these products."

After selling to Beijer Electronics, Inc., QSI became Beijer's North American subsidiary, offering not only exceptionally rugged, handheld, pedestal-mount and panel-mount terminals, graphics, full-color, etc., but also Beijer's robust hardware and innovated HMI software.

Like all business owners, Jim and John learned as they went along. One of their first and most important lessons was to ensure that their board of directors is composed of people with experience relevant to industry, rather than consumer, medical or military experience, and who understand industrial challenges.

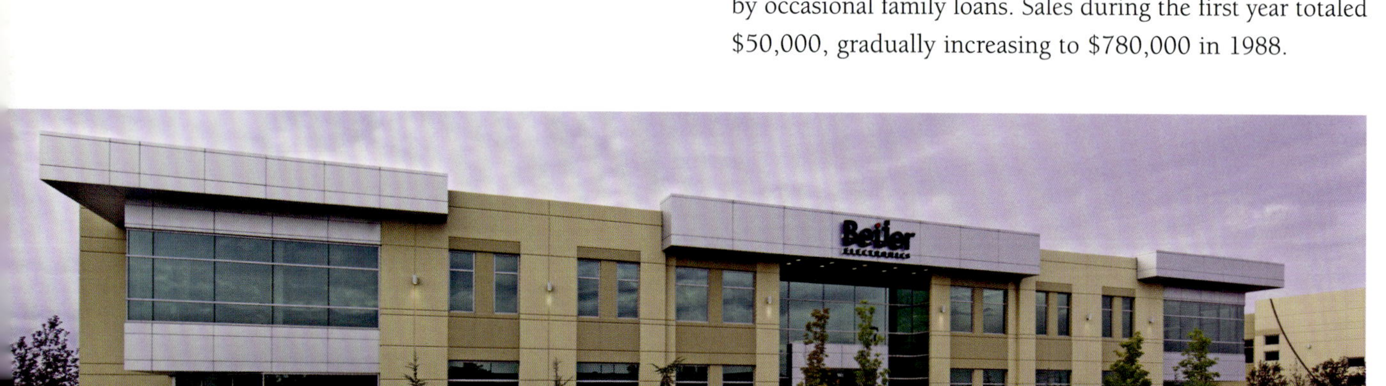

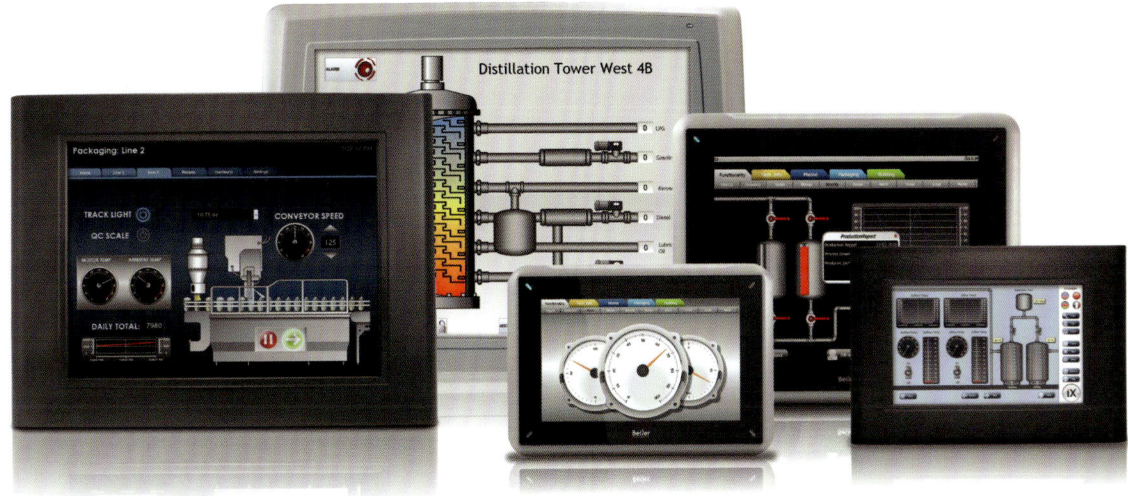

competency is designed to ensure that they can operate in challenging environmental conditions. It has allowed Beijer to diversify into products for use in the oil and gas, medical, energy, trucking, transportation, process control, packaging and other industries, with current annual sales of approximately $30 million, and over 250,000 terminals shipped to over 2,000 customers.

Beijer was among Utah's fastest-growing firms in 1995-2000, with a majority of its raw materials sourced from Utah companies. The company takes pride in its environmental advancement, including a green team focused on reducing waste and recycling. In addition, the company's new building is equipped with automatic lights that will also increase energy conservation.

"We have recently expanded into Brazil," Jim says. "We plan to expand into the medical and mining markets where dependable and rugged products are essential. Outlook for the future is projected at $100 million in the next five to six years, through organic and acquisition growth. Other future plans include an increase in market share in the industrial HMI market, continued focus on environmentally rugged buildings, and the introduction of soft PLC into the Americas."

Additional information is available on the Internet at www.beijerelectronics.com.

In September 2013, Beijer Electronics North America moved to a much larger facility at 1865 West 2100 South, Salt Lake City, to help accommodate its growth and better represent its technical competence. With Malmo, Sweden, as the site of its headquarters, Beijer Electronics has sites in twenty-two countries—Austria, Belgium, Brazil, China, Denmark, Estonia, Finland, France, Germany, India, Latvia, Lithuania, Malaysia, Norway, Singapore, South Korea, Sweden, Switzerland, Taiwan, Turkey, United Kingdom and the United States.

The company sells products including automation software, operator panels, industrial/panel PCs and environmentally-rugged QSI™ HMIs and TREQ® mobile data terminals. These panels or touch screens control machinery and visually communicate machine performance. Their "rugged" core

SYSCO INTERMOUNTAIN

Sysco Intermountain strives to be its customers' most valued and trusted business partner. Our mission of marketing and delivering great products while providing exceptional service is at the heart of what we do. Throughout its history, Sysco has built its reputation on providing quality products, unmatched service, strong relationships, outstanding operations and logistics, and sound financials.

The company employs associates who live in communities across its distribution area. The high retention level and tenure of associates speaks to the quality of career experience offered. The team of talented and creative foodservice professionals is dedicated to making sure customers get what they need, when they need it. This starts by listening and being responsive to customers' needs, while focusing on making every experience easy and enjoyable.

Over the past four decades, Sysco has grown to encompass more than 180 local operating companies with approximately 47,000 employees in the United States, Canada and throughout the world. The common goal of all—from broad line operating companies to local specialty providers—is to provide the best quality, variety and value for every customer, every day, everywhere.

"We live, work, play and dine in the communities we serve throughout the Intermountain region," says President Lisa Gough. "We are also proud to support community programs for hunger relief and general community outreach, as well as agricultural and environmental sustainability. Being a founding member of ProStart, a culinary education program in high schools throughout Utah has helped foster the educational development for students pursuing careers in our industry. At the very heart of our company and our culture, we continuously dedicate efforts toward enhancing the quality of life in the communities where Sysco associates live and work."

Today, food being consumed away from home is consistently changing. We understand the complexity of our business and the customers we serve. "Because our customers demand the very best in terms of quality and variety, Sysco's product mix includes everything from high-end ingredients and specialty items to restaurant supplies and equipment," Gough says. "Our customers also

benefit from one of the largest and most sophisticated temperature-controlled supply chain in the business, ensuring that we deliver at the very highest level of quality, food safety and consistency."

When we talk about the good things that come from Sysco, we are often referring to our variety of services and tools that help our customers' success. We proudly tout the importance of products as seen in our unsurpassed selection of quality in exquisitely marbled steaks and fresh, crisp lettuce to creamy soups, spicy salsas and organic coffees. "It's the variety and uniqueness that matters to our customers. Having the 'right' products and providing a quality and service level that allows our customers to focus on the things that drive

their success is as important as anything we do" says Brian Smith, vice president of Merchandising.

Not only does Sysco service customers across the Intermountain west, but our commitment to the region extends to our suppliers as we seek out local sources for as many products as possible, increasing sustainability and the region's economy in the process.

CHRISTOPHER'S PRIME STEAK HOUSE & GRILL

Right: Our classic filet mignon is a crowd favorite.

Below: Welcome to the comfortable service and amazing food Christopher's has to offer.

Winner of the prestigious Utah "Best of State" award and recipient of an "Excellent" classification by *Zagat* and the Open Table award for "Top Customer Choice," Christopher's Prime Steak House & Grill remains the leader in the Utah fine dining scene. It was founded on the principal that fine dining is about an experience, and from its award-winning architecture to the one-of-a-kind art collection to the warm, comfortable service and amazing food, Christopher's has delivered that experience to guests from around the world.

Christopher Patterson, originally from the Boston/Cape Cod area, founded Christopher's in 1995, assembling a team of the industry's "best and brightest" and retaining his staff over a period of many years. Some chefs have been working with him for ten to fifteen years, and some of the service staff for over seventeen years.

"It was a struggle early on. However, perseverance and hard work eventually paid off," Patterson says. "We invest hundreds of man-hours annually in menu development and sourcing only the best ingredients for every dish. Those featured include Idaho's Snake River Farms American Wagyu beef, twenty-one day aged USDA Prime beef, and organic salmon from Loch Duart, Scotland."

Although every customer has his own favorites, Christopher's is especially noted for its New England Clam Chowder with Ipswich Clams; Crab and Andouille Stuffed Mushrooms with Béarnaise Sauce and Parmesan Crust; Award winning New Orleans Bread Pudding with Kentucky Bourbon Sauce, Whipped Cream and Candied Pecans.

The restaurant's wine list offers hundreds of selections including award-winners across all varietals, vintages and many wines not offered at any other restaurants in Utah.

"Our menus change constantly, evolving with the seasons, markets and food trends. Our chefs have been expertly trained in ingredients and presentations from around the world," Patterson says. "Although the talent and menu selections are diverse, we maintain a stringent policy of sticking to the core principle of all menu items, using only top-notch ingredients to create outstanding flavors. If either component is missing, it doesn't make the cut."

At Christopher's, every menu item must go through an extensive process, with all these steps involving Patterson:

- An extensive description of the item is written.
- A full recipe is written, adhering to Christopher's portion and ingredient minimum standards.
- A tasting with the chefs preparing the item as presented for a guest. Patterson will personally taste the item, and/or have a panel of diners taste it.
- Release of the item as a special, to get feedback over the course of a month. Those that receive a ninety-five percent or better favorable rating go on the next menu.

"We have experienced modest growth through the years and have endured ups and downs with the economy, including the latest recession," Patterson says. "We have always focused on not changing our model. Levels of pricing, service, and portion size have remained consistent with the market throughout all economic turmoil."

❖

Left: Simply breathtaking views from every angle of our one-of-a-kind art collection.

Below: Plenty of charm and classic architecture in the heart of Downtown Salt Lake City.

One key to Christopher's early and sustained growth has been its off-site catering and on-site banquets. Consistently one of the top destinations in Utah for wedding events, it has hosted thousands of such events affecting hundreds of thousands of memories.

"We are also one of the top corporate destinations for special events, dinners and "after-parties," Patterson says. "Both of our locations feature a combined 14,000 square feet of available meeting space. From intimate boardroom meetings to customer appreciation dinners to the all-important company holiday party, Christopher's has done—and cooked—it all.

It is the exclusive caterer for Salt Lake City International Airport's private and charter aircraft, on which dignitaries, sports figures, entertainment stars and business executives eat Christopher's food. Patterson and his staff take pride in providing some of the best food Utah has to offer.

Christopher's also serves VIP dinners featuring entertainment and sports stars as well as visiting executives and dignitaries. One of the restaurant's most memorable moments was hosting the entire Russian Olympic team after the closing ceremonies. On arrival, they brought over 200 one-ounce containers of caviar. As a top destination for Olympic spectators from abroad, Christopher's airline catering traffic increased by 500 percent during the Olympics.

Patterson credits the success of his restaurant to his great staff and loyal Utah customer base that has supported Christopher's since 1995. Christopher's is poised to remain a mainstay in the Utah dining market for years to come, creating thousands more memorable experiences and delicious meals.

The downtown Christopher's restaurant is located at 134 West Pierpont Avenue in Salt Lake City; and the Draper site is at 1122 East Draper Parkway and on the Internet at www.christophersutah.com.

ALSCO INC.

Above: Alsco's first processing facility, located on 130-138 West 100 South.

Below: Alsco's second processing facility, located at 33 East 600 South.

From restaurants and healthcare clinics to processing, repair, and manufacturing facilities, Alsco provides its clients with freshly laundered and pressed linens and uniforms as well as a wide variety of washroom and mat products for lease or purchase.

George A. Steiner made his first foray into the linen business when he was only fourteen years old. Working odd jobs to help support his family, George was hired part-time to deliver cloth towels in Lincoln, Nebraska, for three dollars per week. Less than a year later, George jumped at the opportunity to purchase the business for $50.80. On August 15, 1889, George became the new owner of a towel route connected with the Lincoln Steam Laundry, and by 1891 his

younger brother, Frank M. Steiner, became an equal partner in the business, which they called the Lincoln Towel and Apron Supply Company. The purchase included few assets—an armful of roller and hand towels and a few ten cent wooden rollers that were hanging on customers' walls. However, George and Frank were enterprising and frugal, and their business began to grow.

During the 1890s, the worst economic depression so far in the history of America hit. Corn prices dropped considerably, which greatly affected Nebraska's economy. With the early frosts, droughts and blizzards, the company suffered more. Banks and crops failed. The Lincoln Towel and Apron Supply Company in Nebraska began to struggle, along with most other businesses, as customers reduced their accounts. The young Steiner brothers met hard times head-on—by looking to expand.

Undaunted by their difficulties, George acted on information from friends, who had told him that Salt Lake City, Utah, was a beautiful and prosperous place. George was further encouraged by his college friend, George Dern, a past Utah governor and U.S. Secretary of War, who operated a business in Utah and was doing well. Thus, with Frank running their company in Nebraska, George moved to Salt Lake City to start up a new business.

In Salt Lake City, the new company, named American Linen, rapidly thrived. By 1899 it was large enough for George to rent his first plant, which was located on First South long before Abravanel Hall was built there to host the

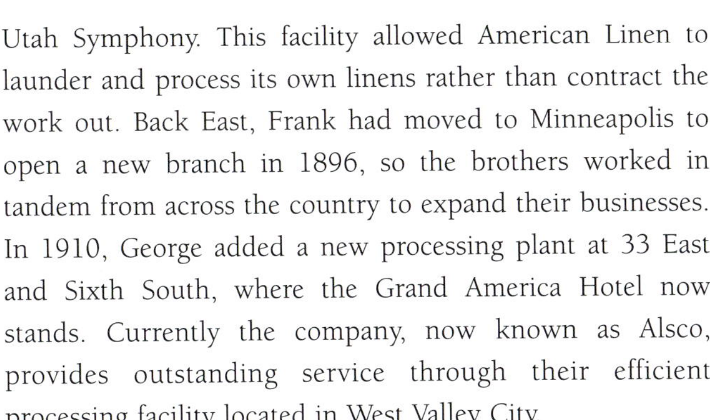

❖

Left: Alsco's global headquarters in Salt Lake City.

Utah Symphony. This facility allowed American Linen to launder and process its own linens rather than contract the work out. Back East, Frank had moved to Minneapolis to open a new branch in 1896, so the brothers worked in tandem from across the country to expand their businesses. In 1910, George added a new processing plant at 33 East and Sixth South, where the Grand America Hotel now stands. Currently the company, now known as Alsco, provides outstanding service through their efficient processing facility located in West Valley City.

Today Alsco has expanded worldwide to 150 plus locations in fourteen countries, including the United States. In addition to its two headquarters in Salt Lake City, other Utah sites include Ogden and St. George.

From being the first towel supplier to add bib aprons to their product line to being recognized by the renowned Hohenstein Institute in Germany in 2009 for inventing the linen and uniform rental industry, Alsco has always looked for innovative ways to enhance its business and improve its products.

Today, Alsco continues to lead by advancing new green technologies using recyclable fabrics and cutting-edge technology to save water and energy in its processing plants.

Now, 125 years later, Alsco remains family owned and operated. Frank G. Steiner, George's son, took over the company's development and growth following the founders, George and Frank. Frank G. was followed by his son, Richard R. Steiner, and subsequently by two grandsons, Robert C. and Kevin K. Steiner, who currently serve as Alsco's co-CEOs.

As a family company in its fourth generation, Utah owned and operated, Alsco remains committed to its family roots and local community. In 1962 the company created the Steiner American Foundation, which later became the Steiner Foundation. Since that time, both Alsco and the Steiner Foundation have made substantial contributions to local organizations that support the arts, education, physical fitness, and healthcare within local communities.

Founded by a young teenager who was constantly creating and adopting new technology, new ways of marketing and new techniques of management, Alsco continues to pioneer the linen and uniform rental-services industry. Alsco leads with high quality products, innovative technologies, and a relentless drive to provide the best customer service in the industry.

For additional information on Alsco or for a facility near you, please visit www.alsco.com.

Peak Alarm Company, Inc.

Headquartered in Salt Lake City, Peak Alarm serves nearly 14,000 customers in a variety of residential, commercial, and industrial markets within its five state service area. It has become a national leader in the security alarm industry, with 250 employees providing electronic and onsite security services including high-performance and custom home audio and video systems from facilities located in Idaho and Utah.

Jerry Howe founded the company in 1969 with limited funds, saved from working technical positions at two Oakland, California alarm companies, a family loan, and two used Volkswagen trucks.

A veteran of four years' U.S. Navy service, Jerry incorporated Peak Alarm in 1972, after his commercial security business grew through knocking on doors and referrals from satisfied customers.

Although he often worked all night, Jerry was a devoted father to his two young children. Since he had scant "family time" in the early days, his wife, Gayle, would prepare a bed in his van for the children to sleep while Jerry installed and serviced alarm systems, and the two of them would take Rick, 5, and Julie, 2, with them on calls.

"Gayle would play with the kids in the back while I was inside, and the kids could go to sleep there," Jerry recalls. "When I was driving we were all together." After a typical twelve hour day, Jerry would return home to monitor his alarms and run service calls. Working from their home basement, Gayle handled billing and correspondence on her grandmother's 1930 Underwood typewriter.

When the owner of Day and Night Alarm Company announced that he wanted to sell his business, Jerry quickly agreed to purchase the company's commercial accounts, making Peak Alarm a significant part of the Salt Lake business community. Over the next forty-five years, he bought many more companies and accounts, and soon new offices in St. George, Utah, Idaho Falls and Boise, Idaho, displayed the Peak Alarm name.

Starting with one employee, who remained after the Day and Night acquisition, Peak's revenues from commercial alarm services then totaled approximately $50,000. Today the company serves almost 14,000 accounts in the Intermountain West and beyond, and approached $15 million in gross sales in 2013.

Peak opened its own central station in 1977 with nine dispatchers working around the clock, establishing its headquarters at 2182 South West Temple. After several enlargements and improvements, the company built a 20,000 square foot building at 1534 Gladiola Street. Since 1969, Peak has diversified into three companies: Peak Alarm, Peak Security, and Peak Audio Video. All have grown in both stature and size.

Peak purchased General Alarm Corporation, and computerized its billing and alarm monitoring in 1985, becoming the first Intermountain West company to develop and build a fully computerized, Underwriters Laboratory listed central monitoring station. Peak Security, Inc. now has more than 150 officers guarding government, residential, industrial, and commercial sites. Its security officers are trained in emergency procedures, including first aid and fire prevention, electronic security and video monitoring.

Between 2000 and now, the company grew from 9,000 to almost 14,000 accounts, and from seventy-first largest to sixty-eighth largest security company in the country. Its installations include burglar and fire alarms, card access systems, and video security for homes and businesses. Most of its alarm and video security systems are now digital, utilizing full Internet compatibility. Cellular or proprietary wireless systems often enhance alarm security, as wireless systems typically operate even after damage to phone lines. All installations are engineered to fit the client's needs.

Peak Audio Video was launched in 2010, responding to a growing opportunity for high-end home entertainment and automation systems. Experienced professionals staff at Peak Audio Video is why they are the leading designer and installer of in-home entertainment and automation systems.

"Our primary competitive asset is our people," Jerry says. "Over the years we have hired, trained and developed high quality personnel, including over 25 who have been with us for 10 or more years, and 14 who have been employed here for over 15 years." These include Jerry and Gayle's children. Rick ultimately served as president of Peak Alarm. Julie is central station manager and her husband, Don, is president of Peak Security. After holding diverse positions, Jeff is president of Peak Audio Video. The youngest children, Tim, Tyler, and Renee, have worked in supervisory and training positions in the central station.

As a national leader in the security alarm industry, Peak has achieved awards and other recognition from industry organizations.

Efforts to reduce Peak's carbon footprint include utilizing higher efficiency vehicles to reduce fuel use and carbon emissions. Energy efficient LED lighting now replaces incandescent lamps. Energy optimizers installed on HVAC systems help reduce the need for air conditioning.

During Peak's forty-five years of family ownership, management has strategically positioned the company by focused capital investing, strategic divestitures and numerous opportunistic acquisitions. This strategy has dramatically changed Peak's size, scope, product offerings, customer mix, and geographic coverage, preparing the company for continued growth and performance.

Salt Lake Chamber

For more than 125 years, the Salt Lake Chamber has stood as the voice of business, supported its members' success and championed community prosperity. With its strategic partners, the Downtown Alliance and World Trade Center Utah, the Salt Lake Chamber is Utah's largest business association and business leader.

On March 2, 2012, the Salt Lake Chamber honored the Church of Jesus Christ of Latter-day Saints for the recent completion of City Creek Center, the mixed-use development in the heart of downtown Salt Lake City. Many prominent business leaders gathered at Abravanel Hall to celebrate the completion of the crown jewel thus far in the Downtown Rising vision statement, announced almost exactly five years earlier. Far from complete, the business-led Downtown Rising endeavor continues to move forward with signature projects to enhance our capital city.

Business associations were nothing new in Salt Lake City when the Salt Lake Chamber of Commerce was organized under the laws of Utah Territory on April 23, 1887. Territorial Governor Caleb West hoped that the new organization could help bring competing elements together on common ground—with an eye toward statehood. Fifteen years later, Utah was indeed a state, but the chamber of commerce was in shambles—the victim of a depression and state partisan politics. Important issues of the day, however, required a strong business organization, and so on February 11, 1902, Salt Lake's business leaders reorganized as the Salt Lake City Commercial Club. It was not long before they reverted to the name

"Salt Lake Chamber of Commerce." This time, however, "Utah's Business Leader" was here to stay.

The chamber is involved in almost every major economic and quality of life issue—from developing a solid infrastructure to promoting tourism. Throughout the years, the Salt Lake Chamber has spurred thousands of improvements in the Salt Lake area, including downtown growth and development, the birth of a transit system, the creation of an international airport, the securing of the Utah Jazz basketball team, continued economic expansion, and effective government and public affairs work. At one time, the Salt Lake Chamber even had its own baseball team and its own vigilante security force. The Salt Lake Chamber's involvement in the past is matched by its current programs and involvement.

As Utah's largest business association, the Salt Lake Chamber has been consistent in representing the interests of Utah's businesses to government. In 2006 the big issue was transportation. The Salt Lake Chamber supported giving voters a choice to expand transportation infrastructure by way of a sales tax increase. The Salt Lake Chamber took this position after an extensive study, which showed that Salt Lake's congestion would triple if action was not taken. Voters agreed—approving Proposition 3 to increase funding for light rail, commuter rail and roads. This was only the beginning of addressing huge transportation needs and finding solutions. The Salt Lake Chamber recognized that to keep the economy growing, transportation must keep flowing.

First published in 2008, the Chamber's annual *Public Policy Guide* sets the stage for legislative initiatives and policy changes, including clean air, education and immigration. Similar to the way it acted as a catalyst to bring solutions to Utah's transportation crisis, the Salt Lake Chamber will continue to be a place where business, government and community leaders come together on common ground to find ways to improve Utah and its business climate.

The entrepreneurial spirit of Salt Lake Chamber members is impressive. These individuals and corporate members—who are at the helm of many of Salt Lake's best and finest businesses—work very hard and very smart. In addition to the Salt Lake Chamber representing their interests to government, they know that it provides excellent opportunities to expand their companies through networking and training. The Salt Lake Chamber is about helping businesses grow, make more profit and hire more people. It is through member involvement and a pool of dedicated volunteers that the Salt Lake Chamber is able to make this possible.

Through seminars, workshops, conferences and other education opportunities, Salt Lake Chamber members can remain current and competitive in the marketplace. Through various events such as Business After Hours, Networking Without Limits and Business Women's Forum, members can network and develop business relationships. Involvement can also be found in Salt Lake Chamber committees and task forces, which address many matters, from events to intensive business and community issues. The Salt Lake Chamber provides additional information on its website at slchamber.com.

For the present and the future, everything is looking promising for the Salt Lake Chamber, its members and the state.

Top, left: Lane Beattie and Curt Dousett at the Chamber's 125th Anniversary Gala.

Top, right: Business After Hours at Rico's Mexican Market.

Left: Honoring the Church of Jesus Christ of Latter-day Saints and their recent contributions to downtown Salt Lake City are (left to right) Governor Gary R. Herbert of the State of Utah, Bishop H. David Burton of the LDS Church, City Creek Reserve President Mark Gibbons, and Salt Lake Chamber President and CEO Lane Beattie.

NICHOLAS & COMPANY

❖

Right: William Mouskondis.

Far right: Peter Mouskondis.

Bottom, left: William and Elyce Mouskondis.

Bottom, right: The Mouskondis Family.

Founded in 1939 by Nicholas William Mouskondis and now in its third-generation leadership, Nicholas & Company has received many honors for the high quality of its products, its outstanding service to customers, and its relationship with team members. These include the *Utah Business* Magazine "Best of State for Food Distribution" in 2003, 2006, 2009, 2010, 2011, 2012 and 2013, and "Best Company to Work For" in 2005, 2011, and 2013.

"We have a business culture focused on creating mutual success with our customers," says Peter Mouskondis, the company's current steward. "Our team of food service experts utilizes state-of-the-art facilities, cutting edge technology, and exemplary food safety practices as we practice "Philotimo," a Greek word meaning the love of honor, every day. We think this captures the true importance of hospitality. We value our genuine partnerships and have a passion for serving people. That's our family recipe for success!"

Nicholas & Company was founded by Nicholas, who left his home in Crete, Greece, to forge a better life in the U.S., "the land of promise and opportunity." With an eighth grade education, no knowledge of the English language, and a sign on his back reading "Utah," Nicholas began his long journey to Salt Lake City. He started the business by collecting discarded, dented cans at the railroad station. After he and his family relabeled them, he sold them to customers on his bread route. Bootstrap tenacity, long hours, and great fortitude kept Nicholas and his wife, Anna, moving ahead, following their vision and realizing the American dream.

Under the progressive leadership of its second president, their son, William (Bill) Mouskondis, the company expanded past Salt Lake City, joined buying groups for purchasing power and distribution partnerships, and increased its customer base. Working with his wife, Elyce, and many dedicated employees, Bill secured larger facilities in the Salt Lake International Center. He placed great emphasis on technology, and was the first foodservice distributor to invest in computers for the delivery fleet, upgraded office systems, and provided laptop computers for the street sales team, receiving numerous awards for its outstanding operations and business practices.

Peter Mouskondis and his wife, Nicole, third generation leaders, have a strong commitment to customer partnerships and the Nicholas & Company team. They invest in building infrastructure and developing the tools needed for success,

more than doubling the size of the company's facility, forming national alliances for product development, and further investing in technology. Additionally, the transportation fleet has been expanded and updated to capitalize on innovation and become more streamlined for safety and efficiency.

Each generation has unique challenges and opportunities. The family's vision and commitment incorporate integrity, honesty and opportunity for all associates and partners. These are guideposts in meeting customers' needs while never forgetting the history and the things that have helped make Nicholas & Company the Intermountain West's largest independent broadline foodservice distributor.

Nicholas & Company has been honored for its achievements by food companies and distributors, magazines, chefs' organizations, culinary and dining groups, the International Foodservice Manufacturers Association, Utah Department of Work Force Services, Salt Lake Chamber of Commerce, Utah Highway Patrol and Utah Department of Agriculture. Its charitable/community work has been lauded by various local and national philanthropic entities.

Thanks to a carbon footprint reduction plan, created in partnership with the SWCA Environmental Performance Group, the company is implementing environmental changes to reduce its environmental footprint. In 2008 its facility was expanded and upgraded to maximize efficiencies, utilizing sustainable practices and products. It provides customers with many options for local, sustainable and green products in all categories it stocks, and is committed to sustainable operations in its warehouse, office and delivery fleet.

"We are committed to sourcing realistic options for the environmentally-conscious foodservice operator, making it easier for our customers to green their operations," Peter says. "The Envirable™ collection of products represents recycled, recyclable and compostable options to traditional paper products, disposables, take-out containers and more.

We are a member of Utah's Own and support many local companies and distribute many local products.

Those at Nicholas & Company are proud of what has been accomplished toward being a sustainable business and a responsible member of the Utah economy and are excited about our continued development. The industry is changing and growing rapidly. Foodnetwork® has been a huge influence, changing the public's perception about dining out and making customers more savvy about food quality and safety.

Nicholas & Company currently has facilities in the Salt Lake City Distribution Center and is now a adding a Las Vegas, Nevada, Distribution Center using the industry's newest technology and best practices. With double-digit growth leading the company into the twenty-first century, it currently employs more than 550 team members.

For more information about the company, find it on Facebook and Twitter and at www.nicholasandco.com.

KIRTON MCCONKIE

Founded in 1964, the firm has a longstanding tradition of excellence for advising and representing clients in Utah, the country and around the world on business and legal issues.

A COMMITMENT TO MEETING CLIENT EXPECTATIONS

Providing exceptional legal skills is merely the starting point to become a client's law firm. How well the attorneys apply and deliver information, advice or strategies is what really makes the difference in client satisfaction and what leads to long business relationships. Kirton McConkie clients know they can count on their attorneys to translate the complexity of legal and business issues into practical information. The resulting insights and perspective help clients take more confident action.

As the largest law firm in Utah, Kirton McConkie offers a broad scope of practice areas benefitting clients in two ways. First, the interrelationships cultivated between areas allow a multifaceted approach to a client's situation. The firm can shape a legal team with the right people, at the right time, based on a client's stage of development or legal needs. Second, based on extensive legal and industry knowledge, the attorneys can spot marketplace trends to offer real-world guidance. Whether it is corporate or real estate transactions, commercial litigation, intellectual property protection, employment concerns or tax planning, Kirton McConkie mixes business value with their legal advice to help clients resolve problems and achieve their long-term goals.

Though based in Utah, much of the firm's business is national and international. Kirton McConkie represents multinational and foreign companies with business interests in the United States and assists American companies in global markets. At last count, the firm has done work in 150 countries and every state in the U.S.

A QUIET DEDICATION TO EXCELLENCE

Since Kirton McConkie has maintained a rather low-key profile over its fifty years, preferring a quiet dedication to client service, many people are unaware they have crossed paths with the firm's work in their daily lives. For instance, visitors to and residents within City Creek Center may be surprised to find the firm participated in all aspects of this mixed-use development, the largest ever undertaken in Utah—including the shopping center, residential condominium projects, 5,000 stall parking structure as well as the retail and commercial office leasing.

Other facts about the firm include:

* Experience across a wide range of industries such as biotechnology/bioengineering, construction, consumer products, direct sales/MLM, education, energy, financial, franchising, healthcare, information technology, insurance, medical devices, natural resources, nonprofits, pharmaceutical/nutraceutical, real estate, sports, technology, telecommunications and transportation.

❖

Above: Offices are located at 50 and 60 East South Temple in Salt Lake City.

Right: Reception area of the Kirton McConkie Building.

- Intellectual property protection for over 500 trademark applications worldwide for the 2002 Olympics as well as protecting and defending the intellectual property assets of many well-known brands.
- Franchising experience from start-up strategies to compliance and franchisee relationships for widely known restaurant, sports, consumer product and fitness brands.
- Extensive knowledge of constitutional and civil rights issues related to free speech, free press, protests, defamation defense and the rights of religious organizations.
- Representation of 31 school districts, 50 charter schools and 14 universities in areas such as purchase, construction, financing and refinancing, leasing, bond issues, employment, mobile phone tower leases, policies and compliance, immigration and litigation.
- Involvement in the sports industry in areas such as assisting a high profile Utah sports figure with immigration, developing a doping policy for the USOC, representing clients in front of the International Federation for Bobsled and Skeleton and to the Court of Arbitration for Sport on matters related to chess, cycling and football.

Founded in 1964 by Wilford (Bill) W. Kirton, Jr., the firm has enjoyed steady growth for fifty years. Oscar W. McConkie, Jr., joined in 1967. The firm was originally formed as an independent legal advisor for The Church of Jesus Christ of Latter-day Saints. As the work increased, the firm grew and had several name changes before and after 1964, but came to settle on Kirton McConkie in 1994.

While the Church remains a large institutional client, the firm has always had an eye toward growing a multi-faceted clientele to ensure its attorneys were challenged to provide the most advanced counsel possible for all clients. From the earliest days, Kirton McConkie has had a commitment to provide high-quality, cost-effective solutions to help clients achieve their organizational objectives, to have a workplace where all are respected and find personal satisfaction and to encourage excellence in all aspects, professionally and personally. The depth and breadth of the firm's combined experience and success underscores this vision.

The firm has a Utah County office in Thanksgiving Park (Lehi).

To learn more, scan this code.

ConsultNet

Founder and Chief Executive Officer Don Goldberg.

As an IT and engineering staffing and technology solutions company, ConsultNet pair's highly skilled technical and business professionals with successful companies to support and provide solutions for their business challenges. It has met the growing complexity of its clients' talent needs by developing a suite of consulting services and scalable staffing methodologies that help clients size their workforce for maximum efficiency.

Consultative and contract staffing is no longer a strategy reserved for high-peak needs or labor shortages. All industries and market sectors have adopted our services as part of their long-term talent acquisition strategy. Whether the demand is for individual contributors or project services, ConsultNet supports all phases of development from initial planning to implementation for successful product launches and internal information technology systems.

Founded by Don Goldberg on September 16, 1996, in Salt Lake City, Utah, the company was soon expanded to Phoenix, Arizona; Seattle, Washington; and Irvine, California. After a high growth strategy was implemented, the company was further expanded to Denver, Colorado; Philadelphia, Pennsylvania; Boston, Massachusetts; and most recently New York, New York.

Attributable to ConsultNet's reputation for pristine customer service and high quality talent ConsultNet was named the principal staffing provider for the 2000 Winter Olympic Games, providing over 625 consultants over the span of that project. As the games ended the Olympic Committee recognized ConsultNet for exceeding all expectations for high quality talent and "best in class" customer service.

This high growth enterprise has been honored by numerous groups, including the Blue Chip Enterprise Award presented by Mass Mutual and the United States Chamber of Commerce; was a finalist for the Ernst and Young Entrepreneur of the Year Award; and was one of the "Top 100 Privately Held Businesses" recognized by the State of Utah's Office of the Governor. It also received the Entrepreneurial Success Award from the Salt Lake Area Chamber of Commerce; the Utah 100 Award presented by the Wasatch Venture Capital Group; and was listed in Southwest Airlines' *Spirit* magazine as one of the ten "Most Dependable Staffing Agencies of the West."

Providing a service that delivers skilled technologists to companies who are struggling for market share, profits, milestones and breakthroughs is a thoughtful and purposeful enterprise. Each day it is our purpose to employ technologists, support our clients and create a work environment of respect, dignity and collaboration. Lofty goals, but a simple purpose: finding work for talented professionals, finding talent for dynamic, leading-edge clients.

ConsultNet has been growing at an industry leading rate of thirty-five percent, year over year for the past four years. Projections indicate that this growth will continue in 2014, 2015, and beyond. It is positioned for sustainable profitable growth as it continues to develop leading-edge talent acquisition services and consultative human resource solutions, partnering with a dynamic portfolio of clients in the technology, financial services, energy, pharmaceuticals, and emerging industries sectors of the U.S. economy. Both ConsultNet and its employees are involved with a number of community and charitable activities, led by the board of directors of the Ronald McDonald House of Utah, the Young Endurance Athletics Foundation, and the Utah Technology Council.

If you are a technologist seeking employment, a company that needs superior technical talent, or a staffing professional looking for significant growth opportunities the choice is clear, the choice is ConsultNet. If you would like to learn more about ConsultNet, please visit us at www.consultnet.com.

Above: Senior Vice President of Enterprise Recruiting Meredith Kaley and Senior Vice President of Enterprise Sales, and Chief Financial Officer Dave Jones.

Below: Chief Financial Officer Mike Malan and Director of Human Resources Sarah Brown.

Mountain West Small Business Finance

Right: Working in tandem with the State of Utah's Economic Development Division, in 1980 Scott Davis helped create a resource for small businesses looking to secure SBA 504 financing, now known as Mountain West Small Business Finance.

Below: Mountain West Small Business Finance has helped more than 4,000 businesses in Utah grow and meet marketplace demands including Schmidt's Pastry Cottage, a company employing more than eighty people at four locations across the Wasatch Front.

Mountain West Small Business Finance (MWSBF) is a private, nonprofit corporation, created in 1980 as an initiative of the State's Office of Economic Development to support small businesses in Utah. Mountain West administers the Small Business Administration's 504 Loan Program, a rural revolving loan fund and a small business working capital fund.

One of MWSBF's first loans was to Gastronomy, Inc. Business partners Tom Guinney and John Williams used the financing to open the Market Street Broiler, an eatery that is today both a Utah institution and a vital component of the partners' Gastronomy family of restaurants.

Since then MWSBF has provided SBA financing to more than 4,000 Utah small businesses representing well over $1 billion. Other well-known Utah businesses MWSBF has secured SBA financing for include Papa Pita Bakery, a 200,000 square foot state-of-the-art, fully automated bakery in West Jordan; Schmidt's Pastry Cottage with four Utah locations in Sugar House, downtown Salt Lake City, Taylorsville and South Jordan; and CSB Nutrition, a Spanish Fork-based nutritional supplement manufacturer. Thousands of new jobs in every corner of Utah and surrounding states have been created as a direct result of MWSBF's efforts. "Mountain West was amazing. I didn't have to spend much time with paperwork—they basically handled everything for me and stepped me through the process. They made (securing an SBA loan) easy," says Steve Borg, Schmidt Pastry Cottage owner and manager.

Mountain West President Scott Davis and its staff believe that a diverse and vibrant community supports success and growth in business. Since it was founded, MWSBF has supported many organizations that help make our communities better places to live including SEED Dixie; SEED Cache Valley, the Utah Microenterprise Fund; TURN, the United Way's preeminent advocate for Utah's disabled community; Clark Planetarium and Discovery Gateway Children's Museum; the Utah Shakespeare Festival; Utah Chamber Artists; and the Utah Food Bank to name a few.

For more information about MWSBF SBA loan and financing services, visit www.mwsbf.com.

A specialized machine manufacturer with three business units, Wintersteiger leads the global market in all three. In Sports, the company provides service and rental solutions for skiing and snowboarding. Customers include sports and rental shops, mountain resorts and ski/snowboard manufacturers. The company's Seedmech business leads the way in agricultural field research equipment, plot combines and planters used in seed research by private seed companies, universities and government research stations. The Woodtech division offers thin cutting solutions for the wood industry, with thin cutting frame and band saws used in producing engineered flooring, doors, furniture, and other applications.

Wintersteiger produced the first plot seeder and seed thresher for plant breeding in 1954, followed ten years later by production of the first stone grinder used in ski production, and in 1970 by the first thin cutting frame saw then used for ski production.

Founded in Austria in 1953 by Johann Wintersteiger, a subsidiary office was opened in Salt Lake City in 1989. The company's mission is to turn customers' requirements into solutions, offering sustainable success with innovative products and services, lean processes and qualified employees.

Almost all national ski teams now use the company's computer-controlled, precision stone grinder. A ceramic disc grinder for edges sets a new standard, giving racers the best possible skis. Almost all ski and snowboard manufacturers now apply disc finish on their edges.

Wintersteiger is an official partner of the U.S. Ski Team and the Team's Center of Excellence in Park City is equipped with state-of-the-art ski and snowboard tuning equipment from Wintersteiger that provides athletes with the best equipment possible.

During the 2002 Olympics, the company hosted a reception with the Austrian and Utah Chambers of Commerce and was honored to welcome the Austrian vice chancellor among the 500 guests.

"Over the years we have expanded our business from ski and snowboard service machines to include storage and software solutions for rental shops," says Fritz Hoeckner, company president. "Our latest additions are high-end ski lockers and boot fitting products. We will continue to bring innovative products to the market, giving more comfort and enjoyment for skiers and snowboarders on the mountain."

The company plans to continue launching innovative products for snow sports, Hoeckner says, adding that today's skiers and snowboarders are better educated and demand better equipment and improved comfort.

"They expect better rental equipment that is properly maintained, a clean shop environment, fast service, and better fitting and dry boots. Wintersteiger can help rental and sport shops fulfill these needs. The company's latest success is the fully automated tuning center Mercury, which sets the standard for high quality ski and snowboard tuning."

For additional information on Wintersteiger, please visit www.wintersteiger.com.

A&Z Produce Company

Above and right: The A & Z Produce Company owners in 2010.

The A&Z Produce Company's motto, "A satisfied customer is our first consideration," mirrors its commitment to supply its valued customers with the finest fresh fruits and vegetables at competitive prices, and the highest customer service and food safety standards.

As the premier independent wholesale distributor of fresh fruits and vegetables across the Intermountain West for almost seventy-five years, A&Z has supplied grocery stores, restaurants, institutions and families, earning the industry's highest integrity and credit ratings.

Founded in 1939 by Dale Atkinson and Lloyd Zesiger, A&Z is a family operation that has always relied primarily on verbal agreements rather than signed contracts. In the high-tech world of the twenty-first century, A&Z stands out as an example of old-fashioned values on which the business was built, while incorporating the latest in technology and food safety.

Clifton Clark, who joined the company in October 1940 bought into it in January of 1941. He left the business during World War II, returning in 1946. With his reputation with suppliers and customers still intact, he soon helped establish A&Z as one of Utah's largest produce wholesalers. As other partners eventually left, Cliff's three sons, Jay Dee, Steve and Scott, became his partners in 1971.

As a child of the Depression and part of a large family where everyone contributed to the family's welfare, Cliff began work at age five, picking onions with his brother, always working, even when he was in school. He was extremely resourceful and incredibly creative, finding ways to make money while keeping his ethics intact, giving his word as bond, and instilling this high standard in his new partners.

As his sons joined in company ownership, A&Z Produce became the largest independent wholesaler in Utah and a leader in the Intermountain West. With growth came new technologies and new ways of doing business, but Cliff's core values always served as the basis of the company's operations. Each of Cliff's sons had a son who wanted to be in the business, and third generation family members, Jeff, Ryan and Spencer Clark, are now its principles.

A&Z offers same-day service, highly unusual in the produce industry, delivers in refrigerated trucks, allows customers a twenty-four hour ordering opportunity, and leads in strict food safety programs.

Located at 366 West 500 South in Salt Lake City, A&Z continues to build its success upon its founding principles, as well as adapting to an ever-changing industry. More information about A&Z is available at www.azproduce.net.

A casual dining restaurant in the heart of downtown Salt Lake City, Himalayan Kitchen transports customers into the heart of Nepal, incorporating Nepalese, Indian and Tibetan cuisines. Everyone at HK believes the keys to winning a customer's heart are excellent food and a warm, friendly environment.

"We use local—and when possible, organic—products and authentic spices from Nepal," says Surya Bastakoti, who learned to cook simple dishes from his mother and is the man behind the restaurant's success. "Every dish is made from scratch by our kitchen staff. By 11 a.m., passersbys can enjoy mouth-watering aromas and hear the familiar chopping sounds of a true kitchen."

HK's most famous dishes include Himalayan Momos—a steamed dumpling with ground meat or mixed vegetables and fresh spices; and mouth-watering Goat Curry–slow-braised, free-range goat meat cooked in Himalayan spices and curry broth. Vegetarians favor Quanty Masala, made with nine varieties of beans and legumes, tomato, onion, ginger, garlic and Himalayan herbs. HK also serves vegan and gluten-free dishes.

After sixteen years as a mountain guide, paraglider and owner of Mt. Pumori Trekking and Expeditions, and a community mentor and leader, Bastakoti came to the U.S. in 2004. Unable to find food similar to that in Nepal, he established his own Nepalese restaurant. His connection to the outdoors continues. Many HK patrons are world-class climbers and mountaineers.

When Surya's friend, Apa Sherpa, reached the twenty-first and final summit of Mount Everest, he carried both the Nepalese flag and one from HK. Surya and his wife, Carmen, threw a huge welcome back party for Apa who presented Surya with the flag he had taken to the summit of Mount Everest. That day, Surya dedicated a wall containing Apa's oxygen tank, expedition photos and messages from Apa's friends. Surya considers "Apa's Wall" one of HK's most precious parts.

HK's early days were challenging, as people unfamiliar with Nepal's cuisine were often hesitant to try it. Starting with just three loyal employees, HK now employs twenty. The average daily income has increased from $450 to $4,000, thanks in part to word-of-mouth from local climbers, friends, paragliders and Nepalese locals. From its original site at 73 East 400 South, HK moved in 2009 to a venue triple its size at 360 South State.

Surya's future plans include renovating the site's top floor, opening a larger banquet hall, a high-end, Indian-themed bar, and an Asian Arts gallery where local artists can display their work.

HK's mission is to serve outstanding and flavorful Himalayan cuisine, crafted traditionally with the finest ingredients, yet with an understanding of modern food, décor and ambience preferences. It seeks to be a community hub for exposure to Nepalese culture and traditions, while giving back to the local community, and is active in dozens of community and charitable activities.

The Salt Lake Tribune

Above: Tribune Building, 2005.

Below: The Salt Lake Tribunes's newsroom, 2013.

Utah's independent source of news for more than 140 years, *The Salt Lake Tribune* is where Utahns go when they need to know.

The Tribune was started in 1871 by William Godbe, a dissident Mormon who broke from Brigham Young over Young's attempts to close Utah's economy to non-Mormons. Its early years were marked by defiance of the church and its leaders, but that gave way to a more accommodating era in the mid-twentieth century that still fostered *The Tribune's* fierce independence.

In 1957, *The Tribune* won a Pulitzer Prize for coverage of a mid-air plane collision over the Grand Canyon that killed 128 people. The planes went down in an isolated canyon nearly 400 miles from the newsroom, but that did not prevent reporters and photographers from getting a complete report in the next day's paper.

Today *The Tribune* operates a sophisticated news-gathering operation, delivering information to readers of the print edition, the website sltrib.com and mobile apps. The paper is delivered throughout Utah, and the site is viewed by more than 2.4 million unique visitors each month.

A consistent award winner for investigative reporting, *The Tribune* keeps Utah politicians and power players under public scrutiny while providing a comprehensive news report encompassing politics, crime and courts, business, entertainment, sports and opinion.

The Tribune website, sltrib.com, is a multimedia and interactive powerhouse, offering photo galleries, videos and interactive graphics. "Trib Talk" live chats invite readers to engage both reporters and newsmakers, and more than 40,000 readers post comments on stories each year. *The Tribune* also maintains a vibrant presence on Facebook, Twitter and Pinterest.

In 2012, sltrib.com was honored by *Editor and Publisher Magazine* with an Eppy award as the best news website worldwide (tying with the Toronto Globe and Mail site).

As part of its commitment to open government, *The Tribune* operates UtahsRight.com, a website dedicated to publishing government information such as court proceedings, childcare and restaurant inspections and public employee salaries. The site receives more than ten million page views annually and is the clearinghouse in Utah for public data.

Through it all, *The Tribune* has maintained its high standards for accuracy and professionalism. Telling it right for all of Utah. That is *The Salt Lake Tribune* way.

Agricultural irrigation systems may seem an unlikely beginning for an IT solutions provider, but it was exactly where Rich Linton, VLCM founder and president, got his start in the brand new world of personal computing. IBM rolled out the world's first-ever personal computer and immediately began looking for qualified dealers to sell and service their exciting new product. In 1983, Linton was one of just three selected from 300 applicants to represent IBM in the state of Utah.

"I think what made us stand out was that IBM had an understanding of the complexity of what we specialized in at the time, which was center-pivot irrigation systems," Linton says. "Since we were well established in rural Utah, they believed we had an advantage marketing to that segment of the state," he says.

Since Linton was selling a product new to the public, technical support became a critical part of the VLCM business model from the very beginning. Linton immersed himself in building a company based on superior customer service and relationships. "We were the ones to step in when other companies failed and have outlasted many of our competitors," Linton said.

Significant milestones in VLCM's thirty year tenure include buying Computerland in 1997, landing the TRAX software and hardware contract in preparation for the 2002 Olympic Winter Games in 1999, expanding operations to Idaho in 2007, opening VLCM Orem in 2009, and achieving VMware Premier Partner status in 2010. (VLCM is the first Utah headquartered reseller to receive this distinction.) VLCM now services organizations small, medium, and large, both in the public and private sector, and employs over 100 people in Utah.

Business success aside, one of Linton's proudest VLCM projects is the Huntsman Cancer Classic. This annual golf tournament benefits the Huntsman Cancer Foundation. "Our contribution helps other people become aware of the amazing work they are doing at Huntsman," Linton says. VLCM also donates all IT support to the Huntsman Cancer Foundation on an ongoing basis. In 2010, VLCM efforts were recognized with the Huntsman Cancer Institute's Giving Circle Award.

For more information about VLCM products and services, please visit www.vlcmtech.com.

Left: Rich Linton, VLCM founder and president, was one of Utah's first IBM dealers, a platform he used to build a company that now employs more than 100 people servicing the IT needs of businesses both large and small.

Below: Giving back to the community is a large part of VLCM's mission and values. The company not only donates all IT support to the Huntsman Cancer Foundation, but is also chief organizer of the Huntsman Cancer Classic, an annual golf tournament benefiting the Huntsman Cancer Foundation as well.

RHODES BAKE-N-SERV™

Customers love Rhodes Bake-N-Serv™ for the aroma and flavor of fresh baked bread and rolls from their own oven. Founded in 1958 by Herbert Cecil Rhodes, Jr., inventor of baking and freezing equipment, Rhodes is now a family-owned business headquartered in Murray, Utah.

Rhodes produces three high quality types of frozen product including "Traditional" frozen bread and roll dough; "AnyTime!" sweet rolls and "Warm-N-Serv" partially baked rolls. They are found in the frozen food section of grocery stores across America. Many restaurants and schools also proudly serve Rhodes, which they bake on premise providing fresh baked rolls.

The versatility of Rhodes "Traditional" frozen bread, roll, and cinnamon roll dough makes it a staple since it is perfect for creating many recipes such as pizza, calzones and breadsticks. These recipes are made by thawing the dough, shaping it, letting it rise and baking to perfection.

"AnyTime!" Cinnamon, Orange, and Caramel Rolls are convenient because they thaw, rise, and bake in an aluminum pan, which saves preparation and cleanup time. There is a packet of real cream cheese frosting that is applied as the rolls come hot out of the customer's oven…absolutely delicious!

Using time-honored baking techniques; Rhodes Bake-N-Serv recently introduced "Warm-N-Serv" Artisan French Crusty Rolls and Mini Baguettes. All "Warm-N-Serv" rolls offer great convenience for today's busy lifestyle as they are partially baked and need only a few minutes in the oven to be ready to enjoy.

Rhodes Bake-N-Serv helps customers to learn a variety of uses on its website. Rhodesbread.com offers free recipes and baking tips. It even offers live chatting with experienced bakers. Rhodes assists families in making unforgettable memories by home baking delicious bread and rolls.

Dedicated to quality, convenience and value; Rhodes is known as "America's Favorite" frozen dough.

In 1987 a small boutique showroom was started in Park City supplying appliances, decorative plumbing, and hardware fixtures to a few builders. Today, Mountain Land Design has become the leader and one of the largest suppliers of kitchen and bath fixtures in Utah.

Dan Devenport has been the president and sole owner for the past seventeen years. "The kitchen and bath industry was not the plan after school." He was convinced there was a career in professional football in his future. Life has a way of creating unusual opportunities, after a short stint playing college football, he found himself working for an appliance distributor. He started delivering appliances with his brother Joe and friend, Steve Stockfish. Out on jobsites he met many contractors where he developed strong relationships. This led to a sales position at Mountain Land Design. In 1993, Devenport bought in as an owner and along with Joe and Steve the business expanded into Salt Lake City in 1997 with a new vision and direction.

Devenport felt the industry was ready for a new type of showroom and purchased a larger building in South Salt Lake. His vision was to display products in kitchen and bath settings as if it was your own home. The concept was very successful and

expanded into Provo and then Layton. Once Devenport was able to acquire experienced key personnel his business grew even more. From here, the company saw a construction boom from 2004 to mid-2008 with a revenue growth of over 250 percent.

In 2009 with the crash of the economy, the company was forced to make cuts in all areas. All three locations remained opened, but expenses and personnel were drastically cut. In 2011, Devenport, knowing that the economy would turn around and having faith in his team, undertook an extensive remodel of Mountain Land Design's plumbing department. This was a bold move but panned out. Weathering the storm and seeing an increase in construction in 2012, Devenport again wanted to show that Mountain Land Design would be the leader in the industry. He remodeled a large portion of the showroom with a living kitchen that features Wolf and Sub-Zero products.

Mountain Land Design does not want to just be a business in Utah; it wants to help make a difference in the community. Employees volunteer their time to several local organizations and participating in these organizations creates a stronger community and helps build a successful business.

To tour our showroom and see our staff, please visit www.mountainlanddesign.com.

PHOTOGRAPHS COURTESY OF CHAD BRAITHWAITE.

Adam Barker Photography

Raised amongst Utah's Wasatch Mountains, internationally acclaimed photographer Adam Barker has a passion for photography matched only by his zest for life. Known for bold landscape and active lifestyle imagery, his love affair with exceptional imagery has translated into stirring editorial work for *Outdoor Photographer*, *Skiing*, *SKI*, *Powder*, *Flyfish Journal*, *American Angler*, *USA Today*, *Fitness*, *Men's Journal*, *The Drake*, *Mountain Magazine* and many more publications.

Widely recognized as one of Salt Lake City's most prolific photographers, Barker's only formal training was gleaned from a black and white photography class at Highland High School. Years later he attended the University of Utah, graduating in Communications with an emphasis in Public Relations. His work has taken him from Asia to Antarctica, but his love for Salt Lake City runs deep. According to Barker, the best part of every journey is coming back home to his family and beloved Wasatch Mountains.

He has drawn praise for his teaching style at workshops both domestic and abroad, and has drawn similar accord for his instructional DVDs. Barker has produced imagery for a varied array of commercial clients including Nike, Volkswagen of America, Deer Valley Resort, Deutsche Grammophon Inc., Manfrotto, Mountain Khakis and many more. When not shooting, Barker can be found spending time with his wife and three sons, or "product testing" in the mountains, on the river, or wherever else nature happens to call. Visit www.adambarkerphotography.com to see more of Barker's work from Salt Lake City, and around the world.

As the premier global quality institute and testing laboratory for filled textile products, IDFL Laboratory and Institute test certifies, inspects, consults, and audits and manages quality assurance programs for companies around the globe. Services are cost effective, client support is the industry best, and its reputation assures accuracy and integrity.

IDFL developed many of the global standards for down and feather testing, and has the world's largest testing database. It created traceability systems for raw materials and uses its reputation for integrity to develop product and factory inspection in Asia. Partnering with the University of Utah, IDFL provides country-of-origin verification on natural textile products. Services include: down and feather testing, inspection and audit services, fabric testing, consulting and research, and natural and synthetic testing.

While working for the government of Utah in the 1950s, Wilford Lieber, Sr., noticed a large variance in the quality of down and feather products, trending toward increasingly inferior down. In 1978 Wilford and Mary Jean Lieber established IDFL, an independent laboratory. Their work in this privately-held family company became the worldwide foundation for all technical testing of jackets and bedding. IDFL consulted with North American governments and industries and helped fledgling industries in Japan and China develop standards. Its reputation is based on absolute integrity and honesty, refusing to alter results or reports.

Susan Morrow and Joyce Mikkelson soon became key partners in the work. Joyce, a globally recognized testing trainer, worked well past her eighty-fifth birthday.

In addition to the Salt Lake City headquarters, IDFL sites include Hangzhou, China; Taipei, Taiwan; and Frauenfeld, Switzerland. Work orders have increased from 1,000 annually in 1978-94 to 20,000 in 2013. Currently, seventy-five percent of IDFL revenue comes from outside North America, with 8,000 clients in seventy countries, and future expansion in Europe, Japan, Korea, Southeast Asia and Latin America. IDFL plans to grow as the premier quality assurance partner in the $20 billion filled textile product sector, and to expand to areas including wool, cotton, polyester, etc.

Global same-day courier service and instant global communications have allowed a small company such as IDFL to become the global leader in quality assurance of filled textiles, providing services to large global retailers and manufacturers of brands including IKEA, GAP, H&M, Zara, Macy's, Costco, Columbia, North Face, Adidas, Puma, Nike, Eddie Bauer, Moncler, Bosideng, and JYSK.

IDFL staff members participate in many charitable activities and are active in recycling and energy conservation. Recycling is practiced in all areas. Wilf Lieber, CEO, sets the example, riding a bike to work in all four IDFL offices.

Harmons Grocery

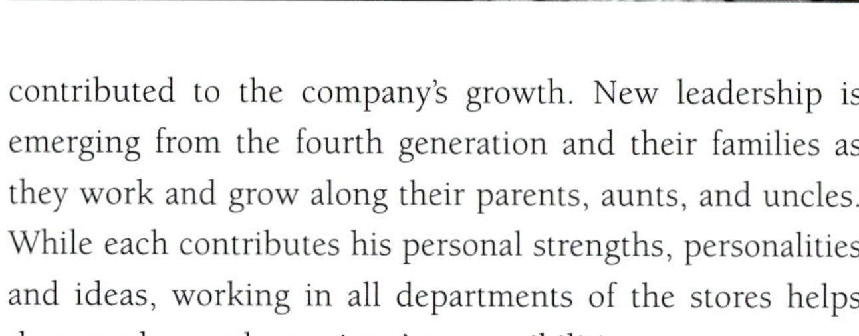

A passion for perpetual learning, growth, and innovation has been the cornerstone enabling Harmons Grocery to expand from a single fruit stand opened in 1932 to sixteen stores by 2012. The Harmons Grocery history began when Jake and Irene Harmon opened The Market Spot at the corner of 3300 South and Main Streets. Harmons Grocery, which is still family owned and operated, now has over 3,000 associates who continue striving to provide a unique shopping experience, offering the freshest and finest quality products, local partnerships, exceptional value, and unequaled customer service.

The Market Spot's 24-hour a day, 7-day a week service, plus the convenience of stocking grocery items along with fresh produce, quickly established the reputation and popularity that would remain over the years. Jake and Irene's values, quality, innovations and integrity have continued into the Harmon family's fourth generation. Son Terry and his wife Doreen maintained the original concepts and values and cultivated standards that would solidify the Harmons vision. Their children, Randy, Bob and Jamie, who grew up in the family business, have all

contributed to the company's growth. New leadership is emerging from the fourth generation and their families as they work and grow along their parents, aunts, and uncles. While each contributes his personal strengths, personalities and ideas, working in all departments of the stores helps them understand associates' responsibilities.

As Harmons continues to grow, so does the desire to learn and innovate and a commitment to valuing associates, customers, and the community. While Bob and Randy are Harmons public face, they credit everyone from the board of directors and continuation of the traditions, values, and expectations established in 1932 to the newest associate with Harmons growth and success.

The Harmon family and its associates believe in helping others. By involving customers and vendors, and community groups, they have raised over $2 million for local charities and nonprofits through projects that are fun and fulfilling.

"Harmons carries a large variety of products—both local and from around the world—including many that are unique," Bob says. "We have worked to provide what the customer is looking for. People tell us what they need, and it is our job to find it. We provide clean, healthy, fresh food that equates to high flavor and great taste. We are about people, people, people, and without them, we are not in business. We feel we are the best at always getting better, and we're never done."

For additional information on Harmons Grocery, please visit www.harmonsgrocery.com.

Rocky Mountain Water Company is Utah's premier locally owned and operated bottled water company, founded by R. Clay Groesbeck, Robert L. (Lee) Jensen and Ronald (Ron) C. Jensen. Serving the Salt Lake and surrounding metropolitan areas since 1986 in the traditional home and office bottled water and office coffee industry, as well as branded and private label product throughout the Intermountain Region in retail and other distribution. Rocky Mountain Water Company strives for excellence in quality water products, customer service and innovation while remaining committed to our natural resources.

Our specialties include Natural Mineral Spring, Distilled and Purified waters in 3 and 5 gallon returnable and recyclable plastic as well as 100 percent recyclable 1 and 2.5 gallon packaging. We also specialize in unique packages such as glass, emergency storage bag-in-box, bulk and 100 percent RPET (remanufactured PET) small package. We have maintained innovative strides with our bag-in-box as provided to the Utah 2002 Winter Olympics and ongoing as represented by our proprietary dispensing systems.

Our Natural Mineral Spring Water comes from a pristine underground source in Millcreek Canyon, located in the Wasatch Range of the Rocky Mountains. The spring is fed by fracture and fault zones in the quartzite along the south slope of Millcreek Canyon. The quartzite rock aquifer provides a unique blend of minerals consisting of calcium, magnesium, potassium, chloride, sodium, sulfate and bicarbonates that create natural electrolytes and slightly alkaline water for a healthy balanced hydration.

We also produce purified steam distilled water which meets the U.S. Pharmacopeia standards established for purified water. Essential for use with medical, dental and other equipment, distilled water also provides for many health benefits, including use with powdered beverages and dietary supplements. Distilled water has many home and commercial applications. Additionally, we offer a premium drinking water processed by Reverse Osmosis.

Rocky Mountain Water Company has maintained excellence in manufacturing, receiving multiple industry awards. Maintaining operations with local ownership and management has provided for excellent customer service and quality water products.

While providing service to the surrounding community, we recognize the importance of contributing to charitable organizations. Over the years Rocky Mountain Water Company has supported such organizations as March of Dimes, AIDS Foundation, American Diabetes and Muscular Dystrophy.

Our quality water products support a healthy life and lifestyle. All our water containers are reusable, recyclable and recycled in disposal. Rocky Mountain Water Company is your local source for Natural Mineral Spring, Distilled and Purified waters in Utah and the surrounding Intermountain Region.

Additional information is available on the Internet at www.rockymtnwater.com.

ROCKY MOUNTAIN WATER COMPANY

Building a Greater Salt Lake City

Salt Lake City's real estate developers, construction companies, heavy industries, and manufacturers provide the economic foundation of the region

ATK Aerospace Group 268
Rio Tinto Kennecott 272
LCG Facades 276
SME Steel 278
Burton Lumber Company 280
Monsen Engineering of Salt Lake City 282
Major Drilling Group International, Inc. 284
Architectural Nexus, Inc. 286
FLSmidth 288
Paulsen Construction 290
Boart Longyear 292
Woodbury Corporation 294
Beacon Metals, Inc. 296
City Creek Reserve, Inc. 298
US Magnesium, LLC 300
Utility Trailer Sales of Utah 302
Alpha Transport, Inc. 303
Hamilton Partners, Inc. 304
Walker Center 305
Cushman & Wakefield | Commerce Real Estate Solutions 306
JBR Environmental Consultants, Inc. 307
Cementation USA, Inc. 308

ATK Aerospace Group

Embarking on a seven-year journey to begin a four-year mission some 746 million miles away, a highly instrumented spacecraft roughly the size of a 30-passenger school bus launched from Cape Canaveral Air Force Station, Florida, October 15, 1997. On the record books as the third heaviest spacecraft ever, *Cassini*, named for the famed eighteenth century Italian astronomer, was on its way to the jewel of the solar system—the mysterious ringed planet, Saturn, and its largest moon, Titan.

Today, some sixteen years since taking to the heavens, *Cassini* is operating on a second mission extension. The orbiting spacecraft is still sending daily data streams, providing clues to some of our most perplexing questions about our universe.

While *Cassini's* longevity has been an unanticipated treasure to the scientific community, it is no surprise ATK Aerospace Group, located in the western Salt Lake valley, played a significant role in this, and many other monumental missions, among the stars. Twin booster rockets, manufactured right here in Utah, delivered a collective 3.4 million pounds of thrust to help boost *Cassini-Huygens* on the first leg of its extraordinary journey.

What began as a dynamite manufacturing plant near the foothills of Salt Lake's west side a century ago, now stands as a world-class aerospace and defense manufacturing facility regarded as a national asset. The first structures were erected on an eight-thousand-acre parcel of land acquired by Delaware-based Hercules Powder Company.

The year was 1913—when both stainless steel and the crossword puzzle were invented. It was the time of railroad expansion. The mining trade was strong and the demand for explosives high. So high, in fact, that Hercules had reached capacity at its California plant. A plant capable of producing 12 million pounds of dynamite a year was needed. With robust dynamite sales in San Francisco and Salt Lake City, the Rocky Mountains made for the ideal location.

Over the years, the company transformed from an explosives production plant to a chemical company to a leader in the aerospace propulsion industry. That transformation accelerated after Russia launched the world's first orbiting satellite, *Sputnik*.

Expanding on its propulsion expertise, the company developed a method to produce lightweight rocket motor cases. The technique involved a combination of filaments and resins to produce composite case structures that were stronger yet lighter than steel. In the launch business, where the correlation between weight and cost is high, a real weight advantage was key. This pioneering work on lightweight structures progressed several generations—from fiberglass, to Kevlar, to complex carbon-composite materials.

Concurrently, the allure of the burgeoning space satellite business drew intense interest from the company's research and development arm. Expertise in fabricating lightweight composite structures for deep space applications was developed in an effort to grow into an adjacent market with great potential. Notable contracts included optical support structures for Hubble Space Telescope and numerous earth-orbiting satellites serving government and commercial customers.

ATK, a young defense company with roots to Honeywell Corporation, acquired Hercules Aerospace Company in 1995. The acquisition positioned ATK as an up-and-coming player in the aerospace and defense industry.

As part of an aggressive growth strategy, ATK made a second landmark acquisition in 2001, looking ninety miles north to Brigham City-based Thiokol Corporation, maker of the space shuttle solid rocket boosters. The bold undertaking added human space launch capability to the company's growing portfolio, making ATK the undisputed world leader in solid rocket propulsion systems. A series of other acquisitions and key contract wins have continued to increase the company's presence in the aerospace, defense and sporting markets, which includes ammunition, firearms and accessories.

ATK has produced and launched more than 2,300 commercial solid rocket motors to date for a wide variety of launch vehicles. Partnered with prime contractors including Lockheed Martin, Orbital Sciences and United Launch Alliance, ATK's solid rocket motors are used on *Athena*™, *Pegasus*®, *Taurus*®, *Minotaur*, and *Antares*™ launch vehicles and as strap-on boosters for the *Delta II* and *Delta IV* family of launch vehicles. Of particular note is ATK's CASTOR® 30, developed in response to a market need for a high-performance, upper-stage motor.

Above: ATK is producing lightweight composite fuselage stringers and frames for the Airbus A350 XWB program at the company's Aircraft Commercial Center of Excellence (ACCE) manufacturing facility just north of Salt Lake City. The twin-engine jetliner is designed to offer up to twenty-five percent greater fuel efficiency over current commercial airplanes.
PHOTOGRAPH COURTESY OF AIRBUS.

Left: ATK's newest rocket motor from the CASTOR® 30 family marks the company's entry point into commercial deliveries to the International Space Station. The CASTOR 30 family of motors is established on a legacy of innovation and reliability that are part of the company's fifty-year heritage in solid rocket systems.

Below: The next-generation military stealth fighter jet, the F-35 Lightning II, takes to the skies in flight testing. Automated fiber placement technology, pioneered by ATK in the early 1980s, provides for lightweight, composite aircraft components with complex contours to be manufactured. The fifth-generation multirole fighter is being developed for the U.S. Air Force, Marine Corps, Navy, and allied nations.
PHOTOGRAPH COURTESY OF LOCKHEED MARTIN.

Technicians complete the center backbone of NASA's James Webb Space Telescope at ATK's Salt Lake County facility. Measuring approximately 24 feet tall by 19.5 feet wide by more than 11 feet deep when fully deployed, and weighing only 2,180 pounds, the highly engineered structure is designed to support the telescope's beryllium mirrors, instruments and other elements. It is also designed to hold the 18-segment, 21-foot-diameter primary mirror nearly motionless while the telescope is peering into deep space..

Selected as the upper-stage motor for our nation's newest medium-class launch vehicle, *Antares*, ATK's CASTOR 30 rocket motor helped launch a demonstration mission to the International Space Station September 18, 2013. This flight served as the gate for Orbital Sciences to begin regular cargo resupply missions to the orbiting laboratory through NASA's Commercial Resupply Services contract. Stratolaunch is the newest system to employ ATK's innovative propulsion technology. Founded in 2011 by entrepreneur Paul G. Allen, Stratolaunch Systems is developing an air-launch system that will revolutionize space transportation by providing orbital access to space at lower costs, with greater safety and more flexibility. ATK signed on with Orbital Sciences in 2013 to provide first and second stage propulsion for the Air Launch Vehicle. The contract includes the design, development and flight hardware for initial Stratolaunch missions.

ATK's supporting role to Department of Defense strategic deterrence efforts is well established and continues through support of both U.S. Air Force Minuteman III and U.S. Navy Trident II D-5 missile systems, and missile defense systems including interceptors and targets.

Within the space components industry, ATK is a leading designer and producer of composite bus structures, towers and subsystems that house flight-critical systems for commercial, civil and military satellites. Programs include numerous components for the A2100, Global Positioning System, 702 and Star 2 buses, as well as components for proprietary customers. These essential satellite components feature high strength-to-weight ratios, superior flatness and thermal dimensional stability—factors that are critical in space applications.

Missions featuring Utah-produced optical support structures include critical components for the Chandra X-ray Observatory, Mars Exploration Rovers, and NASA's Deep Impact mission, to name a few.

For *Hubble*'s successor, NASA's James Webb Space Telescope, ATK partnered with Northrop Grumman Corporation to provide key support structures housing the telescope's primary instruments and mirrors. These structures are required to operate flawlessly at temperatures as cold as -406 degrees Fahrenheit. The most powerful space telescope ever built, the Webb Telescope will observe the most distant objects in the universe, provide images of the first galaxies formed and see unexplored planets around distant stars.

For the composite aerospace structures market, ATK's industry leadership in high-strength, lightweight composite materials makes it the partner of choice to develop and fabricate technically complex components for military and commercial aircraft. Housed in state-of-the-art production facilities in Clearfield (just north of Salt Lake City), ATK-patented technologies that feature signature automation are used to manufacture advanced, lightweight aircraft structures.

For the military's next-generation stealth fighter jet, the F-35 Lightning II, ATK manufactures fourteen major composite structures, including the seven-piece upper wing skin, lower wing skins, engine nacelle skins, inlet ducts, and the upper wing strap using both automated fiber placement and hand layup techniques.

ATK is also a major supplier for today's most advanced commercial aircraft for Airbus and Boeing. ATK's patented automated stiffener forming technology is used to produce lightweight composite fuselage stringers and frames for the Airbus A350WXB. And for Boeing's 787 Dreamliner, ATK produces composite components for the center and aft fuselages. At peak production, more than 10,000 parts per month will be produced in Clearfield.

Building on more than a half-century of advanced rocketry and composites technology knowhow, ATK is partnered with

NASA to open and sustain a bold new era of exploration in the decades ahead. ATK provides the solid rocket boosters for the space agency's new heavy lift rocket, the Space Launch System (SLS)—the most powerful rocket ever built. These boosters capitalize on the experience base from 219 boosters on the Space Shuttle program and feature modern materials, technologies and processes for larger, more powerful boosters, providing twenty-five percent more liftoff capacity at 3.5 million pounds of thrust each.

Beyond sheer firepower, ATK is responsible for pioneering the flight avionics and controls essential to first stage performance, delivering a new level of avionics reliability and performance for America's next-generation launch vehicle. As a critical safety feature, ATK has also developed a uniquely engineered launch abort motor that will be used to pull the astronaut crew to safety in case of an emergency during launch or ascent, unleashing half-a-million pounds of thrust within seconds.

The SLS is designed to launch crews and cargo on direct trajectories that will shorten the missions to deep space destinations. To put its power into perspective, consider the *Saturn V* that carried the *Apollo* crews to the moon, and the space shuttle—individually, they each generated seven million pounds of thrust. The SLS will provide ten million pounds of thrust. This power will deliver three to four times more lift capability than all current launch vehicles.

ATK is proud to be part of the Salt Lake community, providing world-class products for the most advanced commercial and military aircraft, and is primed to launch Utah to the moon, Mars and destinations beyond.

ATK is an aerospace, defense, and commercial products company with operations in twenty-two states, Puerto Rico, and internationally. News and information can be found at www.atk.com, on Facebook at www.facebook.com/atk, or on Twitter @ATK.

Above: NASA's new Space Launch System (SLS) provides an entirely new capability for human space exploration, opening astronaut access to deep space destinations. Combined with ATK's twin solid rocket boosters, SLS will produce 8.4 million pounds of thrust at liftoff—ten percent more thrust than the Saturn V. ATK also provides the launch abort motor capability integral to NASA's launch abort system that will safely pull the Orion crew module away during an emergency on the launch pad or during ascent. Design, engineering, and manufacturing efforts are housed at ATK facilities in Salt Lake, Davis, and Box Elder Counties.
IMAGE COURTESY OF NASA.

Left: Whether it is volunteering at science fairs, assisting at model rocket launching events or supporting the United Way, ATK volunteers are found throughout the community leading the way in initiatives to foster greater interest in science, technology, engineering and math (STEM) careers, and lending a hand in a variety of community endeavors.

RIO TINTO KENNECOTT

Right: People throughout the world came to the Bingham Canyon Mine to live and work where more than forty distinct camps and towns were built in the canyon. Pictured is the Highland Boy district in 1910.

Below: Miners at the Bingham Canyon Mine, shown here in 1906, had an early vision to mine and process copper ore using steam shovels and locomotives that laid the foundation for the modern operation today.

Rio Tinto Kennecott is a fully integrated mining, concentrating, smelting and refining company committed to practicing sustainable development in every facet of its business. Like its parent company, Rio Tinto, Kennecott believes that sustainable development is about taking a long-term view of mining. It is about meeting the needs of today's generation without compromising the needs of future generations. Aligning its business strategies and daily practices around the concept of sustainable development strengthens its operations and products, builds enduring communities and provides lasting benefits for its employees and stakeholders.

Kennecott's parent company, Rio Tinto, has its headquarters in London, with a regional center in South Jordan, Utah. The company has five major plants stretching seventeen miles along the Oquirrh Mountains and is a world leader in mining and processing the earth's mineral resources. Kennecott owns the Bingham Canyon Mine, which has provided minerals from its rich ore body for 111 years. Kennecott produces copper, molybdenum, gold, silver and sulfuric acid, and has historically supplied about fifteen to twenty-five percent of the United States annual copper supply.

The U.S. Army is credited with the start of mining in Utah in 1863. Troops under the command of Colonel Patrick Conner are said to have discovered Utah's first mining claim and helped to form the first mining company and mining district in Bingham Canyon. Early mining at Bingham was underground, with the exception of placer mining.

Bingham Canyon was a beehive of activity at the turn of the century. Dozens of small companies dug tunnels and sank shafts in the mountains where they were mining silver and gold ores, but not the abundant low-grade copper ores that were considered a nuisance.

Daniel C. Jackling, a twenty-nine year old metallurgical engineer, with his partner, Robert Gemmell, a mining engineer, studied and assayed ore samples from the operations that dotted the canyon to determine the value of the "nuisance rock" found by early miners. They determined that vast tonnages of low-grade copper ore existed in the main mountain that divided the canyon. This was the kind of ore the mining companies tried to avoid because it interfered with the recovery of the metals they were mining.

Jackling's vision was to mine and process this mountain of porphyry copper ore using steam shovels to remove the ore and waste, and steam locomotives to transport it from the mine to large-scale mills. This marked the first use of mass-production technology in copper mining. Mining experts of the day scoffed at Jackling's crazy idea—especially when ninety-eight percent of the rock was waste. Most investors also agreed that it was a bad idea.

But Jackling took some influential financiers to Bingham Canyon in June 1903 to convince them that his theory would work and that profits could be made by mining low-grade ores containing thirty-nine pounds of copper per ton.

Jackling's determined conviction was good enough for the backers. They invested $500,000 to get him started, giving birth to the Utah Copper Company on June 4, 1903. That was the beginning of what would become one of the greatest mining enterprises in the world.

In its first year of operation, the company showed a profit of $142,000. Some previously skeptical investors now wanted to come on board, and they invested an additional $5 million into the business.

Of about forty companies that were mining underground for lead, silver, zinc and gold in the Bingham District, only a few were interested in mining copper from the surface.

People throughout the world—mostly immigrants from Europe, Asia and Mexico—came to seek work. More than forty distinct ethnic groups lived in camps and towns throughout the mining district. These groups and their work helped drive the business into the future.

Today, the operation is still thriving. What continues to drive Kennecott is its commitment to sustainable development. This commitment within the community is an important part of how it does business and encompasses economic prosperity, environmental stewardship and social well-being.

Supporting and enhancing a sustainable economy in the Salt Lake Valley is important to Kennecott as a valuable member of the community. Its objective is to understand and maximize the benefits it brings to the economy at local, regional and national levels by being a leader in production, exports and revenue.

Throughout the history of the Bingham Canyon Mine, no other single private-sector operation has generated more production, exports, income and employment for as many years in the state, according to the Bureau of Economic and Business Research at the University of Utah.

❖

Above: The Bingham Canyon Mine, situated in the Oquirrh Mountains, has been producing mineral resources that make modern life possible for more than 111 years.

Left: Kennecott produces 99.9 percent pure copper cathodes that are used to make modern life possible. Cell phones, computers, cars and plumbing are a few of the many benefits enjoyed because of this important element.

Right: The Inland Sea Shorebird Reserve, constructed by Kennecott to mitigate wetland impacts when the company expanded its tailings impoundment in 1996, is a thriving biological habitat to nearly 200 species and 120,000 shorebirds and waterfowl.

Below: Kennecott has spent more than $400 million to restore, reclaim, and re-vegetate nearly 10,000 acres of land impacted by historic mining activities.

Another way Kennecott has demonstrated its commitment to sustainable development is through the development of the Daybreak community. A portion of Daybreak was once impacted by historic mining activities, which led to a period of unprecedented remediation, restoration and reclamation through the mid-2000s. Daybreak is now a sustainably developed community that balances the social, environmental and economic needs of residents and local businesses. Important elements of life have been combined to allow residents to live, work, play and learn in a walkable, vibrant community. The unique development also provides multi-modal transportation options and integrates intelligent community design choices.

This approach to environmental stewardship is at the heart of Kennecott's commitment to sustainable development. Wherever possible, Kennecott prevents, minimizes or mitigates potentially harmful effects of the company's operation on the environment. In the last twenty-five years, Kennecott has spent hundreds of millions of dollars to clean up land and water impacted by historic mining operations, which has included the reclamation of about 10,000 acres of land.

Beyond its regulatory requirements, Kennecott sets additional, self-imposed environmental targets to drive continual improvement. Through these actions, it strives to be a leader in environmental performance by demonstrating good management of natural resources, responsibly reducing its environmental footprint and exceeding community expectations for sustainable development.

Supporting community organizations is another way Kennecott exemplifies its commitment to sustainable development. Throughout the decades, Kennecott has supported numerous individuals and organizations through scholarships, partnerships and foundation contributions that enhance the local community while fostering strong relationships.

Above and left: Daybreak is a sustainably developed community in South Jordan, Utah, that allows residents to live, work, play and learn in one place. When completed, the Daybreak community will have preserved more than one thousand acres of open space for residents to enjoy.

Kennecott has a long-term strategy to partner with community organizations that align with its core values. Kennecott believes cultivating these core values through its community partnerships helps strengthen its operations and products, builds enduring communities and provides mutual benefits.

More information about the company, its operation, its history and its many other community activities is available on the Internet at www.riotintokennecott.com.

LCG Facades

❖

Top: Gary and Ronda Dabb, LCG Facades owners. Gary attributes a large portion of LCG Facades success to Ronda's dedication and support. "If not for her, we would have never succeeded," Gary says.

Below: LCG Facades installed the sloped blast proof walls as well as the photovoltaic canopy in front of the Salt Lake City Public Safety Building. The canopy provides approximately 440 volts. This building has a Zero Energy Foot Print and many other cities are modeling there public safety buildings after ours. In a crisis the building is a command center and is fully powered and operational.

Linford Contract Glazing (LCG) Facades is a Utah-based commercial glass and glazing contractor servicing building projects across the Intermountain West. LCG was founded on the principle of Innovation Through Partnerships: LCG works directly with owners, architects, and contractors to help achieve highly energy efficient enclosure solutions that not only meet design goals but cost and schedule requirements as well. The company's 40,000 square foot Salt Lake City production facility features CNC automated machines operated by a skilled staff to fabricate curtain walls, double facades, rain screen facades, blast resistant applications, and other building products. In the field, LCG Facades employs only the most professional and experienced project management teams to install its products.

Sustainable building practices are at the heart of LCG Facades' vision and mission. The LCG team and partners have vast experience and knowledge in energy-responsible products and systems to benefit any project, including ensuring structures meets new government energy codes, ASHRAE and NFRC standards, as well as desired LEED certification. Some of the specific energy performance solutions offered by LCG include: systems made from 100 percent recycled aluminum, using high-performance thermally-broken systems, triple-glazing, providing three Low-E coatings on a single glass unit, and offering rain screen panel systems that work in accordance with revised Utah energy codes. Creating solutions that are inventive, sustainable, effective, and elegant while exceeding client expectations is LCG Facades' ultimate goal.

LCG Facades is owned and operated by Gary Dabb, who offers more than thirty years of experience in every aspect of the commercial glazing industry. Gary and his wife Ronda previously owned Dabb Associates, a commercial facade drafting company servicing subcontractors and manufacturers across the nation. In 2005 the Dabbs were approached by Linford Brothers Glass to rebuild the company's commercial glazing division. The Dabbs converted the failing division into a profit center within just one year. In 2006-2007 the Dabbs partnered with Earl Linford to purchase the division and relaunched it as a stand-alone venture under the name LCG Facades.

As with many business ventures, LCG Facades first year was full of challenges. The Dabbs and Linford began with relatively small staff: six in the office and twenty-two glaziers in the shop and out in the field. Demand for their products and services were vigorous from the start and within three months LCG's staff had expanded to eight office employees and approximately fifty glaziers. "Within a very short time period we built this company from scratch including all company manuals, benefits, our mission statement and core values, job descriptions, accounting, OSHA safety standards, etc. We definitely had our hands full," Gary says.

Two critical personnel additions to the LCG team were made early on to help manage the intense growth: the Dabbs hired Ted Derby and Kris Standiford. Utilizing his forty-plus year glazing industry career, Derby quickly proved to be an invaluable asset in terms of business development and, according to Dabb, was critical in how LCG weathered the 2008 economic downturn. "Projects were pulled from bidding every day and subcontractors were fighting for position in the market. Derby was critical in assisting LCG Facades stay competitive," Dabb says. Standiford filled the role of CFO and Human Resources Director. With an MBA in accounting, Standiford has kept LCG solvent and up to speed in the accounting world by establishing and maintaining critical relationships with banking and bonding companies.

Other personnel changes came in early 2010 when, as planned from the start, the Dabbs bought out Linford's interest in LCG Facades, thereby becoming the company's sole owners and operators.

Dabb feels strongly that rather than eroding his business, economic trials have made it stronger. "A sign of a good company is one that comes out of a recession better than they went in," Dabb says. In the last several years LCG Facades had made significant investments in software and machine system technology and heavy equipment thereby improving overall company efficiency and customer service. "We can service the community faster, with greater accuracy, and most of all adding value," Dabb says.

Today, LCG Facades growth patterns have remained a consistent twenty-five percent per year. The company's work and products are part of some of Utah's most prominent structures including Ogden's Ensign Plaza, O. C. Tanner's flagship store in downtown Salt Lake City, the Digital Learning Center at Utah Valley University in Orem, Utah Valley Regional Medical Center in Provo, the Park City Medical Center, the University of Utah's Museum of Natural History, the Huntsman Cancer Institute, and the Salt Lake City Public Safety Building to name a few.

Dabb's future plans for LCG Facades include creating Architectural Facades Inc. (AFI) a wholesale facade supplier for the western U.S. and maintaining his company's leadership position within the Intermountain West's commercial building community and continuing to explore methods for energy efficiency and design. "Utah is on the forefront of green building and design and we feel very fortunate to be a part helping Utah's architectural community create buildings that are both beautiful and environmentally friendly," Dabb says. "And, of course, if it were not for my generous wife Ronda, I could not have done what it has taken to turn this company around and provide employment for all the people who make LCG Facades possible." For more information about LCG Facades, please visit www.lcgfacades.com and www.architecturalfacadesinc.com.

Above: LCG Facades products are featured on some of Utah's most prominent buildings including the Utah Museum of Natural History located on the campus of the University of Utah.

Left: LCG Facade's 40,000 square foot Salt Lake City production facility features CNC automated machines.

Below: The University of Utah Huntsman Cancer Center.

SME Steel

SME Steel's impeccable reputation for quality steel fabrication and building erection is well known across the entire Western United States. SME provides every aspect of turnkey steel construction from design assist service consultation to detailing, shop fabrication, and field erection and is one of the few companies in the U.S. offering all Division 5 services: structural steel, miscellaneous metals, metal deck, metal stairs, and ornamental metals. Efficient response, immediate service, on time and within budget scheduling, attention to detail, and superior installation are just a few of the reasons contributing to SME's leadership position in the steel industry.

SME's sixty-acre headquarters in West Jordan, Utah, includes an impressive 150,000 square foot, highly efficient fabrication facility. A second 280,000 square foot fabrication facility is located in Pocatello, Idaho. Together, these two fabrication facilities allow the company to strategically service clients across the Western United States. In addition, SME Steel is the operation center for the company's four divisions: Southwest Steel, LLC, with fabrication facilities in Nevada and Arizona, Southwest Architectural Metals, SME Steel Contractors, Inc. and CoreBrace, LLC.

Southwest Steel Nevada and Southwest Steel Arizona, located in Las Vegas, Nevada, and Phoenix, Arizona, respectively, excel in steel stair and miscellaneous iron fabrication and installation. Southwest Architectural Metals creates ornamental metal products in stainless, aluminum, copper, brass, and bronze with state-of-the-art CNC machinery in their 17,000 square foot facility located next to sister company, Southwest Steel Nevada in Las Vegas. SME Steel Contractors, Inc. located at the parent facility in West Jordan, specializes in structural steel framing.

CoreBrace—one of SME's most innovative brands—is a proven buckling restrained bracing system allowing structures to withstand earthquakes and maintain structural integrity following seismic events. CoreBrace's unique steel braces have been independently tested and implemented in large medical facilities, data centers, sports facilities, and production facilities as well as high-rise and low-rise office buildings throughout the world. The CoreBrace technology is technically superior, cost effective, and readily available. CoreBrace, LLC, is honored to be the recipient of *Utah Business Magazine*'s Sustainable Business Award.

Above: CEO Wayne Searle oversees all four SME Steel divisions: Southwest Steel, LLC, Southwest Architectural Metals, SME Steel Contractors, Inc., and CoreBrace, LLC.

Below: SME Steel installed the Skybridge at Salt Lake's City Creek Center within a four hour time period with a mere six inch clearance, an engineering feat featured on the popular television program "World's Toughest Fixes."

SME Steel has completed many notable projects over the years, including: the 505,000 square foot Smith Center for the Performing Arts in Las Vegas; the 498,000 square foot, USGBC LEED Silver-certified San Diego Public Library, characterized by a three story steel dome housing a reading room for the nine story children's library; AT&T Park, home of Major League Baseball's San Francisco Giants, showcasing an incredible 42,000 seat stadium with a total project cost of $357 million; Disneyland California Adventure Park's "Cars Land," a twelve acre theme park representing the largest portion of Disneyland's recent $1 billion expansion. "Cars Land" is the largest attraction in Disneyland or Disneyworld—exceeding the Matterhorn and Splash Mountain; CityCenter, Las Vegas, a sixty-seven acre multiuse community comprised of hotels, casinos, condominiums, retail space, and entertainment space with SME Steel providing 78,000 tons of steel creating the most expensive privately owned construction project in U.S. history; and Levi's Stadium, home of the San Francisco 49ers NFL team, is the first NFL stadium to incorporate buckling restrained braces—526 CoreBrace BRBs in total.

SME Steel's multi-division operation is headed up by Wayne Searle, CEO, who began his career with SME eighteen years ago in structural steel detailing. Prior to ascending to this current post, Searle served the company in various leadership capacities—including SME Steel president for four years. His thirty-four year tenure in the structural steel construction industry includes experience in shop manufacturing, field installation, drafting, detailing, engineering, project management, contracts, estimating, sales supervision, and administration. Craig Moyes, co-founder of SME, passed the mantle to Searle at SME's twentieth anniversary celebration on April 20, 2012. Moyes, along with co-founder and majority shareholder Jerry Moyes, remains on the SME Board of Directors. Both Moyes are actively and vitally involved in the company's strategic planning and international endeavors.

Since it was founded in 1992, SME has enjoyed steady bottom line financial growth. To what does SME Steel's CEO Searle attribute to his company's success? "The people," Searle says. "We use the same steel and offer the same price as our competitors but it's our staff that makes the difference. I am very lucky to work with more than one thousand creative, highly-professional people who are very good at what they do."

Looking to the future, Searle hopes to expand the SME Steel brand, services, and expertise both nationally and internationally. "We'd like to expand our reach across the entire country and are exploring the possibility of opening new plants in several areas, including collaborating with our partner company in South America to create CoreBrace products there," Searle says.

For more information about SME Steel and its divisions, please visit www.smesteel.com.

Left: CoreBrace is a proven, innovative buckling-restrained bracing system (BRBs) designed to allow buildings to withstand seismic events. The Levi's Stadium, home of San Francisco 49ers NFL team, has incorporated 526 CoreBrace BRBs in its facility.

Below: SME Steel has completed distinctive edifices throughout the Western United States, including the San Diego Public Library's iconic dome.

BURTON LUMBER COMPANY

❖

Right: Left to right, Jeff, Robert and Dan Burton.

Below: Entrance to Burton Lumber's facility 1170 South 4400 West.

A fourth generation, family-owned lumberyard in which fifth generation members are now taking an active part, Burton Lumber Company has been helping build Utah for over a century. Its seven locations and twelve divisions from Logan to St. George provide lumber, hardware, doors, trusses, installation and framing to professional contractors throughout Utah.

The company was organized and chartered in August 1911. Soon afterward, Willard C. Burton became its president, and his son, Carl C. Burton, secretary and treasurer. They were joined by another of Willard's sons, Alma G. Burton. Ownership has remained in the Burton family and family members have been controlling officers from that time through the present.

Burton's original lumberyard was built at the edge of the farm acquired by Willard's father, Robert T. Burton, after he came into the valley as a pioneer. The original wood frame store building burned in a nighttime fire in 1939, and was replaced by a new lumber and hardware store that was state-of-the-art for that time.

In the 1920s the Burtons acquired Midvale Lumber and built another yard, which they named Native Lumber, on South Main Street. From which they sold species of locally grown lumber, including posts and pole logs for farm fencing when farms were still prevalent in the Salt Lake valley.

The Midvale and Native yards were closed in 1968, and the growth of Burton Lumber has been nothing short of phenomenal since then. In 2003 the company moved its headquarters into a 200,000 square foot facility on thirty-two acres of land near the Salt Lake City International Airport, and also opened a number of other sites throughout the state.

In the company's early years, delivery was via horse and wagon, and early financial statements listed horses and tack under property plant and equipment, including a fine team

of horses previously owned and used by the fire department. A treasured company anecdote recalls problems when a fire alarm sounded while a load of lumber was being delivered to a building site. It took all the teamster's skills to get the team to go to the proper site without first rushing to the fire, as they had been trained to do.

Changes in time and technology brought the purchase of a brand new, chain-driven Mac truck in 1917, and another mechanical delivery vehicle, a 1923 Mac chain-driven truck, in 1923. The 1923 truck, now fully restored, is displayed in the company's Salt Lake showroom.

In the early years, stocking, storing, loading, delivery, and unloading of lumber, bags of cement, and all other items were done by hand. This involved either hot and hard work or cold and hard work, depending on weather conditions. The "good old boys" who did that were tough, dependable men, such as Dwight, Herb, Doug, Henry, Spike, Nels and Pete.

Excitement ran high at Burton Lumber and throughout the community when the television series, *Touched by an Angel*, which ran on CBS from 1994 to 2003, requested permission to film in one of the warehouse buildings on State Street. Roma Downey, Della Reese, and Randy Travis were the stars who hung out in the Burton Lumber warehouse for the filming.

The Burton family's ownership and management of the company continues today, with Dan and Jeff Burton as owners. Dan is company president, and his brother, Jeff, is vice president of sales. Their brother, Robert Burton, Jr., serves as the company's general counsel, and their father, Robert T. Burton, after sixty-five years of continuous employment, is still chairman of the board. Growth has fluctuated as Burton Lumber opened new branches throughout Utah and in response to the economy. Over the last fifteen years, the company has employed between 250 and 450 employees.

With ninety-eight percent of its sales coming from commercial and residential contractors and owner/builders,

Burton Lumber's 345 employees are now serving the company's facilities throughout Utah. These include five in Salt Lake City: the Salt Lake Branch and Corporate Facility, the Olympus Branch, the Truss, Turn Key and Door Divisions. Others are the St. George, Lindon, Layton and Logan Branches and the newest division, the St. George Truss Plant.

Both family members and company employees support community projects and programs. Burton Lumber donates each year to Primary Children's Hospital, both through direct contributions and by way of the annual Festival of Trees. Burton employees have generously donated to the Utah Food Bank for the past six years.

Although a great deal has changed in the over 100 years since Burton Lumber's formation in 1911, the company's mission remains consistent. Through dedication, cooperation, determination, and leadership of all its employees, it strives to reach a level of service, quality, and competitive pricing that is superior to its competition, and to do so in a manner that is profitable to both its customers and to itself.

The Burtons are proud of how their company has grown and prospered throughout the years and are looking forward to being a part of what the next century will bring.

For additional information, please visit Burton Lumber on the Internet at www.burtonlumber.com.

Top: Lumberyard at Salt Lake facility 1170 South 4400 West.

Above: Left to right, Carl, Taylor and Willard C Burton, founder.

MONSEN ENGINEERING OF SALT LAKE CITY

Above: Left to right, Ali, James, Richard, Emily, Mikel, Paul, David, Jason and Roger Paul Monsen, Jr.

PHOTOGRAPH BY TRISH EMPEY.

Right: Founder, Roger P. Monsen, Sr.

Monsen Engineering of Salt Lake City is the leading supplier of measurement products and solutions to the design and building industries in Idaho, Wyoming, Utah and Nevada. The third generation, family-owned company is excited to be celebrating their fortieth year in business. The moral compass and business policies set by the company's founder, Roger P. Monsen, Sr., created a strong foundation for Monsen Engineering to grow from.

At the age of fifty-seven, Roger found himself out of work after spending more than twenty-five years with the Pembroke Company. This 100 year old, family-owned company was sold and Roger's philosophy no longer fit into the new owner's corporate culture. Roger was determined to remain in the industry and established Monsen Engineering in 1974 with the support of his brother, Kent Monsen.

Roger was joined by three of his loyal previous employees who followed him to Monsen Engineering. A key original employee was his nephew, Paul Monsen who performed the accounting and financing functions. Paul went on to become the company's CFO and a partner in the business. Richard Monsen, Roger's youngest son, assumed a sales position and eventually became its president.

In the 1970s, Monsen Engineering sold hand drafting tools, drafting room furniture and blueprinting machines, as well as survey levels and transits. In the 1980s, Computer

Aided Drafting (CAD) replaced hand drafting tools causing drafting and engineering practices to change. Richard and Paul branched out into large format scanners, plotters and Xerox engineering copier sales. Monsen Engineering opened the first large format xerographic reproduction department in Utah, managed by Roger P. Monsen, Jr.

In 1992, Monsen Engineering was the first to adopt the newest technology for the land surveying industry. Global Positioning Systems (GPS) eventually replaced traditional survey instruments and is the standard for today's land surveyor.

In 1998, Clark County, Nevada became the fastest growing county in the United States. "The strategic addition of stores in Nevada was important to our growth." Richard says. "During a Las Vegas building boom in 1998, we partnered with Mike Grill, who helped us gain a strong foothold in the Las Vegas market. He manages and operates our Las Vegas store to this day."

In 2003, Monsen Engineering had an opportunity to acquire a twenty year old family-owned company in Reno, Nevada. Marty Crook, a well-known supplier and former competitor, became a valuable part of the Monsen Engineering team. He continues to manage Monsen Engineering's Reno store and oversees repair services and equipment sales in Northern Nevada.

Monsen Engineering's talented employees have been another vital component to its success. Many employees have been with the company for a decade or more. "We pride ourselves in growing talent from within and molding them into great contributors of our development and success," Richard said. "For the last thirteen years, the third generation of the Monsen family has been built into its core."

Based on Monsen Engineering's reputation within the industry, manufacturers continue to present them with new opportunities and groundbreaking technologies.

The company recently added a completely new department dedicated to the newest industrial measurement technology, 3D scanning and printing. Opportunities to expand into new markets and geographic locations also continue to present themselves.

Monsen Engineering prides itself in being a valued community partner. The Nevada Association of Land Surveyors has presented multiple "Member of the Year" awards to Monsen Engineering for its supportive role through consistent involvement with NALS, its programs and objectives. In addition, the company offers the Roger P. Monsen Memorial Scholarship to students in both Utah and Nevada, in an effort to promote the land surveying profession among the region's college students.

After forty years in business, Monsen Engineering's products have changed, but their clients within the design and building industry have remained the same. "We have been blessed with many years when the economy and growth within the architectural, engineering, land surveying, mining and construction industries were very strong." Also unchanged is what Richard says was Roger's business plan when he started the company, "Do the right thing, take care of the customers, and the profit will follow." That simple plan is still in effect at Monsen Engineering.

Monsen Engineering, 960 South Main Street.
PHOTOGRAPH BY TRISH EMPEY.

Major Drilling Group International, Inc.

Major Drilling is a specialized drilling company that delivers on even the toughest jobs. The company utilizes knowledge, extensive experience, a focus on safety, and commitment to meeting the local needs of every customer. The focus is on retaining the best team and a modern, diversified drilling fleet, partnering with customers and local communities for outstanding results.

Major Drilling is committed to a proactive and innovative approach to its people, equipment and safety, with its entire working culture based first and foremost on a safe working environment for employees. Safety is also of primary consideration whenever Major Drilling purchases new businesses or equipment or works through new processes. Major Drilling is also committed to a sustainable development policy that ensures drilling programs minimize any impact on the environment.

From its inception in New Brunswick, Canada, in 1980, Major Drilling has grown into one of the world's largest metals and minerals contract-drilling companies. Major Drilling's extensive experience allows it to mobilize to other parts of the globe to meet customers' specific needs.

Drilling services offered include surface and underground coring, directional, reverse circulation, sonic, geothermal, environmental and water-well, coal-bed methane and shallow gas drilling. Priorities include providing quality work for clients, completing each job satisfactorily, and building strong relationships between local communities, clients, and employees. Senior management brings over 1,000 years of experience into the customer relationships.

During its first twenty years, Major Drilling expanded geographically as a conventional drilling company, acquiring several mineral exploration drilling companies in Eastern Canada between 1980 and 1985, buying equipment at a reasonable price, and adding talented and experienced personnel.

The company acquired drilling companies and affiliates in Canada in the 1980s and expanded into Mexico and South America in the early 1990s. In 1997 the focus turned to expanding Canadian operations and looking to Australia with its strong tradition in mining.

In 2000, Major Drilling shifted focus to specialized drilling efforts, building specialized capabilities and fleet, complemented with strategic acquisitions. Equipment, contracts, inventory and other assets were acquired from Eastern Australia and New Zealand, Mongolia, the Western United States, Southern Africa, South America and Canada. Innovations have focused on safety, from driver education to drilling procedures, such as eliminating the use of pipe wrenches under power and conducting field trials using new rig types with full rod-handling capabilities.

Major Drilling is committed to exceeding our customers' needs on every drilling project, and continue to be the world leader in specialized drilling. Through its investment in people, equipment, and the communities where it operates, paired with its fiscal discipline, Major Drilling is well positioned for the future.

ARCHITECTURAL NEXUS, INC.

Top and above: Architectural Nexus Salt Lake City office.

Architectural Nexus believes that both the client and designer create an architectural design. Neither can work alone. Design is an interactive process, with the client defining the needs and the vision. The designer must learn those needs and gain a thorough understanding until the client's vision becomes a clear concept. This is the concept behind the architecture, interior design, landscape architecture and civil engineering services provided by Architectural Nexus.

Two firms, Thompson Peterson Hammond (TPH) and Jensen Haslem Architects (JH) were afforded the opportunity in 1999 to join as associating architects in a design/build competition together with Layton Construction for the new $25 million Critical Care Pavilion at the University of Utah Health Sciences Center. The experience of working together on this project proved to be highly successful, as the combined firms won the design/build competition as constructors and designers of the pavilion. These partners' collaboration to complete the design, document it, and participate in the construction was equally successful and rewarding. It led both firms to agree that they preferred a cooperative arrangement to their previous competitive situation.

After design of the Critical Care Pavilion, the two firms received the programming commission for the new John A. Moran Eye Center II facility and the Emma Eccles Jones Medical Sciences building, both on the University of Utah Health Sciences Campus. Award of the new Mercy Medical Center in Durango, Colorado, in 2003 solidified Architectural Nexus as a dynamic new architectural force in healthcare design in the Intermountain West. The idea of combining into one firm was discussed, and specific efforts to merge the firms into a single corporate entity began within two months.

Members of both firms found the experience of working together enjoyable. They noted that their work ethic and work styles were similar and their technological skills were compatible and complementary. Believing that they would serve their clients better as a single entity than as separate architectural firms, they had corporate documents prepared, and by January 1, 2003, Architectural Nexus was a legal corporate entity. Joint committees worked to decide how to merge the firms' technology, processes and staff, and the committee participants had a great time discovering the talents, tools and individuals of the newly merged firm. Founders of the original companies—Steve Peterson, John (Jack) Hammond and Tim Thomas of TPH and Tom Jensen and Bruce Haslem, founders of JH—remained in leadership at Architectural Nexus. Don Finlayson, managing principal of JH Architects' Salt Lake City office, was chosen as president of the new firm.

Offices of the original firms were about seven blocks apart in Salt Lake City's Sugarhouse area. There was a line of sight, so they could connect "wirelessly." Placement of a transceiver on its building's roof allowed communication except when the wind was blowing or the trees were in full leaf.

Rather than using the names of key individuals, the new firm chose to call itself Architectural Nexus, indicative of their decision to join together. The annual management retreats began in 2002 at the Homestead Resort in Midway, Utah. The firm endures as one of the best-known healthcare design firms in the Intermountain West. To merge the cultures, TPH managing partner Dave Fletcher and Finlayson were given adjacent offices for easy communication. Traditions, such as a costumed annual Halloween bowling day and lunchtime volleyball on Fridays, were established to encourage socializing.

An iconic project that continues to grow is the Huntsman Cancer Institute and Hospital at the University of Utah Healthcare Campus. Finlayson actually began working at the University of Utah Healthcare Campus when he was an architectural medical planner with a large national architectural firm. The relationship has continued into the twenty-first century.

"We have grown our architectural staff and reach to include an office in Sacramento, California" Finlayson says. "All offices are leaders in institutional and large-scale landscape and site design, as well as civil engineering. Architectural Nexus is one of the largest architecture firms in the Intermountain West and Central California."

The firm's 160 employees include 45 LEED Accredited Professionals, 2 civil engineers, 4 landscape architects, 6 interior designers, an in-house graphic design, marketing and administrative division. The headquarters is at 2505 Parleys Way in Salt Lake City's Sugarhouse area, and the central and northern California office is in downtown Sacramento, California.

"We are regularly placed as the largest firm in terms of revenue in industry publications such as *ENR (Engineering News Record*, a McGraw–Hill publication), *Utah Business Magazine, Modern Healthcare, Utah Construction and Design* magazine, *Utah Facilities* magazine, Comstock's magazine, and the *Sacramento Business Journal*," Finlayson notes. "We are cited in these publications for our Sustainable Design, Healthcare Architecture, and design for the Federal Government and Civic Architecture."

Architectural Nexus welcomes opportunities to grow within the Western Region of the United States as opportunities present themselves, he adds.

The firm and its employees are represented on community and charitable boards and organizations throughout the region, including prominent members of AIA Utah, ASLA, SMPS Utah, USHE (Utah Society Healthcare Engineering), various planning commissions, 21st Business District, the Friends of the Children's Justice Center Salt Lake County, Envision Utah, NAIOP (National, Association of Industrial and Office Properties) and many others.

For more information about the firm, please visit www.archnexus.com.

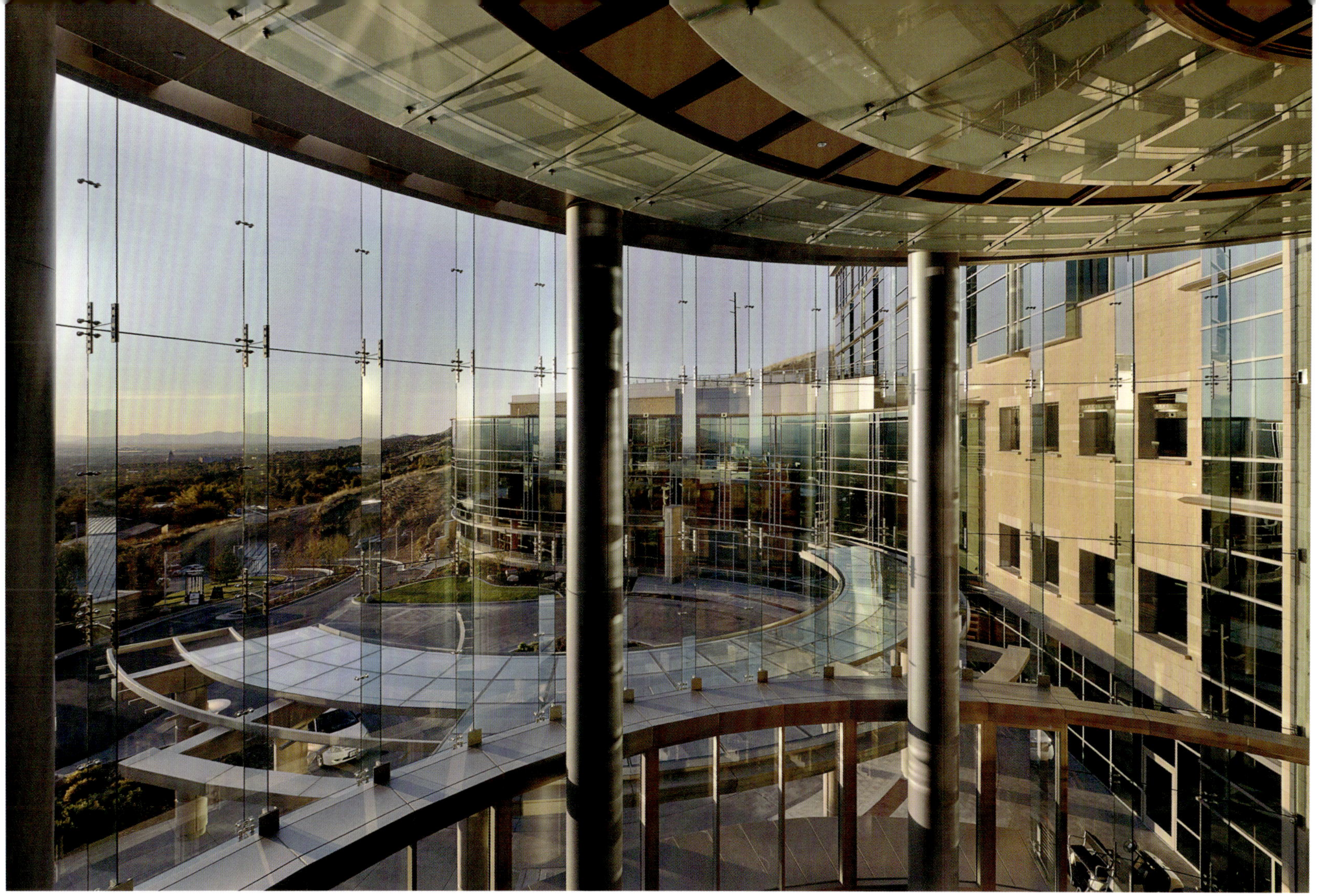

❖

Huntsman Cancer Hospital.

ARCHITECT: ARCHITECTURAL NEXUS. PHOTOGRAPH COURTESY OF DANA SOHM.

FLSMIDTH

❖

Above: FLSmidth's global headquarters for its Mineral Processing division, located in Salt Lake City, supports mining projects throughout the world, including Rio Tinto's Kennecott copper mine in Bingham Canyon.

Below: The Minerals Testing and Research Center on FLSmidth's Salt Lake City campus brings together research and development and pilot testing resources, along with ore characterization and process mineralogy laboratories and a state-of-the-art automated sample preparation system, all in a single facility.

With offices in more than fifty countries and over 15,000 employees worldwide—including its Mineral Processing division here in Salt Lake City—Denmark-based FLSmidth is one of the world's largest minerals industry suppliers. Serving the international mining community as its One Source supplier, FLSmidth has created an unmatched portfolio of accomplishments by combining the proven reliability and quality of the mining industry's leading brands through a number of strategic acquisitions over the last twenty-five years, including: ABON, Buffalo, CEntry, Conveyor Engineering, Dawson Metallurgical Laboratories, Decanter Machine, Dorr-Oliver, EIMCO, Essa, FFE, Fuller-Traylor, KOCH, Knelson, Krebs, Ludowici, MAAG Gear, Mayer Bulk, M.I.E. Enterprises, Möller, MVT, PERI, Phillips Kiln Services, Pneumapress, RAHCO, Raptor, Roymec, Shriver, Summit Valley, Technequip, WEMCO, Vecor and Ventomatic.

FLSmidth's deep connection with Salt Lake City is rooted in EIMCO, founded by Nathan Rosenblatt, a Russian immigrant, in the 1880s. Originally located on the corner of 800 South and State Street, Rosenblatt first opened his scrap metal collection business in downtown Salt Lake. Over the years EIMCO's business ventures evolved, becoming first a brass foundry, then a custom machine shop and eventually a world leader in separation equipment. Today, with EIMCO as part of its diverse brand family, FLSmidth has become a mining industry leading supplier, offering a range of products, tools and services from single machinery to complete cement plants and minerals processing facilities, including services before, during, and after construction.

As the global headquarters for the Mineral Processing division of FLSmidth, the Salt Lake City office supports mining projects throughout the world, including Rio Tinto's Kennecott copper mine in Bingham Canyon. The Salt Lake City office was instrumental in landing FLSmidth a very large project in Mongolia consisting of two contracts with the Mongolyn Alt (MAK) Group; one to supply a greenfield copper concentrator and the other to supply a complete cement plant. This is the first time a project of this magnitude has been undertaken by a single company in the mining industry and shows the success and strength of both the technology and the efforts of the employees who worked on the project.

FLSmidth's current and future development plans include ongoing research with special emphasis on the use of alternative fuels, reducing emissions and waste, improving heat recovery, decreasing power consumption, minimizing water consumption, increasing plant capacity, availability and operating efficiency and minimizing safety risks. The Minerals Testing and Research Center, inaugurated in Salt Lake City in September 2010, is a cornerstone project of these efforts. The center brings together R&D and pilot testing resources, along with the process testing laboratory in a single facility, serving as the springboard for solving customers' processing issues and developing new solutions and products. As a result of the focus on innovation and the R&D investment, FLSmidth files an increasing number of priority patent applications every year.

FLSmidth maintains strong customer relationships through its technology centers and regional sales offices located throughout the world. The company is known locally in many countries for its technical sales, customer services and support staff. A global procurement strategy allows FLSmidth to source equipment and materials competitively, thus creating more opportunities for reduction of cost and delivery schedule optimization. "Customer intimacy is one of the strongest factors uniting us all at FLSmidth. We're focused on coming up with solutions and delivering results for all of our customers, both internally and externally," says Division President of Mineral Processing, Peter Flanagan.

Thomas Schulz, FLSmidth CEO, looks forward to both growing FLSmidth while maintaining its position as an industry innovation and efficiency leader. "It's important for me to meet people, visit them in their local environments and come to know the challenges they face and the demands they have. Only by being close to our customers are we able to really understand what their needs are and how we can best accommodate these needs," Schulz says.

As an industry leader, FLSmidth is proud to consistently provide innovative solutions using the latest in equipment technology, resources and materials. FLSmidth's robust reputation is based on providing customers and partners from around the world with a solid foundation of support and expertise for more than a century. The company's Material Handling division is headquartered in Wadgassen, Germany, and the Cement division headquarters are found in Copenhagen, Denmark. Additional USA offices are located in Washington, Pennsylvania, Arizona, West Virginia and Tennessee.

In addition to FLSmidth's global reach, the Salt Lake City office is committed to supporting the community in which it operates. Some of the local philanthropies to which the company has contributed are: the Utah Food Bank, the Salt Lake affiliate of Susan G. Komen Race for the Cure, Salt Lake County Youth Services' Shelter Kids program, Primary Children's Medical Center's annual Festival of Trees fundraiser and the Boys and Girls Club of Midvale Angel Tree program.

For more information about FLSmidth services and technologies, please visit flsmidth.com.

FLSmidth provides minerals processing equipment for crushing, grinding, flotation, thickening and filtration processes at mining operations around the world including the Esperanza Mine in northern Chile, South America (top, left) operated by Antofagasta Minerals and Marubeni Corporation and the Robinson Copper Mine operated by Quadra Mining in Nevada (top, right).

PAULSEN CONSTRUCTION

"General construction is a contrast between worrying about where the next project is coming from and how to successfully complete the project at hand." This is a truth well known to those at Paulsen Construction, who have successfully made it through ninety years in the business.

Starting in 1924 by Paul Paulsen, who came to the United States from Lofoten, Norway, Paulsen Construction has grown to become one of Utah's most prolific building contractors.

Paulsen, who has been described by his descendants as a hard-working Norwegian who provided estimates on a project by guessing how much it would cost to construct, apparently had a gift for guessing well. The company not only managed to stay in business through the Great Depression, when many others failed, but is still going strong today.

In the 1940s the leadership of Paulsen Construction was assumed by Paul's sons, Herman and Byron, who had been key individuals in the early days. The company was incorporated in 1959, and is now led by Craig and John Paulsen, with members of the family's fourth generation also involved in its activities.

As they always have, those at Paulsen Construction take pride in providing a safe work environment and equal opportunity for all employees and subcontractors while delivering outstanding results for their clients.

"We are general contractors specializing in historical restoration, seismic stabilization, educational facilities and custom residential construction," says John. "The company's mission, 'Building Quality Products with Integrity Since 1924,' remains very much in effect today. Our purpose is to pursue construction projects within our communities while delivering quality buildings for generations to come and restoring buildings from generations past."

Paulsen Construction employs knowledgeable and skilled staff with the opportunity to expand industry skill and techniques while retaining its values of responsive leadership and concern for the industry's future.

The company's long history is a reflection of the area it serves. In the early days, Paulsen Construction built many apartment buildings in Salt Lake City, along with other projects including the "This is the Place" monument, the Daughters of Utah Pioneers Museum, and the second Visitor Center at Temple Square.

After World War II and through the 1970s, the company's projects included many schools, and in the 1980s it constructed numerous wastewater treatment plants. From the 1990s to the present, Paulsen Construction has diversified to include such projects as historic restoration, seismic and custom residential work.

The growth of Paulsen Construction is evident in its current basic statistics, which include an average employee base of twenty-five to thirty and average annual revenue of $10 million for the period from 2008 through 2012.

"We believe that by keeping our company at a reasonable size, we can provide the attention to detail that our clients deserve," John says.

Revenues continue to fluctuate, but continual efforts are made to optimize profits. Despite nationwide financial concerns, Paulsen Construction has experienced continued small growth over the past five years. Hints of financial recovery offer promise for the future. At present the company's customer base is a mix of private and public owners. It plans to continue building on current relationships while also looking to serve new industries.

Attuned to the environmental and conservation concerns so vital to today's business and to the welfare of generations to come, Paulsen Construction addresses these in several different ways. Among them is ownership of a CNG truck that is used to make deliveries in the city and to pick up supplies. The company also encourages the recycling of construction demolition and waste materials, both on its construction sites and in the company's headquarters at 3075 South 230 West, Salt Lake City, Utah.

Throughout its history, Paulsen Construction has been an active partner in a number of community and charitable activities. These include restoration of the Historic Spring City School; service on the board of ABC and on the Utah Executive Residence Commission; as well as support of the Utah Heritage Foundation, Utah Arts and the Traditional Building Skills Institute at Snow College.

With expansion of seismic operations and historical restoration projects currently underway, the company is also planning for the future. Expected highlights in the years ahead are participation in the rural development expected in Utah, plans for celebrating Paulsen Construction's centennial year, and the addition of a fifth generation of family members as participants in the business.

More information about Paulsen Construction is available on the Internet at www.paulsenconstruction.com, along with numerous photographs of past projects.

Boart Longyear

Founded in 1890 by Edmund J. Longyear, Boart Longyear is the world's leading integrated provider of drilling services, drilling equipment and performance tooling for mining and mineral drilling companies globally. Also, Boart Longyear has a substantial presence in energy, mine de-watering, oil sands exploration, and production drilling.

The company aims to be the "One Source" for drilling services, drilling equipment and performance tooling for mining and drilling companies globally by offering customers a comprehensive portfolio of technologically advanced and innovative drilling services and products.

Their Drilling Services division performs contract drilling work for a diverse mining customer base, operating across a wide range of commodities, including gold, copper, nickel, zinc, uranium and other metals and minerals. The division is able to offer the broadest range of drilling technologies in the markets it serves to meet its customers' needs. These technologies include surface and underground diamond coring, reverse circulation, rotary and sonic drilling.

Boart Longyear's Products division is a leading manufacturer, marketer and distributor of a wide range of drilling equipment and performance tooling, including diamond drill bits, drill rods, wireline core extraction systems, drilling rigs and other products used in mineral exploration, mine development, mine production, and environmental and infrastructure drilling. The company's extensive experience in the drilling industry and broad portfolio of patents and innovations have enabled them to develop and deliver a comprehensive line of technologically advanced drilling products to meet the drilling industry's needs for safety, reliability and productivity.

Globally, Boart Longyear's success is a result of the hard work of more than 6,000 employees. From engineers to drillers in the field, Boart Longyear employees set the industry standard for finding solutions in even the most challenging drilling applications.

Right: A Boart Longyear drill crew sets up a LF™130F Heli-portable rig at a remote site in Alaska. Once the LF130F's eleven components are flown to site, the crew will begin drilling to depths up to 5,000 feet for mineral exploration.

Below: Boart Longyear's Drilling Services crew installs a large dewatering well for a mine in Australia. These wells draw water from deep in the earth, reducing the water level and allowing for deeper mining.

Boart Longyear is a global company headquartered in Salt Lake City, Utah, USA, and is listed on the Australian Securities Exchange (ASX: BLY) in Sydney, Australia. Contract drilling services are conducted in 35 countries and drilling products are manufactured in 6 global factories and sold to customers in more than 100 countries.

Safety is a core value at the company. Boart Longyear is committed to the safety of its customers, the environment and making sure each of their employees go home safely every day. All six of the company's global manufacturing plants are ISO 9001, ISO 14001, and OHSAS 18001 certified. In addition, all global drilling services locations are ISO 14001, and OHSAS 18001 certified.

Its presence in the Salt Lake Valley reaches over twenty-five years, beginning with a regional office and manufacturing plant. In 2006, Boart Longyear's global corporate offices were relocated to Salt Lake City. This decision was made to put the company closer to its mining-customer. Since then, Boart Longyear occupies multiple buildings throughout the valley.

Boart Longyear's community efforts are focused on education and opportunities for children; and health and preventive care. The company is committed to sponsoring of the Utah FIRST LEGO League, a global robotics and innovation program that develops an enthusiasm for discovery, science, teamwork and technology.

❖

Top, right: An employee removes finished drill bits from an oven in Salt Lake City, Utah. Boart Longyear manufactures drilling products around the world including Canada, China, Germany, Poland, and the United States of America.

Below: Drillers recover core samples at a site in Africa. These samples are reviewed by geologists to determine the mineral content of an ore body.

WOODBURY CORPORATION

Right: University Mall, Orem, Utah—In the center of it all, University Mall is an award-winning, 1.77 million square foot regional shopping center owned, developed and managed by Woodbury.

Below: The Meadows, American Fork, Utah—Impressive 2 million square foot regional shopping center on Interstate 15 owned, developed and managed by Woodbury.

One of the oldest, most respected commercial real estate companies in the Intermountain West, Salt Lake City-based Woodbury Corporation has a proven record of delivering projects, fulfilling obligations, and finding creative solutions to difficult problems. During its ninety-five year history, it has collaborated with a vast number of tenants, investors, business and community leaders, developing projects with long-term ownership and management in mind.

Among the West's largest and most experienced full-service real estate development firms, Woodbury maintains a talented team of 150 multi-disciplined professionals offering brokerage, management, development, legal, consulting and architectural services for all types of retail, office, hospitality, research park and other land developments throughout the Midwest and Western United States.

With over 150 successful development projects, Woodbury has demonstrated the ability to address any issue, tackle any size project, and efficiently deliver a quality product on time and on budget, thus maintaining their position as a leader in the industry and marketplace.

From vision to completion, Woodbury facilitates all aspects of the design and development process to handle everything from small retail renovations to full-scale master-planned mixed-use developments. Woodbury creates a competitive advantage in leveraging its in-house expertise to complement collaboration with top tier consultants, ensuring high-quality projects.

The firm's legal team handles a broad array of complex legal activities ranging from acquisition, disposition, commercial financing and land-use issues to entity formation and collections, helping create mutually beneficial, long-term relationships with partners, tenants, communities, and companies.

Maintaining integrity of reputation and credit is of primary importance for a company to succeed for nearly a century. Woodbury's reputation and creditworthiness is evidenced by its capacity to finance projects at very favorable terms with a robust pool of commercial banks and insurance companies, with several of those lending relationships extending fifty years and beyond.

From the beginning, Woodbury has believed that property/asset management is the most fundamental and valuable of all real estate activities. Woodbury has managed all major types of investment real estate including retail, office, industrial, residential, and hotels. Its long-term vision is reflected in its investment strategies, land acquisition decisions, building quality, retail partners, and managerial style. Its management outlook focuses on mutually profitable relationships with tenants, contractors, suppliers, and service providers, emphasizing quality over economy and craftsmanship over cutting corners.

Woodbury has the unique ability in-house to develop, design, own and operate its hotels, with its portfolio consisting almost exclusively of Marriott and Hilton brands. Many of its veteran hotel general managers and department heads have worked through the ranks of those national brands for decades. This ensures superior service for guests, a great environment for associates and attentiveness to maximizing financial performance.

Woodbury Corporation and its principals own, control and/or manage over 11 million square feet of retail, office and industrial buildings, 12 hotels comprising over 1,500 rooms, and more than 1,300 residential units in 11 Western and Midwestern states. Continuing to lead in commercial real estate development with complex public-private partnerships and land-use concepts, its original principles and values remain the bedrock of today's organization.

• First Generation–Industrial Era. F. Orin Woodbury entered the real estate business in 1919. Often passing on profitable opportunities in order to build a reputation of integrity over income, the F. Orin Woodbury Company continued to flourish through the Great Depression. In 1935 it was reorganized as Woodbury Corporation. F. O. led in real estate circles locally and nationally, helping develop education programs and professional designations. He served as national president of the Institute of Real Estate Management (IREM) and Counselors of Real Estate (CRE). F. O. brokered many significant land assemblage deals including the Standard Oil refinery and pipeline, Utah State Penitentiary, Veterans Hospital and the Remington Arms Plant.

• Second Generation–Shopping Center Development Era. F. O.'s sons, Wallace and Orin led the development of multiple shopping centers including University Mall in Orem, Utah, over twenty Kmart anchored centers and many grocery anchored shopping centers. Present company chairman Orin R. Woodbury was an aviator and naval flight instructor during World War II, later working for the Woodbury Corporation and founding Practical Building Company, a residential construction business. In 1954, F. O., Orin and Wally founded Richards Woodbury Mortgage Corporation, where Orin served for over thirty years, while continuing his role with

❖

Left: Springhill Suites by Marriott, Draper, Utah—A new, smart, and stylish, 124 suite hotel owned, developed, and managed by Woodbury.

Below: Falcon Hill, Hill Air Force Base, Utah—A 550 acre national aerospace and research park located along Interstate 15 owned, developed, and managed by Woodbury.

Woodbury Corporation. Well into his nineties, Orin continues to work every day contributing to the ongoing success of Woodbury Corporation.

• Third Generation–Diversified Development Era. Rick, Randy, Lynn, Jeff and Guy Woodbury, F. O.'s grandsons, have led the development and acquisition of over 100 office, retail, hotel, and apartment projects including University Mall redevelopment in Orem; The Meadows in American Fork; the University of Utah Research Park; and one of the largest Enhanced Use Lease projects in U.S. history at Utah's Hill Air Force Base.

• Fourth Generation–Innovative Development Era. Two dozen additional family members and other company executives are engaged in projects emphasizing innovative, green approaches to development of new assets and redevelopment of current portfolio assets. Woodbury Corporation focuses on producing properties that are needed in its communities. This diversification helps Woodbury remain strong through fluctuating economies, continuing to seek emerging trends that make real estate equities more profitable.

For additional information, including upcoming projects, services offered and much more, visit www.woodburycorp.com.

Beacon Metals, Inc.

Beginning with the premise that good people could produce great results, Carl W. Buehner and his son-in-law, John C. Riches, founded Beacon Metals, Inc., as a start-up company supplying commercial aluminum windows and hollow metal doors. Their philosophy has positioned the company for tremendous opportunities since its founding in December of 1966. In the company's early days, key individuals in addition to Beuhner and Riches included Hank Ombach and Beulah Knight.

Today, Beacon Metals furnishes commercial and industrial doors and hardware on literally thousands of buildings, which include hundreds of thousands of doors and openings, facilitating public access and security, as well as meeting rigorous life safety and fire codes.

The mission of Beacon Metals is to provide the highest level of value to its customers through competent, certified, licensed professionals and quality products. It strives to be a company of preference, to be financially strong, provide opportunities to its team members and sustain targeted, steady growth.

The company's products and expertise provide beauty and functionality while maintaining the security and safety required for hospitals, schools and universities, government military bases and installations, retail shopping centers and malls, airports, churches and religious houses of worship, industrial treatment facilities, hotels and hospitality, office buildings, prisons and jails, temples, generating plants, sporting and special event arenas, conference centers and numerous other facilities.

The company's founders were surprised when the SBA loan officer reviewing their application commented, "Your business plan will fail in ninety days." Even so, the founders remained committed to the plan, convincing the loan officer to approve the loan. The wisdom of that decision is evident in the company's success, with statistics which today include over fifty employees and over $15 million annually in sales revenues.

When it began, the company's main product line was Steelcraft Manufacturing Company, a leader in the hollow metal door and frame industry, but Beacon struggled with sub-tier hardware lines at that time, as all of the major lines were represented by large, competing door and hardware suppliers in the Salt Lake market. The aluminum window industry, which was extremely competitive, was in the early stages of converting from single pane to double pane windows, rendering most of Beacon's manufacturing equipment obsolete. As a result, the company exited the aluminum window business just a few years after start-up with the commitment to focus its efforts and investment on architectural doors, frames and hardware.

When John was called to serve a mission for the Church of Jesus Christ of Latter-day Saints in South Carolina, Hank became the new general manager. Under his direction, the company purchased property and developed the facility at its current location, 2770 South West Temple, Salt Lake City. During Hank's tenure, the company's revenues doubled prior to his retiring in 1992. Ken Riches, the next generation, became the company's president, a post he still holds. Others who have played key roles in our company include Jim and Larry Butler; Carlos Esparza, Jay Ombach and many other talented and exceptional people.

"Over the years, our company has transitioned from manual processes to computerization," says Ken, president. "Our first computer was an IBM system that required

nine-inch floppy disks." Orders to manufacturers were sent, acknowledged, and returned by mail before manufacturing could begin. All business was transacted this way and was very time consuming. Today, the entire system has changed dramatically. One thing that has remained consistent is the quality of people who have been employed here.

Innovations that have contributed to Beacon Metals' success have included:

- The purchase of a sheer and press providing custom frame manufacturing capability;
- Development of innovative solutions such as: "Stagecraft" under-stage door for the churches and theatres;
- Pre-installment of hardware on doors "in house," to facilitate greater efficiency than when installing at a jobsite;
- Investment in industry software, expanding the ability to manage greater sales revenues.

The company has added a national sales department, a security center team focused on access control, a walk-in counter department, a contract bidding department and an installation team with the ability to provide extraordinary value to its customers.

Beacon Metals, Inc., sites are at 2770 South West Temple, Salt Lake City and 677 North 3050 East Unit 4, St. George, Utah. Additional information is available on the Internet at www.beacon-metals.com.

CITY CREEK RESERVE, INC.

City Creek Reserve, Inc. (CCRI), a real estate arm of The Church of Jesus Christ of Latter-day Saints, is the master developer of City Creek, an urban redevelopment in downtown Salt Lake City that is one of the largest mixed-use projects in the country. A sustainably designed, walkable community of residences, offices, and world-class shopping, City Creek's twenty-three acres span three blocks in the heart of Salt Lake's central business district.

Shortly after successfully hosting the 2002 Winter Olympic Games, leaders in Salt Lake City recognized the need to reinvigorate the city's core. They were concerned about slowing sales and store closures on and near Main Street, a part of Utah's capital city that had always played a vital role in commerce and culture. Working with other downtown stakeholders, President Gordon B. Hinckley, leader of The Church of Jesus Christ of Latter-day Saints, initiated plans to revitalize the three blocks immediately south of Temple Square and Church headquarters.

After four years of study and design, plans for City Creek were announced in October 2006 and construction began. At the peak of activity, more than 1,700 workers were on the job site. More than 300 architects, engineers, consultants and suppliers were involved in the project during five-and-a-half years of construction.

As old buildings were deconstructed, including two enclosed shopping malls, a comprehensive sustainability program reduced waste. More than seventy percent of the debris from demolition was recycled. Steel from an imploded office tower was made into rebar for use in parking garages and foundations of residential and retail buildings. Sustainability in design, construction and operations resulted in the U.S. Green Building Council approving six Leadership in Energy and Environmental Design (LEED) certifications at City Creek.

Most of City Creek's 1.7 million square feet of office space was already occupied when work on the project began. Renewing retail and adding residential properties were project priorities, but so was keeping City Creeks' population of 5,000 office workers productive and well accommodated.

Prior to project construction, the Zions Bank Building was completely reskinned. The 50 South Main tower was imploded to make way for redevelopment, the World Trade Center lobby was remodeled, Temple View Center received a major interior upgrade and was renamed the Deseret Book Building, the base of the KeyBank Tower was substantially reconfigured, and the First Security Building was seismically upgraded and totally renovated. The Kirton McConkie Building, a new office structure on South Temple, brought the number of commercial properties to a total of eight. Today, City Creek office workers enjoy all the conveniences of a live-work-shop downtown community.

Bringing 24/7 residents back to the heart of the city was a primary objective for project planners. 536 new residences were constructed in condominium communities at 99 West, Richards Court and The Regent and in City Creek Landing Apartments. While City Creek's ample underground garages can accommodate 5,000 cars for shoppers, office workers and homeowners, most residents are driving less and living more. A new generation of urban pioneers is enjoying a

refined urban lifestyle with doorstep access to shopping, dining, and Salt Lake's best culture and entertainment venues. A new full service Harmons grocery store makes it easy to call downtown home.

Owned and operated by Taubman Centers, Inc., and anchored by Nordstrom and Macy's, City Creek Center is the project's retail centerpiece with more than 100 stores and restaurants and 2,000 employees. Landscaped walkways set amidst splashing waterfalls, tranquil ponds, a sparkling creek and restful plazas blend to create a vibrant, welcoming place to shop, eat and visit.

Spanning nearly 140 feet over Main Street, a pedestrian sky bridge connects retail galleries where shoppers enjoy climate-controlled comfort under a retractable glass roof. A first in American shopping centers, the sixty-foot roof requires just minutes to open or close. Its innovative design, engineering and fabrication earned national recognition in 2013 from the American Institute of Steel Construction.

The project takes its name from City Creek, the snow-fed stream that sustained early settlers when they first arrived in the arid Salt Lake Valley in 1847. On Main Street, the restored cast-iron façade of Zion's Cooperative Mercantile Institution (ZCMI) reminds shoppers and visitors of the city's pioneering heritage. The first elements of the intricate façade were installed in 1876. Over the years, the signature Main Street face of the ZCMI store became a symbol of industry, commerce and progress and was listed on the National Register of Historic Places. Its painstaking restoration and adaptation as an entrance to Macy's earned a 2013 Heritage Award from the Utah Heritage Foundation.

On March 22, 2012, Church leaders joined retail executives and city and state government officials at City Creek's grand opening. They praised the project's "beautifully landscaped walkways and gathering places, innovative yet timeless architecture, cascading waterfalls, choreographed fountains, and meandering creek."

After nearly ten years of planning and construction and seven million hours of labor, City Creek is fulfilling President Hinckley's vision of renewed vitality at the head of Main Street bringing increased vigor throughout Utah's capital city.

Opposite, top: City Creek at the peak of construction.

Opposite, bottom: Connected by a skybridge spanning Main Street, the retail galleries feature a fully retractable roof—the first in an American shopping center.

Top, left: City Creek Center is the retail centerpiece of the mixed-use project.

Top, right: Courses of water ripple, flow, and fall over City Creek's landscape.

US Magnesium, LLC

Top, right: The US Magnesium production facility at Rowley, Utah, commenced operations in 1972.

Top, left: Magnesium ingots packaged for transportation at the US Magnesium plant.

Top, right: The US Magnesium production facility at Rowley, Utah, commenced operations in 1972.

Opposite, top: Chlorine collection and spray drying equipment utilized in the manufacturing of magnesium.

Opposite, bottom: Crucible hauler used to service the new generation magnesium electrolysis cells at US Magnesium.

As the sole producer of magnesium metal in North America, US Magnesium is one of only three production sites in the world outside China and the former Soviet Union. Magnesium metal is produced as high purity ingots and as alloyed material for specialty applications. The company also produces a family of chloride-based co-products including chlorine for chemical uses, metal production, and water purification. Calcium chloride and iron chloride are also manufactured.

Magnesium metal, which is one-third the weight of steel and two-thirds that of aluminum, is an alloying agent industries use to reduce weight and fuel needs for automobiles and aircraft, and in pharmaceuticals, military flares, high-purity steel manufacturing, nodular iron production, and reduction processes for titanium and zirconium.

The Great Salt Lake magnesium venture was conceived and pursued as early as 1957 by John W. (Jack) Gallivan and James E. Hogle through the H-K Company. After the original production scheme proved technically infeasible, National Lead Industries, led by Jeff Rowley, acquired an eighty-four percent interest in the venture.

In the late 1960s, high purity brines of sufficient strength were produced in the lake's Stansbury Basin segment, using solar energy to evaporate the brines into suitable plant feedstock. Chemical equipment specifically designed for magnesium chloride purification and electrolysis was installed at the plant site northwest of the solar recovery system. The largest spray dryers in the world were designed and installed, and electrolytic cell technology was developed from designs used in Germany in the 1930s.

The magnesium processing scheme in Utah began in 1968, along with solar recovery of magnesium chloride from the Great Salt Lake. In 1972 magnesium production was initiated using a greenfield operating scheme (a proprietary process) and Great Salt Lake-based raw materials.

The original process was difficult to pilot, so the company solved technical problems as they appeared. These difficulties became so extreme that operations ceased in 1975. The company consulted with Norsk Hydro, a Norwegian magnesium operation, reworking the production process and resuming operations in 1976. Four years later, unplanned capital costs and delays in reaching anticipated production rates spurred National Lead to sell the operation to Amax, Inc.

Two plant modifications in the 1970s, related to boron and magnesium oxide removal, improved magnesium chloride purification operations. The direct current electrolytic cells were also modified to accept cell feed available from the Great Salt Lake.

A mid-1980s change in weather patterns led to a rapid rise in the Great Salt Lake's elevation. This resulted in failure of the magnesium operation's solar pond dikes in 1986. Solar evaporation ponds near Knolls, Utah, took advantage of the State of Utah's pumping project, and provided raw materials until the Stansbury Basin ponds were restored in 1992.

Modernization of the magnesium production process, completed in 2001, allowed increased operating capacity and reduced production costs and environmental impact. This program included developing a high amperage, high efficiency electrolyzer and installing a proprietary tertiary cell feed chlorination system, which provided a platform for economic and volumetric growth.

Producing magnesium from waters of the Great Salt Lake is challenging, requiring a unique proprietary operating scheme. In this development, the company achieved production scale operations of anhydrous recovery of magnesium—the only production process that recovered magnesium chloride directly from the original source—followed by dedicated dehydration and electrolysis of the material. Other processes used magnesium oxide or magnesium carbonate feedstock. The anhydrous methodology allowed superior economic performance and provided a broad base of co-product opportunities.

Utah's magnesium production also saw development of the world's largest spray dryers, which were used to dehydrate magnesium chloride from the lake. The process also included development and optimization of continuous chlorination reactors for high purity production of molten magnesium chloride suitable for direct-current electrolysis, resulting in high efficiency production of magnesium metal.

Headquartered in Salt Lake City, US Magnesium has a manufacturing site in Tooele County, Utah. Of its 500 employees, 480 work at the manufacturing plant and 20 at corporate headquarters. Overall sales revenue exceeds $250 million annually. Over thirty major companies purchase magnesium metal and other industries purchase co-products from the chemical segment.

Plant output has grown steadily over the forty years of operations. Major technological advancements completed in 2001 have provided a platform for substantial increases in

production, with the plant currently operating in excess of 70,000 TPY. Future plans provide for the expected escalation in automotive and aerospace demands for weight reduction. The company's energy renewal and conservation efforts generate over twenty-five percent of its electrical needs through gas turbine generators used in magnesium chloride dehydration.

US Magnesium President Ron Thayer describes the company's business future as optimistic, due to ongoing demand and market growth for magnesium compounds, chlorine chemicals, and salts. "We will continue to provide the highest quality magnesium metal and chloride chemicals to our customers, utilizing safe, progressive and responsible production methods," he says.

An active community partner, US Magnesium helps support education and extracurricular activities, including augmented teacher sponsorship in Salt Lake and Tooele counties, music and sports programs, library funding, medical research, and senior services.

UTILITY TRAILER SALES OF UTAH

Wherever reliable truck transportation is needed, operators from throughout North America and a number of foreign countries recognize Utility Trailer Sales of Utah as the place to go. Beginning in the 1960s, Utility Trailer Manufacturing Company supplied trailers in the Utah market to its dealer, Rocky Mountain Utility Trailer Sales.

Growth of the company is reflected in both the number of employees—now about sixty—and the increase in its revenues, which totaled approximately $5 million in 1980 and have risen to about $100 million today.

In its early years, Utility operated from a small shop and office located at 2200 South 400 West, then moved into newly constructed quarters at 1070 West 2100 South. In 1999 modern facilities were built on a fifteen acre tract at 4970 West 2100 South.

James D. Fake, general manager, led the organization and later formed the independent dealership, Utility Trailer Sales of Salt Lake City, which he operated successfully as its president and principal stockholder. After his retirement, the company succeeded to Utility Trailer Sales of Utah, and in 1982 its current owners, Mike Deputy and Clair Heslop, took control of the business.

One of the nation's largest and most successful semi-trailer sales and service companies, Utility Trailer Sales of Utah has earned a reputation for honesty and fair dealing to become a world-class organization that provides excellent quality and value for its trucking industry customers and suppliers.

Brands represented include Utility Trailers, Ottawa Yard Tractors, Kalmar Counter-Balance lifts, Heli Forklifts and Kentucky Trailers. The company operates a fleet of rental trailers and terminal tractors that are available for seasonal use or long-term lease. The company offers financing for trailer purchases.

A professionally trained team of technicians handles repairs and maintenance in the company's large, modern repair shop. A complete line of aftermarket parts is offered for repairs made both on site and for the customer who prefers to repair and service his own equipment. For maximum convenience, mobile service is also available, allowing technicians and service vehicles to travel to each customer's location to perform repairs and scheduled maintenance.

Utility supports a number of community and charitable causes, including the National Kidney Foundation of Utah and Idaho, Salt Lake Rotary Club, American Cancer Society, and the Westminster College Foundation.

More information about the company is available at www.utility-trailer.com.

One of the largest tank truck carriers for delivering fuels in the Western United States, Alpha Transport, Inc., based in Salt Lake City, Utah, has terminals in Utah and Idaho and the ability to service all forty-eight states of the continental United States. Alpha began operations in 1952 as Johnson Oil Company, with the name changed in 1990 to Alpha Transport, Inc., to reflect its most current services.

Alpha's mission is to provide a transportation service of value and to expand the company through customer service and innovation: Right Product, Right Place, Right Time, Every Time!

From its original fleet of 3 trucks and 5 employees, Alpha now has more than 50 trucks and over 80 employees. It specializes in servicing a customer base that distributes virtually every petroleum product, including gasoline, distillates, light motor oils and aviation products. Alpha specializes in hauling bulk petroleum products, with deliveries to multiple locations, such as gas stations, truck stops, bulk plants, refineries and airports. The company's drivers are cleared at nearly every loading terminal in the Western United States, allowing them to go anywhere at any time.

Adam Lindsay, company vice president, noted that the company's drivers are Alpha employees, who are continually trained to recognize customers' needs. Alpha's ongoing safety program minimizes risk to its employees, as well as assuring that the public is served with the highest possible degree of safety.

"In order to maintain these goals, we must promote customer satisfaction through safe and dependable deliveries, modern equipment, and a committed staff," he said.

In 2003, Alpha Transport diversified its fleet, creating the Alpha Express division, a truck load fleet that delivers general commodities such as paper goods, plastics and chemicals to the twenty-four Western states, with the ability to service all other parts of the continental U.S. A licensed and bonded broker, Alpha has decades of brokerage experience and a logistics software system capable of handling any transport order. Its focus is on customer satisfaction that is achieved through safe and reliable services at a reasonable price.

Routine maintenance is essential to provide excellent customer service. With four large bays, over 10,000 square feet and the ability to accommodate LCV vehicles, the Salt Lake City maintenance shop and trained staff ensure that Alpha Transport can offer a well maintained fleet. The shop is cargo tank certified, providing the ability to test and maintain cargo tanks, creating more flexibility with the fleet.

Visit www.alphatransport.com or call Alpha toll free at 1-800-594-8902.

ALPHA TRANSPORT, INC.

HAMILTON PARTNERS, INC.

Hamilton Partners (HP), established in 1987, develops, owns and operates top quality institutional properties including office and industrial buildings, as well as shopping centers, apartment complexes and hotels.

The firm's successful real estate development philosophy includes capitalizing on local operating partners' knowledge, building and operating the highest quality properties, total land development control, and providing great service to lessees.

Management is controlled by twenty partners who have a combined 550 plus years of experience in developing, owning and operating more than 39 million square feet of properties throughout the Midwest and Salt Lake City. Since inception, HP has developed assets worth over $100 million annually, with a portfolio that continues ownership in over 18 million square feet, valued at nearly $2 billion today. The firm's land holdings, over 250 acres, will allow it to continue its annual development volume.

Key individuals in organizing and developing HP include founder Allan Hamilton (who passed away in 2007), Ron Lunt, John Wauterlek, and Jim Sheridan. They and Bruce Bingham, who heads the Salt Lake City office, are managing partners and work together to direct all aspects of development. Hamilton Partners employs over 200 professionals to sustain the firm's reputation for excellent property development and management.

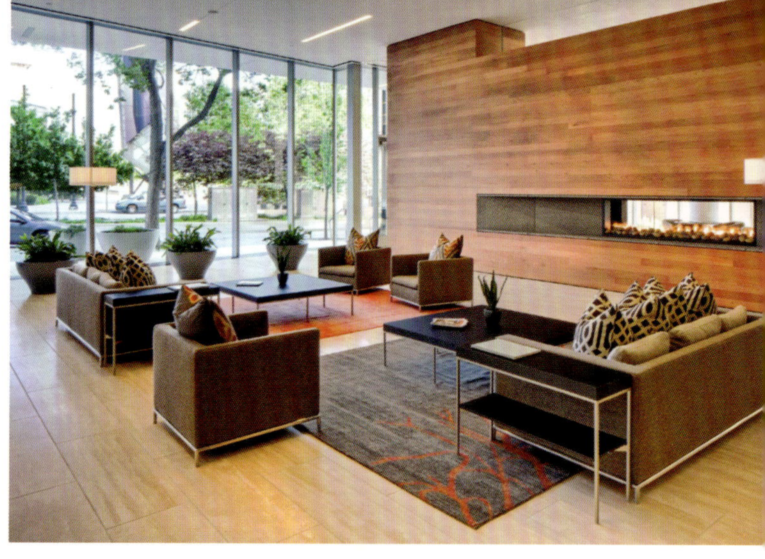

In 2002 this Chicago-based commercial real estate development firm set its sights on Salt Lake City and changed the city's skyline forever.

Not only did Hamilton Partners construct the first Gold LEED certified office tower at 222 South Main Street, located in the heart of the Central Business District, but the company also purchased several downtown landmarks including the Broadway Centre at 300 South and State Street, the Lollin and Karrick Buildings on Main Street, and the Newhouse and Boston Buildings on Exchange Place. Hamilton Partners completed a $10 million renovation to the Boston Building, a 100 year old tower that is considered one of Salt Lake City's first skyscrapers.

The century-old Walker Center at Second South and Main Street marks the geographic heart of Salt Lake City's central business district.

Designed by architects Eames and Young it was originally owned by Samuel, Joseph, David and Matthew Walker. When its grand opening was held in 1912, Main Street was primarily a dirt thoroughfare and construction on the Utah State Capitol building was beginning. When completed, the building was the tallest between the Missouri River and the West Coast. The Walker Brothers' mercantile business, which had opened in the 1800s, moved here, and the building also housed their rapidly growing Walker Bank.

Today Walker Center retains the stately appearance of a bygone era. Its stone façade is adorned with majestic lion medallions, statues of eagles, and other architectural embellishments while it offers modern, state-of-the-art office facilities to its tenants, including AmericanWest Bank, FedEx Office & Print Center, VRx, Smith Hartivgsen and Domo. It provides 110,000 square feet of outstanding office space on 16 floors, a 64 foot Weather Tower, full-floor suites, well over 12,000 square feet of street-level retail space, a dramatic two-story lobby and nearly 4,000 square feet of office space plus a full spa on the lower level.

Walker Terrace, built adjacent to the main tower in 1958, is a 10-story, mixed-use structure that includes a 419 stall parking terrace, a 14,000 square foot office penthouse with spectacular city and mountain views, and street-level retail space. Full renovation in 2006 transformed the building into a Class A office tower while preserving elements of its heritage. This included removal of a 1970s style canopy, restoration of the granite façade, and installation of a historically sensitive canopy above the main entrance.

The Walker Tower is listed on the prestigious National Register of Historic Places, received the Downtown Alliance Achievement Award for Economic Development, and holds the city's second Fallen Officer plaque marking where Chief Andrew Burt was killed in the line of duty in 1883. W. James Tozer, Jr., and Raju L. Shah of Vectra Management Group received the Utah Heritage Foundation's Heritage Award recognizing the all-encompassing renovations to the building in a five year period, and the building and management received the Utah State History's Outstanding Achievement Award.

Its management is actively involved in community projects, such as the Weather Tower's red display in support of the American Heart Association's "Go Red for Women" campaign.

Above: The owners, an investor group led by Raju L. Shah and W. James Tozer, Jr., also had the sixty-four foot Weather Tower rebuilt in 2008. Weather tower colors of constant blue indicate predictions of sunny skies; flashing blue, cloudy skies; constant red, rain forecasts; and flashing red, snow.

Cushman & Wakefield | Commerce Real Estate Solutions

Cushman & Wakefield | Commerce, an independently owned and operated member of the Cushman & Wakefield Alliance, has been the leading provider of real estate brokerage services for more than thirty years. Headquartered in Salt Lake City, the firm offers brokerage, tenant and landlord representation, property and facilities management, consulting and valuation services to corporations, institutions and investors throughout the Intermountain West and Pacific Northwest.

The firm is dedicated, first and foremost, to its clients. With the industry's premier professionals, including over 280 brokers and employees, along with industry-leading technology, its mission is to exceed clients' expectations through service excellence.

Principal Broker/Managing Partner Bill D'Evelyn, along with six others, established Commerce Properties in 1979. In 1999, Commerce merged with Consolidated Realty Group (CRG). In the 1980s interest rates were in the high teens. Savings and loan institutions' challenges during the late 1980s and early 1990s were similar to those recently encountered, with no money available and a bad market situation.

During its more than thirty year history, the firm's name has changed slightly with different international affiliations, but has remained locally owned and operated by President and CEO Michael Lawson; principal Bill D'Evelyn and Chief Operating Officer Rodney Gibson. It is now an independently owned and operated Alliance member of the international firm of Cushman & Wakefield.

As to the future, "Everything we do is strategically and thoughtfully laid out," Lawson stated. "We believe in investing in the firm's infrastructure and services, as well as restructuring departments to run smoother and faster to improve the services the company offers to its brokers and clients."

Key historic events have included: establishment of Commerce Properties (1979); bringing on of Michael M. Lawson as president and CEO (2002); joining of Commerce with Cushman & Wakefield Alliance (2004); acquisition of a Las Vegas, Nevada, firm and folding that operation into the existing office (2010); and acquisition of full ownership of the Provo, Utah, office (2011).

Office openings included Provo, Utah (1998); Northern Utah (1999); Park City, Utah (2001); St. George, Utah (2003); Las Vegas, Nevada (2006); Seattle and Bellevue, Washington (2010); Reno, Nevada (2011); and Boise, Idaho (2012).

The firm is active within industry organizations such as CCIM, SIOR, NAIOP, CREW, etc., and with local economic and business development groups including EDCU, local chambers of commerce and others. On a charitable level, it supports its brokers and staff in such groups as the University of Utah's School of Business, Head Start, Guadalupe School, United Way, Utah Food Bank, and others.

For more information about the firm, property listings, broker information, or market category reports, visit www.comre.com.

JBR Environmental Consultants, Inc., assists companies and organizations in complying with regulatory and environmental standards. JBR supports and assists clients to achieve business and environmental objectives and obtain applicable environmental permits and approvals, while honoring its commitment to staff, clients, and shareholders. It offers an array of products and services, including preparing Environmental Impact Statements (EIS); air monitoring and stack testing; reclamation and remediation services; Environmental Site Assessments (ESA); wildlife and other natural resource surveys; surface water management; and more. Both its commercial and regulatory agency customers applaud the quality and objectivity of JBR staff's work and products.

Two of the five individuals who founded the company in 1985 sold their interest to the other three within a few years of being founded. Joseph (Joe) Jarvis, Robert (Bob) Bayer, and Brian Buck continued to operate and grow the business until Joe retired, followed by Bob years later. Brian still serves as president and board chairman.

Beginning in home offices and basements, with an "all hands on deck" approach, JBR grew rapidly, providing environmental baseline surveys and permitting services for numerous mines being developed in the Western United States. Other clients included electric utilities; federal, state and local governments; manufacturing and retail companies; and various natural resource development companies.

JBR office sites include the Sandy, Utah, headquarters; St. George, Utah; Tempe, Arizona; Denver, Colorado; Boise, Idaho; Butte, Missoula, and Billings, Montana; Elko and Reno, Nevada; Medford, Oregon; and Seattle, Washington. Operated by 150 staff members, JBR continues to grow, based on attention to the quality of the working environment for its staff and the desire of qualified environmental professionals to join the JBR organization. The company focuses on the quality and timeliness of its products and services, validated by its many long-term and repeat clients.

Cognizant of the critical role of environmental issues in the sustained economic growth of the Western United States, the environmental professionals at JBR will continue to provide consulting services in keeping with its reputation and the quality of its work. JBR will continue to grow by hiring additional staff through mergers and acquisitions and by strategically pursuing compatible firms and individuals that share its objectives and goals.

JBR has supported numerous worthy causes, including corporate sponsorship of KUER, the local NPR affiliate; support of St. Jude Children's Hospital; and the Leukemia and Lymphoma Society's Light the Night Walk. JBR supports green initiatives, and is currently piloting a hybrid vehicle program, which allows appropriate vehicles to be implemented as they become available.

JBR Environmental Consultants, Inc.

Left: JBR provides air quality services for the Salt Lake City Department of Airports.

Above: Salt Lake Speed Skating Oval—JBR performed environmental work to assist with events at the venue, 2002.

CEMENTATION USA, INC.

An underground mine contracting and engineering company, Cementation USA, Inc., provides mine development and production services for clients throughout the United States and Mexico. Its parent company is Cementation Canada, Inc., and it is part of the global Murray & Roberts companies. Incorporated in Nevada in 2005, it has a corporate office in Sandy, Utah.

Cementation was originally founded in Great Britain in the 1920s, growing from a small construction company to a global leader in underground mining construction and engineering solutions. After establishing a strong presence in South Africa, a large mining market was purchased in 2003 by Murray & Roberts, a global construction company based in Johannesburg. Cementation Canada, established in 1998, grew swiftly, with increasing demand for services in the U.S., leading to the U.S. entity. Key individuals included Roy Slack, president of Cementation Canada, Inc.; Mike Nadon, promoted from Vice President of Operations in Canada to President of Cementation USA; and Steve Leatherwood, director of finance.

In 2006, Rio Tinto, one of the world's largest mining companies, awarded Cementation a huge project in Arizona involving a vertical shaft—twenty-eight foot in diameter with ultimate depth of 6,943 feet. The company's performance and safety record established its reputation, and it quintupled revenues over the next few years.

The 2008 timing of Cementation's new office opening was unfortunate, as it also marked the mining industry's dramatic downturn, driven by the global economic crisis.

"We managed to hunker down and reduce costs to remain above water," Nadon says. "We negotiated another large project based on our strategy and agreement to reduce our fees

if the project would proceed immediately. This extra revenue launched us into the consistent growth that followed, and to recruiting key individuals, including Bill Tilley, Justin Oleson, Mike Nadon, Mike Condie, Willie Finch, David Sabourin, Brian Still, and Stephen Liu."

Most recently, Nadon has retired and taken on an executive advisory role, and Oleson has been appointed as his successor.

The company's growth is evident in the number of employees—98 in 2008 and 294 in 2013, including 63 corporate office employees, 35 at Utah projects, and 200 in other states. Its revenue has increased from $32 million in 2008 to over $125 million in 2012.

Cementation has received many awards, including the Fast 50, an award given to the fastest-growing companies in Utah. It has also received many Best Employer awards. Its employees are "doers," who actively participate in company and community events. Community and charitable activities include Sandy Kids Club—a club for boys and girls; and Wish Foundation.

For more information, see www.Cementation.com.

1112B
UTA TRAX
TEXAS BRAZIL
City Center
CITY CREEK

About the Photographer

A D A M   B A R K E R

Raised in Utah's Wasatch Mountains, internationally acclaimed photographer Adam Barker's passion for capturing nature's beauty is matched only by his zest for life. His bold landscape and active lifestyle imagery has translated into stirring editorial work for *Outdoor Photographer*, *Skiing*, *Ski*, *Powder*, *Flyfish Journal*, *USA Today*, *The Drake*, *Mountain Magazine*, and many others. Additionally Barker has drawn praise for his hands-on teaching style at workshops around the world, as well as his instructional DVDs. Barker's vast commercial client roster includes Nike, Black Diamond Equipment, Volkswagen of America, Deer Valley Resort and Suunto Watches. When not shooting, Barker can be found spending time with his wife and three sons, or "product testing" in the mountains, on the river, or wherever else nature happens to call.

About the Author

M E L I S S A   F I E L D S

Fifteen years ago native Michigander Melissa Fields drove across the U.S. to spend "just one winter" in Utah. A husband, mortgage and two wonderful kids later she still hasn't managed to make the return move back to the Midwest. Touting Utah's many attributes has made up the core of her career since then; *Sunset*, *Salt Lake Magazine*, *Utah Style & Design*, *Downtown Salt Lake City* and *Ski Utah Magazine* are just a few of the platforms from which she waxes poetic about her beloved adopted home state, and in 2013 she was named editor of *Park City Magazine*. In her free time Fields enjoys skiing, road and mountain biking, hiking, camping and doing all of the above with her family.

Photograph courtesy of Piper Benjamin.

Sponsors

A&Z Produce Company 254
Adam Barker Photography 260
Alpha Transport, Inc. 303
Alsco Inc. 240
America First Credit Union 214
Architectural Nexus, Inc. 286
ARUP Laboratories 190
ATK Aerospace Group 268
Beacon Metals, Inc. 296
Beijer Electronics 234
Boart Longyear 292
Burton Lumber Company 280
Canvas by Instructure 196
Cementation USA, Inc. 308
Christopher's Prime Steak House & Grill...238
The Church of Jesus Christ of Latter-day Saints 198
City Creek Reserve, Inc. 298
ConsultNet 250
Creative Bioscience 220
Cushman & Wakefield | Commerce Real Estate Solutions 306
Davis Hospital and Medical Center 200
Deseret Management Corporation 216
Durham Jones & Pinegar 224
First Utah Bank 222
FLSmidth 288
Hamilton Partners, Inc. 304
Harmons Grocery 262
Himalayan Kitchen 255
Hoopes Vision 202
IDFL Laboratory and Institute 261
Intermountain Healthcare 182
JBR Environmental Consultants, Inc. 307
Jordan Valley Medical Center 200
Judge Memorial Catholic High School 194
Kirton McConkie 248
LCG Facades 276
Lewis Stages 218

Major Drilling Group International, Inc...284
The McGillis School......................203
Monsen Engineering of Salt Lake City.....282
Mountain Land Design 259
Mountain West Small Business Finance 252
Nicholas & Company 246
Paulsen Construction 290
Peak Alarm Company, Inc..................242
Pioneer Valley Hospital 201
Red Iguana 212
Regional Supply 230
Rhodes Bake-N-Serv™ 258
Rio Tinto Kennecott......................272
Rocky Mountain Water Company 263
Royce Industries, L.C....................208
Salt Lake Chamber. 244
Salt Lake City 206
Salt Lake Regional Medical Center 201
The Salt Lake Tribune 256
SelectHealth® 192
SME Steel 278
Sportsman's Warehouse....................232
Strong Automotive Group 228
Sysco Intermountain 236
University of Utah Health Care 184
US Magnesium, LLC 300
Utah Paper Box 226
Utah Transit Authority...................204
Utility Trailer Sales of Utah 302
Visit Salt Lake..........................207
VLCM 257
Walker Center 305
Weber State University 188
Western Governors University 205
Wintersteiger Inc. 253
Woodbury Corporation 294